#		#	
1	八 丨 刂 氵 彡 乛 又	41	丶 卜 丿 亻 丶 丨 彡 韭
2	忄	42	刂 乙 乚 比 七 匕 屯
3	冫 丬 丨 火	43	十 寸 才 斗 半 羊 长 弋 戈 戋
4	讠	44	止 土 士 生 主 立 义 文 亢 方 广 户 少
5	氵 泊 泊 泊 泊 泊	45	尤 龙 尢 也 丨 木 未 末 朱 东 韦 聿
6	泊 泊 …	46	人 入 火 犬 丈 失 夹 力 九 夬 央 专
7	泊 泊 泊 …	47	
8	亻 伯	48	
9	佃 佃 佃 …	49	丁 弓 力 …
10	彳 十 上 止 土	50	欠 尔 乍 勹 勾 包 子 予
11	扌 拍 拍 拍 揩 揩	51	攵 又 反 皮 斤
12	拍 拍 …	52	口 中 虫 由 申 巨 区 凶 西 彐
13	扣 扣 扣 …	53	日 白 丑 艮 良 且 月 肖
14	犭 豸 子 弓 巾 山	54	冂 阝 鸟 鬼 辛 京
15	纟	55	只 支 殳 灵 青 羊 圭 隹 甫
16	木 柏	56	占 各 咼 召 台 合 分 令 仓 仑 它
17	柏 柳 柏 …	57	other
18	禾 釆 米 光 耒	58	丶 丶 丷 丷 ⺌ 羊
19	牛 车 片 丁 工 王 开	59	小 ⺌ 业 ⺍ 八 八
20	饣 矢 缶 立 方 衤 礻	60	一 二 四 禾 不
21	钅	61	⺈ 广 夕 夂 又 マ 丘
22	女 阝	62	亠 亡 去 亦 文 立 言
23	口 呷	63	广 穴
24	叩 叩 叩 …	64	卄 苫
25	日 白 酉 目 耳 田	65	苫 苫 苫 …
26	石 歹 牙 舌 疋	66	竹 收 收 癶 卜 止 山
27	月	67	十 土 士 生 圭 出 木 大 夫 类
28	舟 身 良 艮 区 贝 马	68	口 品 田 田 目 西 雷
29	虫 鱼 角 卓 辛 革 其	69	other
30	other	70	八 八 丿 丨 乙 匕 七 丶 十 寸
31	…	71	八 乂 人 刂 儿 几
32	厂 厂 广 耂 尸 户	72	小 示 小 巛 心
33	广 虍 疒 other	73	一
34	辶	74	丁 干 火 大 天 キ 艹 木
35	走 夊 是 鬼 other	75	土 牛 车 工 王 正 疋 巾 山
36		76	又 夂 女 夕 力 刀 マ 子 手 毛
37		77	水 氺 系 以 仪 衣 厶 见 贝
38		78	口
39	二	79	日 目 且 虫 月 巴 巳 巴
40		80	耳 母 田 皿 other

Chinese
Character
Fast Finder

Laurence Matthews

TUTTLE PUBLISHING
Boston • Rutland, Vermont • Tokyo

Acknowledgements

I have made use of a number of books, websites and dictionaries, primarily the *Han Ying Cidian* ('*A Chinese English Dictionary*,' Commercial Press, Beijing, 1978 and subsequent editions). My thanks also to Flavia Hodges and Nancy Goh at Tuttle for their friendliness and efficiency.

Most importantly, my heartfelt thanks to my wife Alison, for her love, support and encouragement, for numerous suggestions, the many hours shared poring over dictionaries, the computer macros to generate and format the pages of the book, the quality control—a wide spectrum echoing the richness of our life together.

HSK grades in this book are taken from materials published by the HSK authorities. The ultimate rights of interpretations of HSK policies remain with the Office of the PRC HSK State Commission at the following address: HSK Office, 15 Xueyuan Road, Haidan District, Beijing, PRC 100083; Fax 86-10-62311093, 86-10-62311037; Tel 86-10-62317150, 86-10-62317531 x 2685 or 2672.

Published by Tuttle Publishing, an imprint of Periplus Editions (HK) Ltd., with editorial offices at 153 Milk Street, Boston, MA 02109 and 130 Joo Seng Road #06-01/03 Singapore 368357

LCC Card No.: 2004107692
ISBN: 0-8048-3634-5

Printed in Singapore

Distributed by:

Asia-Pacific
Berkeley Books Pte Ltd
130 Joo Seng Road, 06-01/03
Singapore 368357
Tel: (65) 6280 1330; Fax: (65) 6280 6290
Email: inquiries@periplus.com.sg
www.periplus.com

North America, Latin America & Europe
Tuttle Publishing
364 Innovation Drive
North Clarendon, VT 05759-9436, USA
Tel: (802) 773 8930; Fax: (802) 773 6993
Email: info@tuttlepublishing.com
www.tuttlepublishing.com

Japan
Tuttle Publishing
Yaekari Bldg., 3F
5-4-12 Osaki, Shinagawa-ku
Tokyo 141-0032, Japan
Tel: (03) 5437 0171; Fax: (03) 5437 0755
Email: tuttle-sales@gol.com

Indonesia
PT Java Books Indonesia
Jl. Kelapa Gading Kirana
Blok A14 No. 17
Jakarta 14240, Indonesia
Tel: (62-21) 451 5351; Fax: (62-21) 453 4987
Email: cs@javabooks.co.id

08 07 06 05 04
8 7 6 5 4 3 2 1

INTRODUCTION

Chinese characters are fascinating, but can be frustrating. In particular, looking them up in a traditional dictionary can be a nightmare, as there is no 'alphabetical order.'

With this book you can find a character in seconds from its appearance alone. From the finder chart inside the front cover, you can turn to the correct page immediately, and finding the character on that page has also been made as simple as possible. As an optional feature you can make a double thumbnail index (see page xiv) to speed things up even more.

The Fast Finder is designed primarily for serious learners of modern Chinese and serves as a quick reference for experts, but it is also suitable for beginners, or people who wish to dip into characters, browse, or simply discover what a street sign means. With this book you can:

- Find characters quickly, reliably and intuitively—from their visual appearance alone;
- Quickly check the meanings, pronunciations, stroke-counts and radicals of characters;
- Look at traditional characters to see how they have been simplified;
- Look up newly encountered characters or check on those you have temporarily forgotten;
- Find elusive characters more easily in large character dictionaries;
- Simply browse and explore, comparing similar characters.

There are some hints on finding characters on page vii, but the system is so intuitive that you can try it right now: for example, try finding 独 or 空 .

I wish you success, fun and enjoyment in your study of Chinese characters!

Chinese Characters

Several tens of thousands of characters exist, but two or three thousand suffice for almost all purposes, and in many circumstances far fewer are needed. A knowledge of the 500 most common characters covers 75 per cent of Chinese writing, 1,000 gives 86 per cent, 2,000 gives 96 per cent, and 3,000 gives 99 per cent (the numbers depending very slightly on the context).

There is no 'officially approved' set of characters (as exists, for example, in Japan), and so each book or dictionary has to choose its own selection. The Fast Finder contains approximately 3,200 characters. Among these, all the 2,905 characters contained in the Chinese Proficiency Test (the *Hanyu Shuiping Kaoshi*, administered by the office of the HSK State Commission under the Chinese Ministry of Education) are included, and additional characters have been chosen to cover the characters found in well-known textbooks, with an eye also to frequency of occurrence in Chinese as measured by the databases now available on the internet.

This book uses the modern simplified characters, as used in modern China. (Traditional characters, however, are still found in the People's Republic, and are in widespread use in Chinese communities around the world. You can look up traditional characters using the appendix. For more on simplified and traditional characters, see page xiii.)

Pronunciations are given in the 'pinyin' system for modern *putonghua* (or 'Mandarin'). The pronunciation of characters is different in, say, Cantonese, but the meanings of the characters are basically universal.

Modern Chinese dictionaries are often organized alphabetically by the pronunciation of the characters. However, in many circumstances you will want to look up a character you have encountered, and yet you don't know the pronunciation for this character. For this reason dictionaries usually include an index or indexes to help locate characters by their appearance alone.

One type of index uses a system of character components called 'radicals' to classify characters. This is the system long used to organize traditional dictionaries in China, but has many pitfalls for the beginner (and even for native speakers!), even in its modern versions. Another system arranges the characters by stroke-count (the number of pen-strokes, or traditionally brush-strokes, needed to write the characters), but this is very slow to use, and counting strokes is also not without its pitfalls. A few other systems have been devised to help with this problem, notably the 'four-corner' method. This book arose out of my own frustration with these various methods when learning characters, and uses instead the human brain's pattern-recognition abilities directly.

The radical system is basically a good one, but not as logical as one might hope, and experts tend to forget how difficult it was to master the radical system initially. The Fast Finder uses 'intuitive radicals': character components which you think *ought* to be radicals *are* treated as such. However, most symbols in the finder chart are traditional radicals (or their modern equivalents), and so as you become more familiar with radicals and their quirks, you will find it easy enough to use the many books based on more traditional systems.

Information given

The purpose of this book is to *find* characters quickly, and to this end the amount of clutter on each page has been kept to a minimum. Thus the information given for each character is basic. However, it is sufficient to determine the meaning of a character, to check at a glance any characters you have confused or temporarily forgotten, or to look up the character quickly in your favorite dictionary or character guide for fuller information.

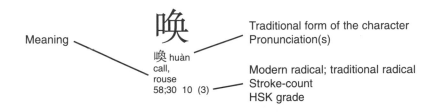

Meaning

唤

唤 huàn
call,
rouse
58;30 10 (3)

Traditional form of the character
Pronunciation(s)

Modern radical; traditional radical
Stroke-count
HSK grade

Below each character are four lines of information. The first line gives the character's traditional form (or forms), and its pronunciation(s). An absence of traditional forms (or an asterisk *) means that the character is a traditional form in its own right. For more details on traditional characters, see page xiii. Pronunciations are separated by spaces if the character has more than one. For more on pronunciations, see page x.

The next two lines give the basic meaning(s) of the character and are meant to be read together; if only one line is needed then the symbol '–' is printed on the following line. For more on meanings, see page xi.

The last line of information gives the modern and traditional radicals, separated by a semicolon (the numbers referring to Tables 4 and 5 at the back of the book); the stroke-count of the character; and finally in parentheses its grade in the HSK (Chinese Proficiency Test).

Hints on finding characters

It is a good idea to start by looking through the book to get a feel for how the characters are organized and displayed. The Fast Finder is organized with many characters to a page, so that you can see at a glance the characters which share a particular radical—and you can profitably browse this way too.

Dividing up a character

Take a look at pages 38, 39, and 40, the 'indivisible' characters. Initially you might find you have a tendency to regard any character which doesn't split left-right as indivisible; but you will see that the characters on pages 38–40 are generally quite simple ones. The vast majority of characters *do* divide into components.

To find a specific character, first look at how it 'naturally' breaks down into components. The split will usually be left-right or top-bottom, and will usually (although not always) be 'clean' with white space on the page between the two components. Having split the character, choose the simpler component as your radical, which you will use to look up the character. If the components look roughly equal in simplicity, choose either; if you already recognize one of the components as a radical, you can use that. The same character may be found in two places: for example you will find 引 under ◧ on page 14, and also under ▢ on page 41.

In fact many characters are to be found in several different locations in the Fast Finder. A consequence of having compact information for each character is that the whole entry can be repeated in each of these locations, thus eliminating the need for cross-references, and avoiding any need to decide which radical is 'correct.'

Although most characters split left-right or top-bottom, don't forget the other patterns (pages 32–37). For these characters, use the enclosing component as the radical.

Sometimes there is a choice of 'how much' of a character to take as the radical. For example, when looking for 雇, is the radical 丶 or 户? In such cases, both radicals will be on the same page to make it easier to find the character (in odd cases where they are not, then the character will be found in both places, or there will be cross-reference of the form 启 ⟶ 32). Character with several reasonable possibilities are listed under all of these. But I rely on you not to make 'unnatural' divisions: 望 is in the ▬ section under 王, not 土.

Finally, if looking for a character which also happens to serve as a radical, treat it as a character in its own right. For example, you would look up 柱 under ◧ on page 16, but 木 itself under ■ on page 38.

Finding the right page

Look for your radical in the finder chart inside the front cover. Remember to look in the correct section (▮ or ▯, etc.) as several radicals appear in more than one section. The arrangement of the radicals in the finder chart is intuitive, with similar radicals grouped together, and the simpler ones generally coming before the complex ones. If you can't find the radical on the finder chart, look on the relevant 'others' page (these are pages such as 30, 31, 57 or 69, which contain radicals which have only one or two characters each.) You will very quickly become familiar with the common radicals, which appear explicitly in the finder chart, and hence sense when to look on the 'others' pages.

As illustrated on the inside front cover, if a radical has many characters then they will be subdivided according to how the remainder of the character divides up. In the case of a few particularly common radicals which flow onto two or three pages, this idea is used in the finder chart too.

For 'indivisible' characters, the shape of the top of the character is used; you can see how this works by glancing through pages 38–40. The same idea is used for the 'others' pages and implicitly elsewhere.

Finding the character on the page

When you turn to the page, check at the top of the page that your chosen radical is there. (The thin vertical gray lines in the finder chart inside the front cover indicate whether to look on the left hand or right hand page.)

The characters for the same radical are grouped together: again, the arrangement is intuitive with the simpler ones coming before the more complex. Characters which are very similar and likely to be confused, such as 何 and 伺, or 勒 and 勤, are placed close together. As mentioned above, if a radical has many characters then they will be subdivided according to how the remainder of the character divides up.

If the character itself is printed in gray, then you were not really looking for it in the right place: never mind, at least you have found it! However, the same character will appear elsewhere in the book, printed in black. As you use the Fast Finder, taking a closer look at these gray characters will help you to appreciate more precisely how character components fit together and to distinguish between similar and easily-confused components. You are bound to find some gray characters where you would not imagine that anyone would look for them, but rest assured that there are people who would, and did!

Important distinctions

If you are new to Chinese characters, then there are several points to watch out for. Make sure you distinguish between radicals such as 宀 and 艹, or 力 and 刀, for example. You will learn these distinctions with time (in fact, pretty quickly).

On the other hand, unfortunately, some variants denote the same character. A few characters have minor variations from one typeface to another, or are slightly different when hand-written. Many traditional characters exist in several variant forms, and some slightly older versions of character components are still around (see the appendix). Fortunately this is not much of a problem for simplified characters.

Characters also incorporate remnants from much earlier times. For example, many traditional radicals have several forms, depending on whether they appear to the left, right, top, bottom, etc. of the characters to which they contribute. Thus:

> 犭 and 犬 are different forms of the 'dog' radical;

> 忄 and 心 are different forms of the 'heart' radical.

To further complicate matters, many of these forms have different stroke-counts, which can sometimes make finding even the radicals a problem! In the Fast Finder these forms are treated as though they are different radicals, in the belief that although such facts about the characters and their historical derivations can be fascinating, they should not frustrate your attempts simply to *find* a character.

Pronunciations

Pronunciations are given in pinyin, with the tones marked by accents above the vowels. All pronunciations for a character are given (even if a subsidiary pronunciation is only used for proper names), and the pronunciations are generally in order of frequency, with the most common pronunciation first. A character may have two or even three common pronunciations, but the vast majority of characters have only one, or at least one dominant one.

Characters can change tones for reasons of euphony (notably a 3rd tone changing if it precedes another), and these changes are ignored. The tones taken by 一, 七 and 不 also depend on the character which they precede; otherwise different tones tend to imply different meanings, or shades of meaning, of the character.

Meanings

The English meanings given are as short and concise as possible; their purpose is to 'suggest and remind' as one book puts it. Current rather than original historical meanings are given. From the meanings supplied, you will usually be able to deduce the meaning of the characters in a given context, but there are some points you should note.

Firstly, characters do not usually correspond neatly to single English words. Also, like an English word, a character may have several distinct meanings. (If so, it is safer not to assume that the meanings correspond in any one-to-one manner with the pronunciations. Although I have tried to list meanings in the same order as pronunciations, this is not always possible. A large character dictionary will make it clear which pronunciations can take which meanings.)

Where several meanings are given, similar meanings are separated by commas and distinct meanings by semicolons. If two meanings are separated by commas then they may qualify each other: thus 'firm, hard' indicates 'firm to the touch' rather than either 'industrial organization' or 'difficult.' Sometimes a character has a large range of meanings depending on context, and the symbol '&' alerts you to the existence of further meanings.

Conversely, several characters may share a common English meaning, so be wary of using this book to translate in the English-to-Chinese direction. Familial relationships and forms of address are particular cases of this: for example the single word 'aunt' in English corresponds to various characters in Chinese with meanings such as 'wife of father's younger brother,' and forms of address such as 'you' similarly depend on relative age, status, etc.

Characters can often serve as several parts of speech (for example acting as both a verb and a noun). Where the English word is ambiguous I have used 'a' to denote a noun and 'to' to denote a verb; for example 飞 is 'to fly' whereas 蝇 is 'a fly.' On the other hand the meaning of 舞 is given simply as 'dance' since it acts as both 'to dance' and 'a dance.'

The following notation and abbreviations are used:

EB, HS   The so-called 'Earthly Branches' and 'Heavenly Stems,' which are used in enumeration, old notation for dates and various astrological purposes (see Table 3 at the back of the book).

[ ]   Brackets [ ] are used when the character is only likely to be encountered as part of a compound word made up of two or more characters; the meaning in brackets is that of the compound. For example 啤 is given as meaning '[beer],' since you will only find it in the compound 啤酒 meaning 'beer.'

( )	Parentheses ( ) are used in explanations, such as 'right (hand)' or '(bus) stop.' The word 'literary' means that the character is confined to written Chinese and is somewhat flowery or bookish. Sometimes a word such as 'particle' is given in parentheses instead of a meaning: some terms used in this way are discussed below.
(particle)	These are words which give a gloss to the sentence as a whole, and are often difficult to pin down concisely. Fortunately, if you are learning Chinese, you will know the common ones already as they are bound to be included in any book or course you are using.
(sound)	Some characters are used mainly to convey sounds, as for example in 'spelling out' the syllables of foreign names: Samoa is 'sa-mo-ya' (萨摩亚); in many cases the syllables in the foreign language have to be shoehorned to fit. Sometimes this phonetic rendering only applies to part of a word: for example 'saxophone' is rendered 'sa-ke-pipe' or 'sa-ke-se-pipe.' (Conversely, of course, Chinese words such as 'Beijing,' familiar to many English speakers simply as sounds, all have meanings which you can discover by using the Fast Finder.)
(surname)	Many characters are used as surnames or family names, and for some characters this is their only modern usage.
(measure word)	Several dozen characters serve as counting units for nouns, analogous to the word 'head' in 'six head of cattle' or 'sheet' in 'three sheets of paper.' Measure words are usually easily recognized in Chinese as they always directly follow numbers.

Many other characters take on roles of 'surname,' 'sound' or 'measure word' in addition to their main meanings. I only list these roles in the Fast Finder if the character has no other (modern) meaning.

Finally, as far as compounds (words made up of two or more characters) are concerned, their meanings can be guessed, more often than not, from the context and the meanings of the individual characters. But of course many derived meanings are somewhat oblique, in the same way that English words such as 'laptop' and 'honeymoon' have meanings not implicit in their component parts. Compounds are listed in large dictionaries under the first character of the compound.

Simplified and Traditional Characters

During the twentieth century simplified characters were introduced in the People's Republic of China. Although the modern characters are all you need to know in many circumstances, you will still see traditional characters around, and the written literature, going back thousands of years, is written in traditional characters. Thus, although the Fast Finder is based on simplified forms, the traditional forms of the characters are given as well. The appendix, which contains all the traditional character equivalents of the characters in the main pages (but not repeating those which are unchanged on simplification), will let you look up a traditional character to find its modern simplified form. It uses the same method as the main book (except there is no thumbnail index) and has its own finder chart. For more details see the notes at the beginning of the appendix.

Chinese characters have evolved (slowly) since time immemorial, but the recent simplification was more drastic. Depending on the character, the radical may simplify (as in 詞 ➝ 词) or the remainder (燈 ➝ 灯), or both. Some characters change completely (頭 ➝ 头), and particularly tricky are cases where simplification changes the apparent radical (葉 ➝ 叶). Many characters remain unchanged (本 ➝ 本), including some surprisingly complex ones.

Several traditional characters can simplify to the same modern character, as in 發, 髮 ➝ 发. Sometimes the traditional forms in question are variants of the 'same' character: in the world of traditional characters these may have more or less equal status, or one may be an 'older' form. I have given some of the more common variants, but there is no hard and fast cut-off point for variants, and dictionaries have been accused of listing too many. In any event, there will be only one simplified form.

Quite often a simplified character is identical to its traditional form, but also acts as the simplified form of another traditional character, e.g. 里, 裏 ➝ 里. This situation is denoted by an asterisk * in the Fast Finder entry for the simplified form.

Only rarely does a traditional character simplify to different simplified forms (the choice depending on meaning and context). There are, however, a few characters which sometimes simplify and sometimes don't (depending on context or to avoid ambiguity). The traditional form thus qualifies as a 'simplified character' in that it will be seen in texts written in simplified characters. Table 1 at the end of the book lists those characters in the Fast Finder to which this applies.

Thumbnail index

A unique feature of this book is the option to make a double thumbnail index, as illustrated in the diagram below. This speeds up the use of the Fast Finder even more (and this is especially noticeable if you are using it repeatedly to look up many characters).

The thumbnail index allows immediate access to any page directly from the finder chart inside the front cover. Simply find the desired radical in the chart as normal, then put your right thumb on the tab with the chosen page number to open the book at the correct page. This tab will be on the same horizontal line as the radical you have found (thus actually bypassing the need to note the page number).

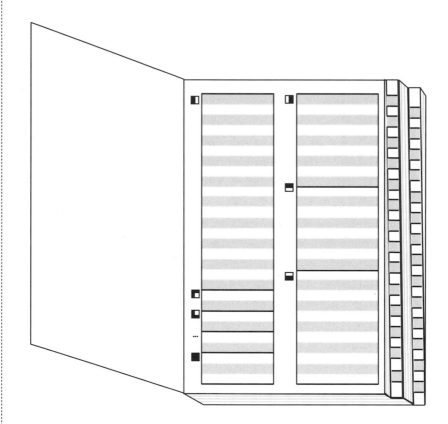

To make the thumbnail index, cut the main pages (1–79) as indicated by the heavy black lines in the block on the right hand side of each right-hand page, as indicated in the diagram below:

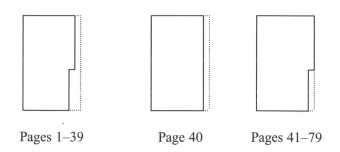

Pages 1–39   Page 40   Pages 41–79

For the main pages it is best to make the horizontal cut first, followed by the vertical cut or cuts. Be careful when cutting the pages; make sure that you are not unintentionally cutting two pages at once.

In order to have the thumbnail index visible from the finder chart, you will also have to cut these introductory pages, including the finder chart itself. Cut along the dotted line marked on the right hand edge of the right hand pages.

■ 丶 八 丶 亅 丿

小 xiǎo
small; young; petty
79;42 3 (1)

办 辦 bàn
manage; set up; punish
28;160 4 (1)

火 huǒ
fire
-
83;86 4 (1)

心 xīn
heart; core; feelings
81;61 4 (1)

必 bì
necessarily; certainly
1;61 5 (1)

州 zhōu
state, prefecture
1;47 6 (4)

刃 rèn
blade; sword, knife; kill
27;18 3 (4)

刁 diāo
cunning
-
6;18 2 (4)

苏 蘇 嘛 sū
revive; ('su' sound)
50;140 7 (4)

亦 yì
also, too (literary)
162;8 6 (4)

尔 爾 ěr
you; like that, that (literary)
79;89 5 (3)

忙□ → 2
灯□ → 3

丫 yā
fork (in tree), bifurcation
24;2 3 (-)

业 業 yè
business; already
140;75 5 (1)

亚 亞 yà
inferior; Asia
168;7 6 (3)

严 嚴 yán
tight; strict, severe
168;30 7 (2)

半 bàn
half, semi-; partly
3;24 5 (1)

米 mǐ
rice; meter (length)
159;119 6 (1)

平 píng
flat, even, level; calm; average
2;51 5 (1)

乎 hū
(suffix; particle)
2;4 5 (2)

来 來 lái lai
come, arrive; do; bring; future; during; approx.; &
94;9 7 (1)

寸 cùn
very small; inch
54;41 3 (2)

勺 sháo
spoon, ladle
26;20 3 (2)

为 為 wéi wèi
do, act, act as; become; be equal to; for the sake of
1;86 4 (1)

归 歸 guī
return; converge; &
70;77 5 (3)

帅 帥 shuài
commander; smart, graceful
57;50 5 (4)

师 師 shī
teacher, expert; lesson; army; &
3;50 6 (1)

临 臨 lín
arrive; about to; copy; to face
3;131 9 (2)

旧 舊 jiù
old, former, outdated; worn
103;134 5 (1)

门 門 mén
gate, door; family; sect; &
46;169 3 (1)

卜 *蔔 bǔ bo
divination; foretell
16;25 2 (2)

以 yǐ
using; so as to; according to; &
23;9 4 (1)

八 bā
eight
-
24;12 2 (1)

儿 兒 ér
child, youth; son; ('r' suffix)
29;10 2 (1)

川 chuān
river; a plain
4;47 3 (4)

顺 順 shùn
obey; suitable; along; in order
170;181 9 (2)

么 麼 me
[what; such as] (suffix)
4;200 3 (1)

从 從 cóng cōng
from; to follow; secondary; &
23;60 4 (1)

◨　丶　彡　フ　又

斗
*鬥 dòu dǒu
fight; dovetail;
dipper; &
82;68 4 (2)

头
頭 tóu tou
head; top; first,
chief; end; &
52;181 5 (1)

须
須鬚 xū
have to, must;
beard
63;181 9 (1)

非
fēi
not, no, non-;
wrong; evil
205;175 8 (1)

永
yǒng
eternal,
forever
1;85 5 (1)

水
shuǐ
water; liquid;
river, lake
125;85 4 (1)

承
chéng
undertake;
indebted; &
5;64 8 (2)

泉
quán
spring,
fountain
150;85 9 (4)

汞
gǒng
mercury
-
48;85 7 (4)

浆
漿 jiāng jiàng
thick liquid,
syrup; starch
125;85 10 (3)

双
雙 shuāng
two, twin, dual,
bi-, double
35;172 4 (1)

劝
勸 quàn
advise; urge,
encourage
35;19 4 (2)

欢
歡 huān
pleased,
happy, joyful
35;76 6 (1)

邓
鄧 dèng
(surname)
-
34;163 4 (4)

对
對 duì
correct, yes; regarding; versus;
to face; towards; deal with; &
35;41 5 (1)

戏
戲 xì
to play; make
fun of; a show
35;62 6 (2)

艰
艱 jiān
difficult
-
35;138 8 (2)

观
觀 guān guàn
observe; view;
Taoist temple
35;147 6 (1)

鸡
雞鶏 jī
chicken,
cock, hen
35;172 7 (1)

难
難 nán nàn
difficult; nasty;
disaster; blame
35;172 10 (1)

1	41
2	42
3	43
4	44
5	45
6	46
7	47
8	48
9	49
10	50
11	51
12	52
13	53
14	54
15	55
16	56
17	57
18	58
19	59
20	60
21	61
22	62
23	63
24	64
25	65
26	66
27	67
28	68
29	69
30	70
31	71
32	72
33	73
34	74
35	75
36	76
37	77
38	78
39	79
40	80

忆 憶 yì
recollect
-
41;61 4 (2)

怀 懷 huái
bosom; cherish;
yearn; pregnant
41;61 7 (3)

忧 憂 yōu
worry, anxious;
grief
41;61 7 (4)

快 kuài
quick; soon;
sharp; happy; &
41;61 7 (1)

性 xìng
quality, nature;
sex
41;61 8 (2)

怔 zhēng
terrified
-
41;61 8 (-)

恨 hèn
hate;
regret
41;61 9 (2)

惟 wéi
solely;
thought
41;61 11 (4)

慨 kǎi
angry; touched;
generous
41;61 12 (4)

惭 慚 cán
ashamed
-
41;61 11 (3)

懒 懶 lǎn
lazy;
sluggish
41;61 16 (2)

惦 diàn
think of;
concerned
41;61 11 (3)

慷 kāng
generous;
vehement
41;61 14 (4)

怖 bù
fear
-
41;61 8 (3)

恢 huī
vast;
resume
41;61 9 (2)

忧 憂 yōu
worry, anxious;
grief
41;61 7 (4)

悯 憫 mǐn
pity,
sympathize
41;61 ˙10 (-)

忙	恼	惊	怕	惶	愧
máng	nǎo	驚 jīng	pà	huáng	kuì
busy; hurried, hasty	angry; worried	startled, alarmed	afraid; worried; possibly	fear -	ashamed -
41;61 6 (1)	41;61 9 (4)	41;187 11 (2)	41;61 8 (1)	41;61 12 (-)	41;61 12 (3)

忧	怯	惋	愤	慎	情
憂 yōu	qiè	wǎn	憤 fèn	shèn	qíng
worry, anxious; grief	timid, cowardly	sigh; sympathize	resent; indignant	cautious -	emotion; love; favor; situation
41;61 7 (4)	41;61 8 (4)	41;61 11 (4)	41;61 12 (2)	41;61 14 (3)	41;61 11 (1)

悼	惜	慌	懂
dào	xī	huāng	dǒng
mourn, lament	cherish; pity; begrudge	flustered; scared	understand -
41;61 11 (4)	41;61 11 (3)	41;61 12 (2)	41;61 15 (1)

悦	恍	悄	憎
yuè	huǎng	qiǎo qiāo	zēng
pleased; to please	sudden; seemingly	quiet; softly	hate, detest
41;61 10 (3)	41;61 9 (-)	41;61 10 (2)	41;61 15 (-)

恒	悟	怪
恆 héng	wù	guài
permanent; persist; usual	realize, understand	strange; very; monster; blame
41;61 9 (4)	41;61 10 (2)	41;61 8 (2)

悍	惕	慢	愣	惯	惧
hàn	tì	màn	lèng	慣 guàn	懼 jù
fierce, brave	vigilant -	slow; postpone; haughty	dazed; reckless	habitual; pamper	fear, dread
41;61 10 (-)	41;61 11 (3)	41;61 14 (1)	41;61 12 (3)	41;61 11 (1)	41;61 11 (4)

悔	惰	憾
huǐ	duò	hàn
regret, repent	lazy -	regret -
41;61 10 (2)	41;61 12 (4)	41;61 16 (3)

怜	恰	愉	怡	惨
憐 lián	qià	yú	yí	慘 cǎn
pity, sympathy; pamper	suitable; exactly	happy -	happy (literary)	pitiful; cruel; seriously
41;61 8 (2)	41;61 9 (3)	41;61 12 (1)	41;61 8 (-)	41;61 11 (3)

次 冰 决 冻 冲

次 cì
sequence; 2nd;
next; inferior
8;76 6 (1)

冰 *冰 bīng
ice
-
8;15 6 (2)

决 *決 jué
decide, resolve;
definitely; &
8;15 6 (1)

冻 *凍 dòng
freeze
-
8;15 7 (2)

冲 *沖 衝 chōng chòng
add water, rinse, flush;
rush; clash; vigorous; &
8;15 6 (2)

冯 况 凉 冶 冷

冯 *馮 féng
(surname)
-
8;187 5 (4)

况 *況 kuàng
situation;
compare
8;15 7 (1)

凉 *涼 liáng liàng
cool, cold;
disappointed
8;15 10 (1)

冶 yě
smelt
-
8;15 7 (3)

冷 lěng
cold, frosty;
rare; deserted
8;15 7 (1)

凌 凄 凑 净 凛

凌 líng
approach; rise;
soar; insult
8;15 10 (4)

凄 *淒 悽 qī
chilly; sad;
bleak
8;15 10 (4)

凑 *湊 còu
get together;
luckily
8;15 11 (3)

净 *淨 jìng
completely; net
(profit); clean
8;15 8 (1)

凛 lǐn
cold; strict;
apprehensive
8;15 15 (-)

准 凝 凋 减

准 *準 zhǔn
allow; quasi-;
definitely; &
8;15 10 (1)

凝 níng
solidify;
concentrate
8;15 16 (3)

凋 diāo
wither;
fade
8;15 10 (-)

减 *減 jiǎn
subtract,
deduct, reduce
8;15 11 (2)

兆 习 羽

兆 zhào
omen; portend;
million, mega-
29;10 6 (4)

习 習 xí
practice; be
used to; habit
6;124 3 (1)

羽 yǔ
feather
-
183;124 6 (2)

 疒 → 33

求 录 隶 救 剥 弱

求 qiú
beg, request;
seek
1;85 7 (1)

录 錄 lù
record;
employ
70;167 8 (1)

隶 隸 lì
subordinate,
servant, slave
124;171 8 (3)

救 jiù
rescue,
aid
113;66 11 (2)

剥 剝 bāo bō
peel off
-
17;18 10 (3)

弱 ruò
weak; inferior;
a bit less
71;57 10 (2)

 状 壮 妆 将

状 狀 zhuàng
form, condition;
certificate; &
42;94 7 (2)

壮 壯 zhuàng
strong, robust;
boost; grand
42;33 6 (3)

妆 妝 zhuāng
adorn;
apply make-up
42;38 6 (4)

将 將 jiāng jiàng
going to, about to; (preposition);
incite; commander; &
42;41 9 (1)

兆 北 乖 乘

兆 zhào
omen; portend;
million, mega-
29;10 6 (4)

北 běi
north
-
39;21 5 (1)

乖 guāi
obedient;
quick-witted
4;4 8 (3)

乘 chéng shèng
ride; multiply;
make use of
149;4 10 (2)

火

灶
zào
kitchen;
oven, stove
83;86 7 (4)

燦 càn
[magnificent,
bright]
83;86 7 (3)

烛
燭 zhú
candle;
watt
83;86 10 (3)

炼
煉 liàn
refine,
smelt, temper
83;86 9 (1)

灯
燈 dēng
lamp, light,
lantern
83;86 6 (1)

炸
zhà zhá
explode; to
bomb; deep-fry
83;86 9 (3)

炊
chuī
to cook
-
83;86 8 (4)

烁
爍 shuò
glittering;
sparkle
83;86 9 (3)

炉
爐 lú
stove,
furnace
83;86 8 (3)

炕
kàng
to dry; kang,
heated bricks
83;86 8 (4)

炒
chǎo
fry, stir-fry;
heat up
83;86 8 (3)

熔
róng
melt, fuse,
smelt
83;86 14 (4)

煌
huáng
bright,
luminous
83;86 13 (3)

熄
xī
extinguish,
(fire) go out
83;86 14 (4)

烧
燒 shāo
burn; fever;
to cook, heat
83;86 10 (1)

烂
爛 làn
mushy; messy;
rotten; worn out
83;86 9 (2)

烘
hōng
bake;
to dry (at a fire)
83;86 10 (4)

煤
méi
coal
-
83;86 13 (2)

烦
煩 fán
vexed; tired of;
bother, trouble
83;86 10 (1)

焊
hàn
weld,
solder
83;86 11 (3)

爆
bào
explode, burst;
quick-fry
83;86 19 (3)

燥
zào
dry,
arid
83;86 17 (2)

焰
yàn
flame,
blaze
83;86 12 (3)

焕
煥 huàn
shining,
brilliant
83;86 11 (-)

燃
rán
burn,
ignite
83;86 16 (2)

烤
kǎo
bake,
roast
83;86 10 (2)

燧
suì
flint;
beacon fire
83;86 16 (-)

炮
pào páo bāo
artillery; to dry;
quick-fry
83;86 9 (2)

烟
*煙 菸 yān
smoke, mist;
tobacco; opium
83;86 10 (2)

1	41
2	42
3	43
4	44
5	45
6	46
7	47
8	48
9	49
10	50
11	51
12	52
13	53
14	54
15	55
16	56
17	57
18	58
19	59
20	60
21	61
22	62
23	63
24	64
25	65
26	66
27	67
28	68
29	69
30	70
31	71
32	72
33	73
34	74
35	75
36	76
37	77
38	78
39	79
40	80

■ 讠 讠 讠 讠 讠 讠

讠

计	让	认	诀	讲
計 jì	讓 ràng	認 rèn	訣 jué	講 jiǎng
compute; plan; meter, gauge	cede, allow; invite; &	recognize, admit; adopt	farewell; know-how	speak, discuss, tell, explain; &
10;149 4 (1)	10;149 5 (1)	10;149 4 (1)	10;149 6 (-)	10;149 6 (1)

许	诈	记	讥	诅	课
許 xǔ	詐 zhà	記 jì	譏 jī	詛 zǔ	課 kè
allow; promise; praise; maybe	cheat, swindle; feign; bluff	recall; a mark; note down	ridicule -	[to curse] -	lesson, course, class; tax
10;149 6 (1)	10;149 7 (4)	10;149 5 (1)	10;149 4 (4)	10;149 7 (-)	10;149 10 (1)

订	证	讶	评	诬
訂 dìng	証 證 zhèng	訝 yà	評 píng	誣 wū
fix; agree on; book (seats); &	prove; evidence; certificate; &	astonished (literary)	comment on, appraise, judge	falsely accuse
10;149 4 (2)	10;149 7 (2)	10;149 6 (3)	10;149 7 (1)	10;149 9 (3)

讠

训	诽	讹	谁	谢
訓 xùn	誹 fěi	訛 é	誰 shuí shéi	謝 xiè
teach, instruct; model, example	slander -	error; extort; blackmail	Who?; anyone	thanks; politely decline; wither
10;149 5 (2)	10;149 10 (4)	10;149 6 (4)	10;149 10 (1)	10;149 12 (1)

讠

讨	讯	词	询
討 tǎo	訊 xùn	詞 cí	詢 xún
discuss; incur; demand; &	interrogate; news, report	words, speech	inquire -
10;149 5 (1)	10;149 5 (2)	10;149 7 (1)	10;149 8 (3)

试	诫	诚
試 shì	誡 jiè	誠 chéng
try, attempt; trial, test	warn, admonish	sincere -
10;149 8 (1)	10;149 9 (4)	10;149 8 (2)

讠

谜	谴	诞
謎 mí mèi	譴 qiǎn	誕 dàn
riddle, puzzle	[condemn, denounce]	birth; birthday; fantastic
10;149 11 (3)	10;149 15 (4)	10;149 8 (3)

讠
讠

诉	讽	调
訴 sù	諷 fēng	調 tiáo diào
inform; accuse; complain	satire; mock	mix; fit in; mediate; provoke; move, transfer; melody; &
10;149 7 (1)	10;149 6 (3)	10;149 10 (1)

 日

议 議 yì	访 訪 fāng	谅 諒 liàng	该 該 gāi	谊 誼 yì	诧 詫 chà
opinion; discuss	visit; inquire, search for	forgive; guess, suppose	ought; deserve; the aforesaid; &	friendship	surprised
10;149 5 (2)	10;149 6 (1)	10;149 10 (1)	10;149 8 (1)	- 10;149 10 (1)	- 10;149 8 (4)

诗 詩 shī	读 讀 dú dòu	谈 談 tán	请 請 qǐng	诸 諸 zhū	谤 謗 bàng
poetry	read, recite; study	discuss; conversation	please; ask, invite	all, every; various	slander (literary)
- 10;149 8 (2)	10;149 10 (1)	10;149 10 (1)	10;149 10 (1)	10;149 10 (4)	10;149 12 (4)

详 詳 xiáng	说 說 shuō shuì	谦 謙 qiān	谱 譜 pǔ
detailed; fully known	speak; explain; theory; scold; &	modest	chart, register; melody; &
10;149 8 (2)	10;149 9 (1)	- 10;149 12 (3)	10;149 14 (4)

诺 諾 nuò	谎 謊 huǎng	谋 謀 móu	谨 謹 jǐn
promise; yes; consent	lie, falsehood	plan; contrive; consult	cautious; sincere
10;149 10 (-)	10;149 11 (4)	10;149 11 (3)	10;149 13 (3)

诵 誦 sòng	译 譯 yì	语 語 yǔ	设 設 shè
recite	translate, interpret	language; say, speak; words	to found, establish; &
- 10;149 9 (3)	10;149 7 (1)	10;149 9 (1)	10;149 6 (1)

识 識 shí zhì	误 誤 wù	课 課 kè	谓 謂 wèi	谭 譚 tán
knowledge; know; opinion	mistake; harm; miss (train)	lesson, course; class; tax	say; to name; meaning	(surname)
10;149 7 (1)	10;149 9 (1)	10;149 10 (1)	10;149 11 (2)	- 10;149 14 (-)

话 話 huà	谣 謠 yáo	诱 誘 yòu	诡 詭 guǐ	谗 讒 chán
speech, word; talk, talk about	song, ballad; rumor	guide, lead; entice	cunning, tricky; weird	slander
10;149 8 (1)	10;149 12 (3)	10;149 9 (4)	10;149 8 (-)	- 10;149 11 (4)

论 論 lùn lún	诠 詮 quán	诊 診 zhěn	讼 訟 sòng	谐 諧 xié	谬 謬 miù
discuss; theory; decide; &	[annotate]	examine (a patient)	dispute; litigate	in accord; humorous	mistaken; untrue
10;149 6 (1)	- 10;149 8 (-)	10;149 7 (3)	10;149 6 (4)	10;149 11 (4)	10;149 13 (4)

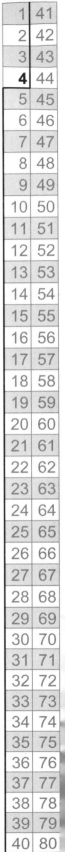

1	41
2	42
3	43
4	44
5	45
6	46
7	47
8	48
9	49
10	50
11	51
12	52
13	53
14	54
15	55
16	56
17	57
18	58
19	59
20	60
21	61
22	62
23	63
24	64
25	65
26	66
27	67
28	68
29	69
30	70
31	71
32	72
33	73
34	74
35	75
36	76
37	77
38	78
39	79
40	80

■ 泊 ： 泊 泊 泊

泊
泊
泊

沪	泣	注	泳	泌	浅
滬 hù	qì	*註 zhù	yǒng	mì	淺 qiǎn
Shanghai -	weep; tears	pour; pay heed; take notes; &	swim -	secrete -	shallow; simple; light (color); &
40;85 7 (4)	40;85 8 (4)	40;85 8 (1)	40;85 8 (1)	40;85 8 (3)	40;85 8 (1)

浪	泊	澳	浦	消	
làng	bó pō	澳 ào	pǔ	xiāo	
wave, billow; dissolute	anchor, moor; lake, pool	bay, inlet, harbor	river bank, river mouth	vanish; dispel; leisurely	
40;85 10 (2)	40;85 8 (4)	40;85 15 (4)	40;85 10 (-)	40;85 10 (1)	

淳	济	流	滚	潦	
chún	濟 jǐ jì	liú	滾 gǔn	liǎo lǎo	
honest (literary)	many (people); aid, relief	stream, current, flow; grade; &	tumble; boil; Get lost!	sloppy, hasty; unlucky; puddle	
40;85 11 (-)	40;85 9 (1)	40;85 10 (1)	40;85 13 (2)	40;85 15 (4)	

液	湾	滴			
yè	灣 wān	dī			
liquid, fluid	gulf, bay, bend in river	drip, drop, trickle			
40;85 11 (2)	40;85 12 (4)	40;85 14 (2)			

浓	淀	滨	演	溶	
濃 nóng	澱 diàn	濱 bīn	yǎn	róng	
dense, thick	sediment; shallow lake	seashore, brink	develop; perform; &	dissolve -	
40;85 9 (2)	40;85 11 (4)	40;85 13 (4)	40;85 14 (1)	40;85 13 (3)	

沾	洁	法	浩	洗	溃
zhān	潔 jié	fǎ	hào	xǐ	潰 kuì
wet; moisten; stain; touch	clean, neat	law; method; model for	vast, great	wash; redress; to loot	overflow; break through; ulcer
40;85 8 (3)	40;85 9 (3)	40;85 8 (1)	40;85 10 (4)	40;85 9 (1)	40;85 12 (4)

沙	涉	清	渣	漆	滞
shā	shè	qīng	zhā	qī	滯 zhì
sand; granules; hoarse	wade; involve; to experience	clear; settle up; quiet; fully; &	shards; dregs, sediment	paint, lacquer	stagnant -
40;85 7 (2)	40;85 10 (3)	40;85 11 (1)	40;85 12 (3)	40;85 14 (3)	40;85 12 (4)

浅	浇	淡	淹		
淺 qiǎn	澆 jiāo	dàn	yān		
shallow; simple; light (color); &	to water, irrigate	insipid; pale; indifferent	inundate; drown; sweaty		
40;85 8 (1)	40;85 9 (3)	40;85 11 (2)	40;85 11 (3)		

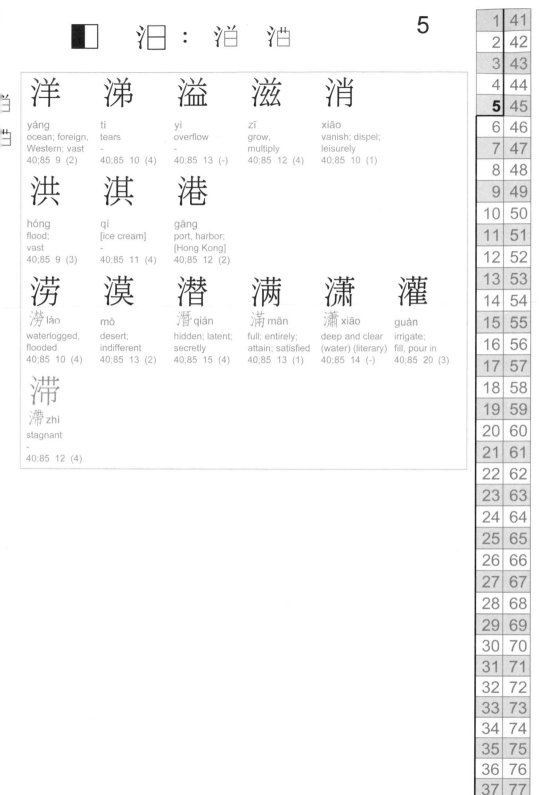

■□　　汩　：　沿　洎

洋	涕	溢	滋	消
yáng	tì	yì	zī	xiāo
ocean; foreign, Western; vast	tears	overflow	grow, multiply	vanish; dispel; leisurely
-	-	-		
40;85 9 (2)	40;85 10 (4)	40;85 13 (-)	40;85 12 (4)	40;85 10 (1)

洪	淇	港
hóng	qí	gǎng
flood; vast	[ice cream]	port, harbor; [Hong Kong]
-		
40;85 9 (3)	40;85 11 (4)	40;85 12 (2)

涝	漠	潜	满	潇	灌
澇 lào	mò	潛 qián	滿 mǎn	瀟 xiāo	guàn
waterlogged, flooded	desert; indifferent	hidden; latent; secretly	full; entirely; attain; satisfied	deep and clear (water) (literary)	irrigate; fill, pour in
40;85 10 (4)	40;85 13 (2)	40;85 15 (4)	40;85 13 (1)	40;85 14 (-)	40;85 20 (3)

滞
滯 zhì
stagnant
-
40;85 12 (4)

泪

污	添	泽	涌	涵
*汙 污 wū	tiān	澤 zé	湧 yǒng	hán
dirt, filth; smear; corrupt	add, increase	pond, marsh; damp; luster	gush, surge; emerge	contain; culvert
40;85 6 (2)	40;85 11 (2)	40;85 8 (3)	40;85 10 (3)	40;85 11 (-)

没	沿	沼	浸	涩
沒 méi mò	yán yàn	zhǎo	jìn	澀 sè
[not]; sink, submerge	along; follow; border, edge	pond, pool	soak, immerse	astringent; rough; difficult
40;85 7 (1)	40;85 8 (2)	40;85 8 (4)	40;85 10 (3)	40;85 10 (-)

涡	滑	澡	漂	潭
渦 wō	huá	zǎo	piāo piǎo piào	tán
eddy, whirlpool	slide; slippery, smooth; crafty	bath -	to float; rinse; beautiful; &	pond, pool
40;85 10 (-)	40;85 12 (2)	40;85 16 (1)	40;85 14 (1)	40;85 15 (4)

温	湿	混	渴	漫	瀑
wēn	濕 溼 shī	hùn hún	kě	màn	pù
warm; thermo-; review	wet, damp	mix up; pass for; &	thirsty -	overflow; freely; everywhere	waterfall -
40;85 12 (2)	40;85 12 (2)	40;85 11 (2)	40;85 12 (1)	40;85 14 (3)	40;85 18 (4)

泪

沃	泛	活
wò	*氾 汎 fàn	huó
irrigate; fertile	general, vague; to flood	alive; moving; work, labor; &
40;85 7 (4)	40;85 7 (2)	40;85 9 (1)

浮	淫	滔	溪	潘
fú	yín	tāo	xī	pān
to float; hollow; fleeting; &	excessive; lewd	flood; torrential	brook, small stream	(surname) -
40;85 10 (2)	40;85 11 (4)	40;85 13 (4)	40;85 13 (4)	40;85 15 (4)

沉
chén
to sink; lower;
profound; heavy
40;85 7 (2)

瀉 xiè
flow swiftly;
torrent; diarrhea
40;85 8 (4)

渾 hún
muddy; foolish;
simple; entire
40;85 9 (3)

深
shēn
deep; very; late;
intimate; &
40;85 11 (1)

汽
qì
vapor,
steam
40;85 7 (1)

海
hǎi
sea;
huge
40;85 10 (1)

*淨 jìng
completely; net
(profit); clean
8;15 8 (1)

漁 yú
fishing
-
40;85 11 (3)

洛
luò
(a river)
-
40;85 9 (-)

滌 dí
wash, cleanse
(literary)
40;85 10 (4)

洽
qià
harmonious;
discuss
40;85 9 (4)

滄 cāng
deep blue
(sea)
40;85 7 (-)

淪 lún
sink;
be reduced to
40;85 7 (-)

塗 tú
rub on, smear;
erase; scrawl
40;32 10 (2)

浴
yù
bath,
bathe
40;85 10 (3)

治
zhì
control; peace;
cure; study; &
40;85 8 (1)

滲 shèn
seep, ooze,
leak
40;85 11 (4)

淆
xiáo
confuse;
mix up
40;85 11 (3)

滯 zhì
stagnant
-
40;85 12 (4)

濫 làn
excessive;
overflow
40;85 13 (3)

澄
chéng
clear,
transparent
40;85 15 (4)

澀 sè
astringent;
rough; difficult
40;85 10 (-)

溜
liū liù
glide; smooth; slip away; row of;
flow of water; gutter; locality
40;85 13 (3)

1	41
2	42
3	43
4	44
5	45
6	46
7	47
8	48
9	49
10	50
11	51
12	52
13	53
14	54
15	55
16	56
17	57
18	58
19	59
20	60
21	61
22	62
23	63
24	64
25	65
26	66
27	67
28	68
29	69
30	70
31	71
32	72
33	73
34	74
35	75
36	76
37	77
38	78
39	79
40	80

汁	江	汇	汗	汪
zhī	jiāng	huì	hàn hán	wāng
juice	river	gather, meet; remit (money)	sweat	form puddles; (dog's) bark
-				
40;85 5 (4)	40;85 6 (1)	40;22 5 (3)	40;85 6 (2)	40;85 7 (4)

沐	沫	沛	池	泄	浅
mù	mò	pèi	chí	xiè	qiǎn
wash (hair), [bathe]	foam	copious	pond; sunken area	release, let out, to vent, to leak	shallow; simple; light (color); &
-	-	-			
40;85 7 (-)	40;85 8 (4)	40;85 7 (4)	40;85 6 (2)	40;85 8 (4)	40;85 8 (1)

沃	汰	沈	波	泌
wò	tài	shěn	bō	mì
irrigate; fertile	clean out; discard	(surname)	a wave	secrete
		-	-	-
40;85 7 (4)	40;85 7 (4)	40;85 7 (3)	40;85 8 (3)	40;85 8 (3)

汉	汝	汤
hàn	rǔ	tāng
Chinese (lang); Han; man	you (literary)	hot water; soup
40;85 5 (1)	40;85 6 (-)	40;85 6 (1)

津	沸	浦
jīn	fèi	pǔ
ferry; moist; sweat; saliva	boil (water)	river bank, river mouth
40;85 9 (4)	- 40;85 8 (3)	40;85 10 (-)

浊	油	泪	沮
zhuó	yóu	lèi	jǔ
turbid, muddy; chaotic	oil, grease, fat; to paint	teardrop	dispirited; prevent
40;85 9 (4)	40;85 8 (2)	- 40;85 8 (2)	40;85 8 (-)

洒	酒
sǎ	jiǔ
sprinkle; spill	wine, liquor
40;85 9 (2)	40;164 10 (1)

洲 zhōu	泌 mì	淮 huái	滩 tān	涨 zhǎng zhàng
continent; shoals, islet	secrete	[Huaihe river]	beach, sands; shoals, rapids	rise, go up; swell
40;85 9 (4)	40;85 8 (3)	40;85 11 (4)	40;85 13 (3)	40;85 10 (2)

沏 qī	浙 zhè	渐 jiàn jiān	游 *遊 yóu	渊 yuān	润 rùn
infuse	Zhejiang	gradually	swim; wander; reach (of river)	deep; profound	moist; lubricate; adorn; profit
40;85 7 (4)	40;85 10 (3)	40;85 11 (2)	40;85 12 (1)	40;85 11 (-)	40;85 10 (3)

溯 sù	湖 hú	潮 cháo	澎 pēng péng	淋 lín lìn	淑 shū
go against flow; trace back	lake	tide, upsurge; damp	splash; sound of waves	drenched; filter	virtuous (literary)
40;85 13 (-)	40;85 12 (3)	40;85 15 (1)	40;85 15 (-)	40;85 11 (3)	40;85 11 (-)

渺 miǎo	溉 gài	激 jī	鸿 hóng	测 cè	溅 jiàn
vast (lake, sea); hazy; negligible	[wash, irrigate]	violent; arouse; annoy; chill	swan, goose; grand	to measure; predict, infer	splash
40;85 12 (4)	40;85 12 (3)	40;85 16 (2)	40;196 11 (-)	40;85 9 (2)	40;85 12 (3)

沥 lì	涯 yá	源 yuán	渡 dù	滤 lǜ
trickle, drip	limit, margin; shoreline	source	cross (a river); ferry	filter
40;85 7 (4)	40;85 11 (-)	40;85 13 (2)	40;85 12 (2)	40;85 13 (4)

派 pài	波 bō	泼 pō	涛 tāo	泥 ní nì	漏 lòu
clan, faction; style; send	a wave	sprinkle; unreasonable	great waves, billows	mashed (food); mud, plaster	omit; leak; divulge
40;85 9 (1)	40;85 8 (3)	40;85 8 (2)	40;85 10 (4)	40;85 8 (2)	40;85 14 (2)

汛 xùn	河 hé	沟 gōu	泡 pào pāo	淘 táo
flood	river	ditch, ravine, channel, groove	bubble; soak; dawdle; spongy	rinse, clean out; bothersome
40;85 6 (4)	40;85 8 (1)	40;85 7 (3)	40;85 8 (3)	40;85 11 (4)

润 rùn	洞 dòng	汹 xiōng	涵 hán
moist; lubricate; adorn; profit	hole, cave; thoroughly	[turbulent]	contain; culvert
40;85 10 (3)	40;85 9 (2)	40;85 7 (4)	40;85 11 (-)

1	41
2	42
3	43
4	44
5	45
6	46
7	47
8	48
9	49
10	50
11	51
12	52
13	53
14	54
15	55
16	56
17	57
18	58
19	59
20	60
21	61
22	62
23	63
24	64
25	65
26	66
27	67
28	68
29	69
30	70
31	71
32	72
33	73
34	74
35	75
36	76
37	77
38	78
39	79
40	80

伯 :   伯 伯

 伯
伯
伯

仪 yí	代 dài	伐 fá	伏 fú	优 yōu	伪 wěi
apparatus; gift; rite; appearance	substitute for; era, generation	cut down (tree); attack	prostrate; hide; confess; &	excellent -	fake; bogus
21;9 5 (2)	21;9 5 (1)	21;9 6 (4)	21;9 6 (4)	21;9 6 (2)	21;9 6 (4)

仿 fǎng	位 wèi	住 zhù	依 yī	信 xìn	傅 fù
imitate; resemble	place, seat, throne	live, reside; stay; cease	according to; comply; rely on	true; believe; letter, news; &	teach, teacher; apply (paint)
21;9 6 (2)	21;9 7 (1)	21;9 7 (1)	21;9 8 (2)	21;9 9 (1)	21;9 12 (1)

伯 bó bǎi	倍 bèi	停 tíng	傍 bàng	偏 piān	傻 shǎ
uncle; earl	double; multiple	stop, halt, stay; park (car)	draw near; close to	leaning; biased; perverse	stupid, dumb; mechanically
21;9 7 (2)	21;9 10 (1)	21;9 11 (1)	21;9 12 (2)	21;9 11 (2)	21;9 13 (2)

估 gū	侍 shì	佳 jiā	债 zhài	值 zhí	
to estimate -	attend, wait on	beautiful, fine	debt -	value, price; on duty; happen to	
21;9 7 (2)	21;9 8 (4)	21;9 8 (3)	21;9 10 (3)	21;9 10 (2)	

侦 zhēn	催 cuī	倚 yǐ	僚 liáo		
spy; scout; detect	to urge; expedite	lean on, rely on	official -		
21;9 8 (4)	21;9 13 (2)	21;9 10 (3)	21;9 14 (3)		

 佲
佲

倦 juàn	僧 sēng	俏 qiào	倘 tǎng	偿 cháng	伴 bàn
tired -	Buddhist monk	handsome; in demand	if -	compensate; fulfil	partner; accompany
21;9 10 (3)	21;9 14 (-)	21;9 9 (3)	21;9 10 (3)	21;9 11 (3)	21;9 7 (3)

供 gōng gòng	借 jiè				
supply; confess; &	*藉 borrow; lend; pretext				
21;9 8 (2)	21;9 10 (1)				

仁
rén
benevolence;
kernel
21;9 4 (4)

侄
zhí
nephew
-
21;9 8 (4)

佰
bǎi
hundred
-
21;9 8 (-)

儒
rú
Confucian
-
21;9 16 (-)

僵
jiāng
numb; stiff,
rigid; impasse
21;9 15 (3)

侯
hóu
marquis
-
21;9 9 (4)

侵
qīn
invade; intrude;
approaching
21;9 9 (2)

侣 lǚ
companion,
mate
21;9 8 (4)

保
bǎo
protect;
ensure
21;9 9 (2)

促
cù
to urge;
urgent; hurry
21;9 9 (2)

但
dàn
but, yet;
merely
21;9 7 (1)

倡
chàng
initiate
-
21;9 10 (2)

俱
jù
all,
complete
21;9 10 (2)

偶
ǒu
mate; in pairs;
idol; by chance
21;9 11 (3)

低
dī
low;
to lower
21;9 7 (1)

侨 qiáo
live abroad,
expatriot
21;9 8 (3)

俘
fú
capture;
prisoner
21;9 9 (4)

伤 shāng
wound; harm,
hurt; get sick of
21;9 6 (2)

侮
wǔ
to bully;
to insult
21;9 9 (3)

侈
chǐ
extravagant;
prattle (literary)
21;9 8 (4)

像
xiàng
shape; be like;
(see Table 1)
21;9 13 (1)

价 jià jie
value,
price
21;9 6 (2)

伦 lún
series; peer;
(feudal) ethics
21;9 6 (-)

伶
líng
actor (archaic);
[clever; bereft]
21;9 7 (4)

俭 jiǎn
thrifty,
frugal
21;9 9 (4)

偷
tōu
steal;
stealthy
21;9 11 (2)

份
fèn
portion,
share
21;9 6 (2)

俗
sú
custom, habit;
popular; vulgar
21;9 9 (2)

俊
jùn
handsome;
talented
21;9 9 (4)

倪
ní
[inkling];
(surname)
21;9 10 (-)

1	41
2	42
3	43
4	44
5	45
6	46
7	47
8	48
9	49
10	50
11	51
12	52
13	53
14	54
15	55
16	56
17	57
18	58
19	59
20	60
21	61
22	62
23	63
24	64
25	65
26	66
27	67
28	68
29	69
30	70
31	71
32	72
33	73
34	74
35	75
36	76
37	77
38	78
39	79
40	80

仆	亿	化	仅	什	仕
*僕 pú pū	億 yì	huà huā	僅 jǐn	*甚 shén shí	shì
servant; fall prostrate	a hundred million	alter; -ise, -ify; melt; spend; &	merely; barely	[what?]; sundry; ten	an official -
21;9 4 (4)	21;9 3 (1)	21;21 4 (1)	21;9 4 (2)	21;9 4 (1)	21;9 5 (-)

件	仟	任	伍	作
jiàn	qiān	rèn rén	wǔ	zuò zuō zuó
thing; letter, document	thousand -	appoint; allow; despite; &	five; 5-man platoon	do, make, write; act as; pretend; regard as; get up (from bed); &
21;9 6 (1)	21;9 5 (-)	21;9 6 (1)	21;9 6 (2)	21;9 7 (1)

仙	仗	仇	仔	仍	伊
xiān	zhàng	chóu	zǐ zī zǎi	réng	yī
immortal being; fairy	hold (weapon); rely on; battle	hatred; enemy	young animal; [careful]	still, yet	he, she; ('i' sound)
21;9 5 (4)	21;9 5 (3)	21;9 4 (3)	21;9 5 (2)	21;9 4 (2)	21;9 6 (3)

休	体
xiū	體 tǐ tī
to stop; to rest; Don't!	body; in person; style; system
21;9 6 (1)	21;188 7 (1)

你	他	伟	传
*妳 nǐ	tā	偉 wěi	傳 chuán zhuàn
you, your	he, him; other, another	great -	pass on, transmit; &
21;9 7 (1)	21;9 5 (1)	21;9 6 (1)	21;9 6 (2)

付	代	伐	伏	优	伪
fù	dài	fá	fú	優 yōu	偽 僞 wěi
pay, hand over	substitute for; era, generation	cut down (tree); attack	prostrate; hide; confess; &	excellent -	fake, bogus
21;9 5 (2)	21;9 5 (1)	21;9 6 (4)	21;9 6 (4)	21;9 6 (2)	21;9 6 (4)

伴	侠	佛	俩	俄
bàn	俠 xiá	*彿 fó fú	倆 liǎ liǎng	é
partner; accompany	[chivalrous] -	Buddha -	two, both, several (colloq)	soon, presently
21;9 7 (3)	21;9 8 (-)	21;9 7 (2)	21;9 9 (1)	21;9 9 (3)

仲	伸	使	便	佣
zhòng	shēn	shǐ	biàn pián	傭 yòng yōng
go-between; middle (of 3)	stretch, extend	send; envoy; use; enable; if	convenient; informal; &	fee; servant, hired labor
21;9 6 (-)	21;9 7 (2)	21;9 8 (1)	21;9 9 (1)	21;9 7 (4)

伙
*夥 huǒ
partner; group;
provisions
21;9 6 (2)

似
sì shì
similar;
seem; than
21;9 6 (2)

仰
yǎng
face up;
admire; rely on
21;9 6 (2)

们
們 men
(plural suffix)
-
21;9 5 (1)

候
hòu
await; ask after;
time, season
21;9 10 (1)

修
xiū
repair; amend;
build; study; &
21;9 9 (2)

例
lì
example; rules;
precedent
21;9 8 (1)

俐
lì
[clever]
-
21;9 9 (4)

侧
側 cè
side;
to lean, incline
21;9 8 (3)

倒
dǎo dào
topple, collapse; exchange;
pour; invert; go back; &
21;9 10 (1)

做
zuò
make, do, write;
be, become; &
21;9 11 (1)

傲
ào
defy; proud,
arrogant
21;9 13 (2)

假
jiǎ jià
fake; borrow;
vacation; &
21;9 11 (1)

僻
pì
secluded,
eccentric
21;9 15 (4)

倾
傾 qīng
collapse; lean,
incline; pour out
21;9 10 (3)

储
儲 chǔ
store up
-
21;9 12 (4)

佐
zuǒ
assist
-
21;9 7 (-)

佑
*祐 yòu
help; protect;
bless
21;9 7 (-)

俯
fǔ
condescend;
bow one's head
21;9 10 (3)

何
hé
What?, Who?
etc. (literary)
21;9 7 (1)

伺
sì cì
to watch; await;
serve
21;9 7 (3)

付
fù
pay,
hand over
21;9 5 (2)

健
jiàn
healthy, strong;
invigorate
21;9 10 (1)

佩
pèi
admire; wear
(sword, badge)
21;9 8 (3)

伪
偽 僞 wěi
fake,
bogus
21;9 6 (4)

彳

律	征	很	往	彷	彼
lǜ	*徵 zhēng	hěn	wàng wǎng	páng	bǐ
law, rule	travel; solicit; sign; evidence	very -	towards; go; previous	[hesitate, waver]	that; the other; he, she
62;60 9 (2)	62;60 8 (2)	62;60 9 (1)	62;60 8 (1)	62;60 7 (-)	62;60 8 (3)

径	役	得	後	徐
徑 jìng	yì	de dé děi	hòu	xú
path; directly; diameter	compel; battle; service; servant	(particle); fit for; get; need; must	after (see Table 1)	slowly, gently
62;60 8 (3)	62;60 7 (4)	62;60 11 (1)	62;60 9 (-)	62;60 10 (4)

待	徒	德	循	徊
dài dāi	tú	dé	xún	huái
await; about to; to treat; stay; &	walk; merely; bare; in vain; &	virtue; kindness	follow; comply with	[hesitate, waver]
62;60 9 (2)	62;60 10 (3)	62;60 15 (2)	62;60 12 (3)	62;60 9 (4)

衍	衔	街	衡	行
yǎn	銜 xián	jiē	héng	xíng háng
redundant; spread (literary)	hold (in mouth); rank, title	street -	scales; weigh, measure	go; do, perform; capable; OK; for now; line; (business) firm
62;144 9 (4)	62;167 11 (4)	62;144 12 (1)	62;144 16 (3)	62;144 6 (1)

徘	彻	御	微	徽
pái	徹 chè	*禦 yù	wēi	huī
[hesitate, waver, linger]	thorough; penetrate	drive (vehicle); resist; imperial	micro-, tiny; wane; subtle	emblem -
62;60 11 (4)	62;60 7 (2)	62;60 12 (3)	62;60 13 (2)	62;60 17 (4)

十

协	博
協 xié	bó
together, jointly; assist	plentiful; to gain, win
12;24 6 (3)	12;24 12 (3)

上

比	切	顷
bǐ	qiē qiè	頃 qǐng
compare; than; to gesture; &	slice; eager to; accord with; &	just now; (unit of land area)
123;81 4 (1)	27;18 4 (1)	39;181 8 (3)

止

此	歧	雌
cǐ	qí	cí
this -	fork (in road); diverge	female -
102;77 6 (2)	102;77 8 (4)	208;172 14 (4)

土

址 zhǐ	地 dì de	块 塊 kuài	坡 pō	坪 píng	坏 壞 huài
site, location	earth, soil; place; &	clod, lump; yuan (colloq)	slope	level ground	bad, evil; spoil, ruin
49;32 7 (2)	49;32 6 (1)	49;32 7 (1)	49;32 8 (2)	49;32 8 (-)	49;32 7 (1)

坤 kūn	埔 pǔ	埋 mái mán	圾 jī	场 場 chǎng cháng
feminine	[Huangpu]	bury	[garbage]	site, spot, field; &
49;32 8 (-)	49;32 10 (4)	49;32 10 (2)	49;32 6 (2)	49;32 6 (1)

堆 duī	圳 zhèn	墩 dūn	疆 jiāng
heap, pile	irrigation ditch; [Shenzhen]	mound; block	boundary, frontier
49;32 11 (2)	49;32 6 (-)	49;32 15 (-)	71;102 19 (3)

垃 lā	坟 墳 fén	坑 kēng	坊 fáng fāng	埠 bù	坯 pī
[garbage]	grave, tomb	hole, pit; tunnel; entrap	workshop, mill; lane, alley	jetty, port; city	semi-finished product
49;32 8 (2)	49;32 7 (3)	49;32 7 (3)	49;32 7 (4)	49;32 11 (4)	49;32 8 (4)

培 péi	境 jìng	壤 rǎng	填 tián	堵 dǔ	墙 牆 qiáng
cultivate, train, foster	boundary; place; situation	soil, earth, place	fill up; fill out (form)	block up, stifle, obstruct	wall
49;32 11 (3)	49;32 14 (2)	49;32 20 (3)	49;32 13 (2)	49;32 11 (2)	49;90 14 (1)

垮 kuǎ	埃 āi	堪 kān	塔 tǎ	增 zēng	坝 壩 bà
collapse, break down	dirt, dust	able to; bear, sustain	tower, pagoda	increase, grow	dyke, dam, embankment
49;32 9 (3)	49;32 10 (4)	49;32 12 (4)	49;32 12 (2)	49;32 15 (1)	49;32 7 (3)

坦 tǎn	堤 dī	塌 tā	埋 mái mán	坛 壇 壋 罎 罎 罎 tán
level, smooth; calm; candid	dyke, dam, embankment	collapse, cave in; calm down	bury	altar, platform; jar, jug
49;32 8 (3)	49;32 12 (3)	49;32 13 (3)	49;32 10 (2)	49;32 7 (4)

均 jūn	域 yù	城 chéng	坡 pō	塘 táng	墟 xū
equal, even, balanced; all	region, territory	(city) wall; city	slope	embankment; pool, pond	ruins; mound; market
49;32 7 (2)	49;32 11 (3)	49;32 9 (1)	49;32 8 (2)	49;32 13 (4)	49;32 14 (3)

1 41
2 42
3 43
4 44
5 45
6 46
7 47
8 48
9 49
10 50
11 51
12 52
13 53
14 54
15 55
16 56
17 57
18 58
19 59
20 60
21 61
22 62
23 63
24 64
25 65
26 66
27 67
28 68
29 69
30 70
31 71
32 72
33 73
34 74
35 75
36 76
37 77
38 78
39 79
40 80

拍
拍
拍

拍
pāi
clap, beat time;
bat, racquet; &
55;64 8 (1)

dǎo
to pound, beat;
harass
55;64 10 (4)

rǎo
harass, disturb;
trouble
55;64 7 (2)

找
zhǎo
seek; call on;
give change
55;64 7 (1)

我
wǒ
I, me, my,
we, our
101;62 7 (1)

hù
protect,
guard
55;149 7 (2)

拄
zhǔ
lean on
(walking stick)
55;64 8 (4)

捕
bǔ
catch, seize;
arrest
55;64 10 (2)

搏
bó
to fight;
throb; pounce
55;64 13 (4)

拉
lā lá lǎ
pull; lengthen;
cut; chat; &
55;64 8 (1)

抗
kàng
resist, defy,
anti-
55;64 7 (2)

jǐ
squeeze; jostle;
crowded
55;64 9 (1)

掠
lüè
plunder;
sweep past
55;64 11 (3)

摔
shuāi
fall, tumble;
fling; break
55;64 14 (2)

搞
gǎo
make, do; set
up; procure; &
55;64 13 (1)

接
jiē
receive; accept;
catch; connect
55;64 11 (1)

摘
zhāi
pick, pluck,
select
55;64 14 (2)

撞
zhuàng
rush; collide,
bump into
55;64 15 (2)

擅
shàn
excel at;
unilaterally
55;64 16 (4)

挖
wā
dig,
excavate
55;64 9 (2)

控
kòng
accuse;
control
55;64 11 (2)

按
àn
push; restrain;
according to; &
55;64 9 (2)

擦
cā
rub, wipe;
erase; &
55;64 17 (1)

níng nǐng nìng
wring, screw;
differ; mistake
55;64 8 (3)

技
jì
skill, ability;
talent
55;64 7 (1)

持
chí
hold, support,
maintain; &
55;64 9 (1)

guà
hang; to phone;
worry; register
55;64 9 (1)

指
zhǐ zhī zhí
finger; point at;
rely on
55;64 9 (1)

掉
diào
fall; drop, lose;
swap; turn back
55;64 11 (1)

抄
chāo
copy; shortcut;
confiscate; &
55;64 7 (2)

搏
bó
to fight;
throb; pounce
55;64 13 (4)

摧
cuī
break,
destroy
55;64 14 (3)

搜
*蒐 sōu
search
-
55;64 12 (3)

xié
carry, bring,
take along
55;64 13 (4)

捷
jié
victory;
quick, nimble
55;64 11 (3)

náo
scratch; hinder;
disturb; yield
55;64 9 (4)

掩
yǎn
cover, conceal;
shut
55;64 11 (3)

挎
kuà
carry (on arm
or shoulder)
55;64 9 (4)

揍
zòu
hit, strike
(colloq)
55;64 12 (4)

捧
pěng
flatter; hold in
both hands
55;64 11 (2)

拦
攔 lán
block,
obstruct
55;64 8 (2)

拼
*拼 pīn
piece together;
go all out
55;64 9 (2)

拌
bàn
mix
-
55;64 8 (4)

挡
擋 dǎng dàng
block, ward off;
gear (cars)
55;64 9 (2)

捎
shāo shào
take,
bring; &
55;64 10 (4)

撑
chēng
support, prop
up; fill; unfurl
55;64 15 (3)

搂
摟 lōu lǒu
extort; gather
up; embrace
55;64 12 (3)

搅
攪 jiǎo
stir, mix;
disturb
55;64 12 (3)

拱
gǒng
arch; encircle;
nudge; &
55;64 9 (4)

捞
撈 lāo
dredge, fish for;
get illicitly
55;64 10 (2)

措
cuò
arrange;
manage
55;64 11 (2)

搭
dā
build; join;
carry; travel; &
55;64 12 (2)

摸
mō
feel; grope for;
sound out
55;64 13 (2)

描
miáo
to trace, copy,
retouch
55;64 11 (2)

1	41
2	42
3	43
4	44
5	45
6	46
7	47
8	48
9	49
10	50
11	51
12	52
13	53
14	54
15	55
16	56
17	57
18	58
19	59
20	60
21	61
22	62
23	63
24	64
25	65
26	66
27	67
28	68
29	69
30	70
31	71
32	72
33	73
34	74
35	75
36	76
37	77
38	78
39	79
40	80

扌

择
擇 zé zhái
pick, choose
55;64 8 (2)

投
tóu
fling; leap into; send; deliver; &
55;64 7 (2)

招
zhāo
beckon; invite; recruit; incur; provoke; confess; a trick
55;64 8 (2)

拯
zhěng
rescue, save
55;64 9 (-)

抒
shū
express (an opinion)
55;64 7 (-)

捅
tǒng
poke, stab; disclose
55;64 10 (4)

揉
róu
rub, knead
55;64 12 (3)

捉
zhuō
grasp; seize, capture
55;64 10 (2)

拐
*拐 guǎi
to turn; abduct; swindle; limp
55;64 8 (2)

损
損 sǔn
decrease; loss; harm, damage
55;64 10 (2)

捐
juān
forsake; donate; tax
55;64 10 (4)

操
cāo
grasp; operate; exercise; &
55;64 16 (1)

担
擔 dān dàn
undertake; burden
55;64 8 (2)

捍
hàn
defend, guard
55;64 10 (4)

捏
niē
hold; knead; fabricate (lie)
55;64 10 (3)

揭
jiē
remove; uncover
55;64 12 (3)

提
tí dī
carry; lift, raise; to extract; mention; put forward; &
55;64 12 (1)

摄
攝 shè
absorb; act for; take (photo)
55;64 13 (3)

摆
擺 襬 bǎi
put, arrange; sway, wave; &
55;64 13 (1)

扌

括
kuò
include; to contract
55;64 9 (2)

插
chā
insert
-
55;64 12 (2)

捶
chuí
bang, thump; to cudgel
55;64 11 (4)

抵
dǐ
resist; prop up; compensate; &
55;64 8 (3)

摇
搖 yáo
shake, sway, wave, flutter
55;64 13 (2)

授
shòu
give, confer; teach
55;64 11 (2)

援
yuán
grasp; help, aid; cite
55;64 12 (2)

播
bō
sow, scatter, broadcast
55;64 15 (1)

口 扫 : 拍 … 把

拖
tuō
pull, drag;
delay
55;64 8 (2)

探
tàn
explore, scout;
visit; lean out
55;64 11 (2)

挥 huī
to wave, wield;
wipe; scatter; &
55;64 9 (2)

换 huàn
exchange
-
55;64 10 (1)

挽
wǎn
pull; coil up;
redeem; lament
55;64 10 (3)

搀 chān
support, help;
mix, blend
55;64 12 (4)

掐
qiā
nip, pinch,
choke; sever
55;64 11 (4)

挣 zhèng zhēng
struggle free;
earn
55;64 9 (3)

扮
bàn
disguise,
dress up as
55;64 7 (2)

抬
tái
raise,
lift
55;64 8 (1)

挨
āi ái
abut; in turn;
suffer; dawdle
55;64 10 (2)

掺 chān
mix,
blend
55;64 11 (4)

拾
shí
pick up, collect;
ten
55;64 9 (1)

抡 lūn lún
brandish;
choose
55;64 7 (4)

捡 jiǎn
pick up, glean,
collect
55;64 10 (2)

拴
shuān
tie, fasten,
to tether
55;64 9 (3)

抢 qiǎng qiāng
snatch; vie for;
to rush; scrape
55;64 7 (2)

捻 niǎn
twist
(with fingers)
55;64 11 (4)

擒
qín
capture
-
55;64 15 (-)

撼
hàn
shake
-
55;64 16 (-)

挫
cuò
thwart;
to lower
55;64 10 (3)

携 xié
carry, bring,
take along
55;64 13 (4)

揽 lǎn
clasp; tie rope
to; to take over
55;64 12 (4)

撵 niǎn
drive out,
expel
55;64 15 (4)

攒 zǎn cuán
save, hoard;
assemble
55;64 19 (4)

撰
zhuàn
write,
compose
55;64 15 (-)

摺
zhé zhē shé
bend, fold; &
(see Table 1)
55;64 14 (-)

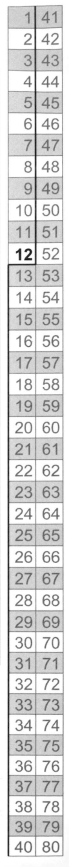

扣 扣 扣 扣

扣

扑 撲 pū	扶 fú	抹 mā mǒ mò	扯 chě	扎 *紥 紮 zhā zhá zā
rush at, attack; to flap, flutter	hold on to; help	to plaster; wipe, erase; to skirt	pull, to tear; chat	prick, stab; encamp; tie up
55;64 5 (2)	55;64 7 (2)	55;64 8 (3)	55;64 7 (3)	55;64 4 (2)

扩 擴 kuò	拙 zhuō	拌 bàn	扰 擾 rǎo	找 zhǎo	我 wǒ
expand, extend	clumsy; my (humble)	mix -	harass, disturb; trouble	seek; call on; give change	I, me, my, we, our
55;64 6 (2)	55;64 8 (4)	55;64 8 (4)	55;64 7 (2)	55;64 7 (1)	101;62 7 (1)

抉 jué	披 pī	挟 挾 xié	拣 揀 jiǎn	执 執 zhí
pick, single out (literary)	drape over; unroll; split	coerce; hold (under the arm)	choose, select	hold; manage; persist; abide by; capture; receipt
55;64 7 (-)	55;64 8 (2)	55;64 9 (4)	55;64 8 (2)	55;32 6 (2)

挫 cuò	拂 fú	抽 chōu	拽 zhuài zhuāi	捕 bǔ
thwart; to lower	wipe, flick, brush away	to extract; to smoke; whip; &	pull, drag; hurl, fling	catch, seize, arrest
55;64 10 (3)	55;64 8 (-)	55;64 8 (1)	55;64 9 (4)	55;64 10 (2)

扛 káng gāng	抚 撫 fǔ	拒 jù	打 dǎ dá
to shoulder, lift, carry	pacify; caress; nurture	resist, reject, refuse	hit; make; tie up; send; fetch; buy; shoot; calculate; dozen; &
55;64 6 (2)	55;64 7 (4)	55;64 7 (2)	55;64 5 (1)

托 *託 tuō	扔 rēng	扬 揚 yáng	扫 掃 sǎo sào	扭 niǔ	拇 mǔ
entrust; pretext; support; &	hurl; throw away	raise; winnow; publicize	clear away, sweep	turn round; roll; wrench; grapple	thumb; big toe
55;64 6 (2)	55;64 5 (2)	55;64 6 (1)	55;64 6 (2)	55;64 7 (2)	55;64 8 (4)

扣 kòu	押 yā	把 bǎ bà	报 報 bào	拥 擁 yōng
arrest; fasten; knot; deduct; &	detain; escort; mortgage; &	to hold; control; a handle; &	report; reply; newspaper	swarm, crowd; embrace; &
55;64 6 (2)	55;64 8 (3)	55;64 7 (1)	55;32 7 (1)	55;64 8 (2)

扣 扣 扣

拒 jù	抠 摳 kōu	抓 zhuā	搁 擱 gē gé	捆 kǔn
resist, reject, refuse	root out; carve; delve into	scratch; seize; arrest; &	put; put aside; endure	tie, bind; bundle
55;64 7 (2)	55;64 7 (4)	55;64 7 (2)	55;64 12 (2)	55;64 10 (2)

扒	**批**	**挑**	**排**		
bā pá	pī	tiāo tiǎo	pái pǎi		
cling; to dig up, rake; to stew; &	slap; criticize; batch	choose; carry; poke; stir up	line up; row, line; platoon; rehearse; raft; eject; push; pie		
55;64 5 (3)	55;64 7 (1)	55;64 9 (2)	55;64 11 (1)		

抑	**拟** 擬 nǐ	**捌**	**推**		
yì	draft; intend; imitate	bā	tuī		
repress; restrain		eight	push; grind; to clip; deduce; shirk; postpone; elect; esteem		
55;64 7 (3)	55;64 7 (4)	-	55;64 11 (1)		
		55;64 10 (4)			

挪	**掷** 擲 zhì zhī	**揪**	**摊** 攤 tān		
nuó	throw	jiu	spread out; booth, stall; &		
move	-	hold tight; seize; pull			
-	55;64 11 (4)	55;64 12 (3)	55;64 13 (3)		
55;64 9 (4)					

掀	**撕**	**搬**	**撒**	**撤**	**撇**
xiān	sī	bān	sā sǎ	chè	piē piě
lift (lid or cover)	rip, tear	move (house); remove; &	let go; scatter, spill, drop	remove, withdraw	abandon, cast off; fling; skim
55;64 11 (2)	55;64 15 (2)	55;64 15 (2)	55;64 15 (2)	55;64 15 (3)	55;64 14 (4)

扩 擴 kuò	**抓**	**拆**	**折** 摺 zhé zhē shé		
expand, extend	zhuā	chāi cā	bend; fold; break; lose; rebate; be convinced; amount to; &		
55;64 6 (2)	scratch; seize, arrest; &	tear apart, dismantle	55;64 7 (2)		
	55;64 7 (2)	55;64 8 (2)			

振	**扳**	**披**	**拔**	**拨** 撥 bō	**拢** 攏 lǒng
zhèn	bān	pī	bá	stir, poke; allocate; batch	approach; sum; tie up; comb
shake, wave; rouse; boost	pull; to turn	drape over; unroll; split	root out; select; seize; &	55;64 8 (3)	55;64 8 (3)
55;64 10 (3)	55;64 7 (4)	55;64 8 (2)	55;64 8 (2)		

拓	**掂**	**搓**	**掘**	**据** 據 jù jū	**握**
tà tuò	diān	cuō	jué	seize, occupy; according to; &	wò
make rubbing; open up (land)	heft, weigh up (in the hand)	rub (with the hands)	dig, excavate	55;64 11 (2)	grasp
55;64 8 (4)	55;64 11 (4)	55;64 12 (4)	55;64 11 (4)		-
					55;64 12 (1)

拘	**抱**	**掏**	**抖**	**抛**	**挺**
jū	bào	tāo	dǒu	pāo	tǐng
arrest; restrict; inflexible	cherish; adopt; embrace; &	pull out; scoop; pick-pocket	tremble, shake; rouse	throw, fling; leave behind	erect; stick out; very; endure
55;64 8 (4)	55;64 8 (1)	55;64 11 (2)	55;64 7 (2)	55;64 7 (3)	55;64 9 (1)

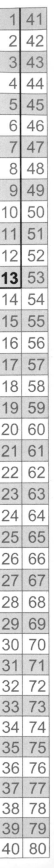

1 41
2 42
3 43
4 44
5 45
6 46
7 47
8 48
9 49
10 50
11 51
12 52
13 53
14 54
15 55
16 56
17 57
18 58
19 59
20 60
21 61
22 62
23 63
24 64
25 65
26 66
27 67
28 68
29 69
30 70
31 71
32 72
33 73
34 74
35 75
36 76
37 77
38 78
39 79
40 80

犭 豸

犭

狂	犯	独	狸	狠	狼
kuáng	fàn	獨 dú	lí	hěn	láng
crazy; violent; wild; arrogant	offense; attack; criminal	single, alone, only	raccoon, wild cat	ruthless; resolute	wolf
69;94 7 (3)	69;94 5 (2)	69;94 9 (2)	69;94 10 (4)	69;94 9 (3)	- 69;94 10 (2)

犹	狭	狡	猿
猶 yóu	狹 xiá	jiǎo	yuán
still, yet	narrow	crafty, sly	ape
69;94 7 (3)	- 69;94 9 (4)	69;94 9 (3)	69;94 13 (3)

狄	狱	猴	狮
dí	獄 yù	hóu	獅 shī
(surname)	prison, jail; lawsuit	monkey	lion
- 69;94 7 (-)	69;94 9 (3)	69;94 12 (2)	69;94 9 (2)

猜	猪	猎	猫	猛
cāi	豬 zhū	獵 liè	貓 māo máo	měng
guess, suspect	pig, swine	hunt	cat	fierce, violent; brave; abrupt
69;94 11 (2)	69;152 11 (1)	69;94 11 (3)	- 69;153 11 (2)	69;94 11 (3)

狸	猩	猖	猾
lí	xīng	chāng	huá
raccoon, wild cat	orangutan, chimpanzee	[wild, savage, rampant]	sly, cunning
69;94 10 (4)	69;94 12 (-)	69;94 11 (4)	69;94 12 (3)

狗	狈	狐
gǒu	狽 bèi	hú
dog	[legendary wolf; dire straits]	fox
- 69;94 8 (2)	69;94 7 (4)	69;94 8 (4)

豸

豹	貌
bào	mào
leopard, panther	view; face, appearance
198;153 10 (-)	198;153 14 (2)

子 弓 巾 山

孔
kǒng
hole,
aperture
74;39 4 (2)

孙
孫 sūn
grandchild
-
74;39 6 (3)

孩
hái
child
-
74;39 9 (1)

孤
gū
orphan;
alone; lonely
74;39 8 (3)

引
yǐn
to guide, lead;
lure; cite; &
71;57 4 (2)

弘
hóng
great, grand;
enlarge
71;57 5 (-)

弥
彌 瀰 mí
full; more;
redeem
71;57 8 (4)

张
張 zhāng
open; expand;
display; look
71;57 7 (1)

强
*強 疆 qiáng qiǎng jiàng
strong; better;
force; stubborn
71;57 12 (2)

弦
xián
string (of bow,
musical inst.)
71;57 8 (4)

弹
彈 tán dàn
shoot; flick; pluck;
rebound; bullet
71;57 11 (2)

粥
zhōu
gruel,
porridge
71;119 12 (3)

弱
ruò
weak; inferior;
a bit less
71;57 10 (2)

疆
jiāng
boundary,
frontier
71;102 19 (3)

帐
帳 賬 zhàng
canopy, curtain;
accounts
57;50 7 (3)

帕
pà
handkerchief;
turban
57;50 8 (-)

帖
tiē tiě tiè
docile; fitting;
note, card
57;50 8 (4)

帆
fān
a sail;
canvas
57;50 6 (4)

帜
幟 zhì
flag,
banner (literary)
57;50 8 (3)

帽
mào
hat,
cap
57;50 12 (1)

幅
fú
size, width
(e.g. of cloth)
57;50 12 (2)

幢
chuáng zhuàng
stone pillar;
pennant
57;50 15 (3)

屿
嶼 yǔ
small
island
60;46 6 (3)

峡
峽 xiá
gorge,
ravine
60;46 9 (3)

崎
qí
[rugged,
uneven]
60;46 11 (-)

岭
嶺 lǐng
mountain peak,
ridge, range
60;46 8 (4)

峻
jùn
high; steep;
stern, severe
60;46 10 (4)

峰
fēng
peak, summit;
hump
60;46 10 (3)

1	41
2	42
3	43
4	44
5	45
6	46
7	47
8	48
9	49
10	50
11	51
12	52
13	53
14	54
15	55
16	56
17	57
18	58
19	59
20	60
21	61
22	62
23	63
24	64
25	65
26	66
27	67
28	68
29	69
30	70
31	71
32	72
33	73
34	74
35	75
36	76
37	77
38	78
39	79
40	80

纠	纪	红	纯	纤
糾 jiū	紀 jì	紅 hóng gōng	純 chún	纖 縴 xiān qiàn
entangle; rectify	discipline; age, era; chronicle	red; bonus	pure, simple; skilful	tiny, slender; tow-rope
77;120 5 (2)	77;120 6 (1)	77;120 6 (1)	77;120 7 (3)	77;120 6 (2)

练	纬	线	纸	级	纳
練 liàn	緯 wěi	綫 線 xiàn	紙 zhǐ	級 jí	納 nà
silk; practice; experienced	latitude, weft	thread; route, line; brink; clue	paper -	rank, grade; step	receive; accept; pay; enjoy; sew
77;120 8 (1)	77;120 7 (-)	77;120 8 (2)	77;120 7 (1)	77;120 6 (1)	77;120 7 (4)

细	组	纽	绅
細 xì	組 zǔ	紐 niǔ	紳 shēn
tiny, slender; delicate; careful	organize; group	handle, button, knob; fasten	gentry
77;120 8 (1)	77;120 8 (1)	77;120 7 (4)	77;120 8 (4)

维	纵	绑	缴	缎
維 wéi	縱 zòng	綁 bǎng	繳 jiǎo	緞 duàn
hold together; maintain; &	leap; vertical; indulge; release	bind, tie	pay, hand over; capture	satin -
77;120 11 (2)	77;120 7 (3)	77;120 9 (3)	77;120 16 (4)	77;120 12 (4)

绷
繃 bēng bèng běng
stretch taut; rebound; crack
77;120 11 (4)

缠	编	绒	约
纏 chán	編 biān	絨 róng	約 yuē yāo
entwine, tangle; pester	weave; arrange; compile, edit	soft cloth, velvet, flannel	make appointment; agreement; restrict; approx; brief; frugal; &
77;120 13 (4)	77;120 12 (2)	77;120 9 (4)	77;120 6 (2)

继	缝
繼 jì	縫 féng fèng
follow on; afterwards	sew, stitch; seam, fissure
77;120 10 (1)	77;120 13 (3)

绸	纲	纳
綢 chóu	綱 gāng	納 nà
silk -	nub; precis; category	receive; accept; pay; enjoy; sew
77;120 11 (4)	77;120 7 (3)	77;120 7 (4)

纹
紋 wén
wrinkles;
grain (of wood)
77;120 7 (3)

绞
絞 jiāo
twist; wring;
hang (by neck)
77;120 9 (4)

纺
紡 fǎng
spin (cotton);
reel
77;120 7 (2)

统
統 tǒng
unify; all;
system
77;120 9 (2)

缔
締 dì
bind, join;
contract
77;120 12 (4)

综
綜 zōng zèng
sum up;
put together
77;120 11 (2)

缩
縮 suō
withdraw;
shrink
77;120 14 (2)

绪
緒 xù
thread; task;
emotion
77;120 11 (2)

结
結 jié jiē
tie; knot; settle
up; congeal; &
77;120 9 (1)

续
續 xù
continue;
add more
77;120 11 (1)

绩
績 jī
meritorious
achievement
77;120 11 (1)

绵
綿 mián
silk floss; soft;
continuous
77;120 11 (4)

缚
縛 fù
tie up
-
77;120 13 (3)

线
綫 線 xiàn
thread; route,
line; brink; clue
77;120 8 (2)

绕
繞 rào rào
go round; coil;
wind; confuse
77;120 9 (2)

纱
紗 shā
yarn,
gauze
77;120 7 (3)

缕
縷 lǚ
thread; wisp;
detailed
77;120 12 (-)

缘
緣 yuán
reason, cause;
edge; along
77;120 12 (3)

绿
綠 lǜ lù
green
-
77;120 11 (1)

绍
紹 shào
continue
-
77;120 8 (1)

经
經 jīng jìng
go through; manage; constant;
scriptures; longitude; &
77;120 8 (1)

织
織 zhī
weave,
knit
77;120 8 (1)

绢
絹 juàn
silk
-
77;120 10 (2)

缉
緝 jī qī
seize, arrest;
stitch
77;120 12 (-)

绳
繩 shéng
rope, string;
restrain
77;120 11 (2)

缅
緬 miǎn
remote;
far back
77;120 12 (-)

缓
緩 huǎn
slow, relaxed;
delay; revive
77;120 12 (3)

绣
繡 繍 xiù
embroider
-
77;120 10 (3)

终
終 zhōng
end, finish;
death; entire
77;120 8 (2)

络
絡 luò
to coil up;
keep in a net
77;120 9 (3)

绝
絕 jué
absolutely; sever;
use up; hopeless; &
77;120 9 (2)

纷
紛 fēn
in profusion;
confused
77;120 7 (2)

绘
繪 huì
draw,
paint
77;120 9 (4)

给
給 gěi jǐ
give; for (someone);
allow; supply; ample
77;120 9 (1)

缀
綴 zhuì
sew, stitch; put
together; adorn
77;120 11 (4)

幻
huàn
unreal;
changeable
76;52 4 (3)

幼
yòu
young;
child
76;52 5 (3)

丝
絲 sī
silk; thread;
tiny amount
2;120 5 (2)

1	41
2	42
3	43
4	44
5	45
6	46
7	47
8	48
9	49
10	50
11	51
12	52
13	53
14	54
15	55
16	56
17	57
18	58
19	59
20	60
21	61
22	62
23	63
24	64
25	65
26	66
27	67
28	68
29	69
30	70
31	71
32	72
33	73
34	74
35	75
36	76
37	77
38	78
39	79
40	80

柏 ： 柏 柏 柏 栖 栖

柏 柏 柏

柱	柏	棉	槐	栈
zhù	bǎi bò	mián	huái	棧 zhàn
pillar, column	cypress, cedar	cotton -	acacia, locust tree	storehouse; stable; inn
94;75 9 (3)	94;75 9 (3)	94;75 12 (2)	94;75 13 (4)	94;75 9 (-)
杭	校	梳	核	榜
háng Hangzhou -	xiào jiào school; check, collate; &	shū comb	hé hú nucleus, kernel; examine	bǎng announcement; list of names
94;75 8 (-)	94;75 10 (1)	94;75 11 (3)	94;75 10 (3)	94;75 14 (2)
柠	榨	棕	棺	榷
檸 níng [lemon] -	zhà squeeze, wring	zōng palm (tree)	guān coffin -	què discuss
94;75 9 (4)	94;75 14 (4)	94;75 12 (4)	94;75 12 (4)	94;75 14 (4)
枯	枝	桂		
kū withered, dried up; boring	zhī branch, twig	guì laurel, cassia, cinnamon tree		
94;75 9 (3)	94;75 8 (3)	94;75 10 (4)		
桔	柿	棱	植	
*橘 jú jié tangerine -	shì persimmon -	*稜楞 léng edge; ridge	zhí to plant, grow, set up	
94;75 10 (1)	94;75 9 (2)	94;75 12 (4)	94;75 12 (2)	
棒	椅			
bàng stick, cudgel; good, capable	yǐ chair			
94;75 12 (3)	94;75 12 (1)			

栖 栖

栏	样	梯	档	梢	楼
欄 lán railing; column (in newspaper)	樣 yàng sample; shape; appearance; &	tī ladder, stairs; terracing	檔 dàng files; shelves; grade	shāo tip (of twig, branch)	樓 lóu floor, story; tower
94;75 9 (4)	94;75 10 (1)	94;75 11 (2)	94;75 10 (3)	94;75 11 (4)	94;75 13 (1)
棋	横	模	槽	檬	
qí chess, board game	橫 héng hèng horizontal; harsh; &	mó mú pattern, mold, template	cáo trough; groove, slot	méng [lemon] -	
94;75 12 (3)	94;75 15 (3)	94;75 14 (2)	94;75 15 (4)	94;75 17 (4)	

标
标 biāo
label, sign,
symptom; prize
94;75 9 (2)

梧
wú
[phoenix tree,
parasol tree]
94;75 11 (4)

棍
gùn
cudgel;
rascal
94;75 12 (3)

棵
kē
(measure word)
-
94;75 12 (1)

桶
tǒng
bucket,
barrel
94;75 11 (2)

橘
jú
tangerine
-
94;75 16 (1)

桥
桥 qiáo
bridge
-
94;75 10 (1)

杉
shān shā
China fir
tree
94;75 7 (-)

梅
méi
plum
-
94;75 11 (3)

格
gé
grid; standard;
subdivision
94;75 10 (2)

桅
wéi
mast
-
94;75 10 (4)

橡
xiàng
oak;
rubber tree
94;75 15 (4)

枪
槍 qiāng
gun;
spear, lance
94;75 8 (2)

检
檢 jiǎn
check, inspect;
act correctly
94;75 11 (1)

榆
yú
[elm]
-
94;75 13 (4)

松
*鬆 sōng
pine tree; loose;
relaxed; &
94;75 8 (2)

榴
liú
pomegranate
-
94;75 14 (4)

樱
樱 yīng
cherry
-
94;75 15 (4)

1 41 2 42 3 43 4 44 5 45 6 46 7 47 8 48 9 49 10 50 11 51 12 52 13 53 14 54 15 55 **16** 56 17 57 18 58 19 59 20 60 21 61 22 62 23 63 24 64 25 65 26 66 27 67 28 68 29 69 30 70 31 71 32 72 33 73 34 74 35 75 36 76 37 77 38 78 39 79 40 80

杜	材	林	株	朴
dù	cái	lín	zhū	*樸 pǔ pō pò piáo
prevent, shut out	materials; timber; ability	forest, grove; group	tree trunk; a plant	plain, simple
94;75 7 (4)	94;75 7 (2)	94;75 8 (2)	94;75 10 (2)	94;75 6 (2)

枚	杖	枕	栈	栋
méi	zhàng	zhěn	棧 zhàn	棟 dòng
(measure word)	cane, crutch, walking stick	pillow; block	storehouse; stable; inn	supporting beam, ridgepole
-	94;75 7 (-)	94;75 8 (3)	94;75 9 (-)	94;75 9 (4)
94;75 8 (4)				

权	机	杨	极
權 quán	機 jī	楊 yáng	極 jí
rights; power, authority; &	machine; opportunity; &	poplar	extreme, pole, polar
94;75 6 (3)	94;75 6 (1)	-	94;75 7 (1)
		94;75 7 (4)	

杠	朽	杯	杆	枉
gàng	xiǔ	*盃 bēi	桿 gān gǎn	wǎng
bar, pole; delete	decayed, rotten; senile	cup	pole, shaft	crooked; to wrong; in vain
94;75 7 (4)	94;75 6 (3)	-	94;75 7 (2)	94;75 8 (3)
		94;75 8 (1)		

柄	栖	梗	棵
bǐng	棲 qī	gěng	kē
stem, handle	stay; perch (birds)	stalk, stem; obstruct; &	(measure word)
94;75 9 (3)	94;75 10 (-)	94;75 11 (4)	-
			94;75 12 (1)

柜	相	根	栅
*櫃 guì jǔ	xiāng xiàng	gēn	柵 zhà shān
cupboard; (shop) counter	mutual; looks; photo; &	root; basis; thoroughly	railings, fence
94;75 8 (3)	94;109 9 (1)	94;75 10 (1)	94;75 9 (-)

桃	柳	树	彬	
táo	liǔ	樹 shù	bīn	
peach	willow	tree; to plant, set up; uphold	[urbane, refined]	
-	-			
94;75 10 (3)	94;75 9 (3)	94;75 9 (1)	94;59 11 (-)	
椒	棚	椰	概	椭
jiāo	péng	yē	gài	橢 tuǒ
spice plant, pepper, chili	shed, shack; awning	coconut	general, in summary; &	[oval, ellipse]
94;75 12 (3)	94;75 12 (3)	94;75 12 (-)	94;75 13 (1)	94;75 12 (4)
桩	板	析	橱	
椿 zhuāng	* 闆 bǎn	xī	櫥 chú	
stake (in the ground)	board, plank; hard, stiff	divide, dissect, discriminate	wardrobe, cabinet, closet	
94;75 10 (3)	94;75 8 (1)	94;75 8 (2)	94;75 16 (-)	
村	柯	构	械	
cūn	kē	構 gòu	xiè	
village	stalk; handle (literary)	construct, compose	tool, weapon, instrument	
-				
94;75 7 (1)	94;75 9 (-)	94;75 8 (2)	94;75 11 (2)	
枢	柜	框		
樞 shu	* 櫃 guì jǔ	kuāng kuàng		
axis, pivot, hub	cupboard; (shop) counter	frame, rim		
94;75 8 (-)	94;75 8 (3)	94;75 10 (4)		
枫	桐			
楓 fēng	tóng			
maple	tung tree, paulowina tree			
-				
94;75 8 (-)	94;75 10 (4)			

1 41
2 42
3 43
4 44
5 45
6 46
7 47
8 48
9 49
10 50
11 51
12 52
13 53
14 54
15 55
16 56
17 57
18 58
19 59
20 60
21 61
22 62
23 63
24 64
25 65
26 66
27 67
28 68
29 69
30 70
31 71
32 72
33 73
34 74
35 75
36 76
37 77
38 78
39 79
40 80

和

私 sī private; selfish; secret, illicit 149;115 7 (2)	秆 *稈* gǎn stalk, stem 149;115 8 (4)	秤 chèng steelyard, weighing scales 149;115 10 (4)	科 kē area of study; section; branch 149;115 9 (1)	称 *稱* chēng chèn call, name; weigh; suitable 149;115 10 (2)
秩 zhì decade; in good order (literary) 149;115 10 (2)	租 zū rent, hire, lease 149;115 10 (1)	和 hé hè huó huò harmony; mild; with; sum; mix 149;30 8 (1)	秧 yāng seedling; small fry; vine 149;115 10 (3)	种 *種* zhǒng zhòng seed; species, type; cultivate 149;115 9 (1)

和口

利 lì profit, benefit; sharp 149;18 7 (1)	秋 qiū fall, autumn; period, year 149;115 9 (1)	秘 *祕* mì bì secret - 149;115 10 (2)	稚 zhì young, infantile 149;115 13 (3)

和口

秒 miǎo second (of time, arc) 149;115 9 (2)	秘 *祕* mì bì secret - 149;115 10 (2)	秽 *穢* huì dirty; ugly; weeds 149;115 11 (4)	穆 mù solemn 149;115 16 (4)	税 shuì tax 149;115 12 (3)	稍 shāo slightly 149;115 12 (2)
稼 jià sow (grain); crops 149;115 15 (2)	稿 gǎo manuscript, draft; straw 149;115 15 (3)	穗 suì ear (of grain); tassel; Guangzhou 149;115 17 (4)			
积 *積* jī amass, store; long-standing 149;115 10 (2)	程 chéng regulation; journey; & 149;115 12 (2)				
稻 dào rice; paddy field 149;115 15 (2)	移 yí move, change 149;115 11 (2)	稳 *穩* wěn steady, certain, reliable 149;115 14 (2)	稀 xī sparse, scarce, dilute 149;115 12 (3)		

和口
和口

科 kē area of study; section; branch 149;115 9 (1)	稠 chóu dense, thick, crowded 149;115 13 (4)

釆 米 光 耒

释 彩

釋 shì
explain; resolve; release
197;165 12 (2)

cǎi
color; variety; acclaim; prize
63;59 11 (1)

籽 料 粗 粒 粹 粮

zǐ
seed
-
159;119 9 (4)

liào
raw materials; grain; expect
159;68 10 (2)

cū
thick, coarse, rough; careless
159;119 11 (2)

lì
grain, granule
159;119 11 (2)

cuì
pure; essence
159;119 14 (4)

糧 liáng
grain, provisions
159;119 13 (2)

粉 粘 精 糟 糕

fěn
dust, powder; white; pink
159;119 10 (2)

*黏 zhān nián
glue; sticky; paste up
159;119 11 (2)

jīng
splendid; spirit; fine; clever; &
159;119 14 (1)

zāo
rotten; a mess; grain; dregs
159;119 17 (2)

gāo
cake
-
159;119 16 (2)

糊 糖 糠

hú hū hù
paste, gum; plaster
159;119 15 (2)

táng
sugar; candy
159;119 16 (1)

kāng
husk, chaff
159;119 17 (4)

辉 耀

輝 huī
radiance; shine
172;159 12 (2)

yào
dazzle; honor; boast
172;124 20 (3)

耗 耕

hào
use up; dawdle; bad news
176;127 10 (3)

*畊 gēng
plow
-
176;127 10 (3)

1	41
2	42
3	43
4	44
5	45
6	46
7	47
8	48
9	49
10	50
11	51
12	52
13	53
14	54
15	55
16	56
17	57
18	58
19	59
20	60
21	61
22	62
23	63
24	64
25	65
26	66
27	67
28	68
29	69
30	70
31	71
32	72
33	73
34	74
35	75
36	76
37	77
38	78
39	79
40	80

牛　车　片

牛

牡	牲	牧	物	特	牺
mǔ	shēng	mù	wù	tè	犧 xī
male (animal)	livestock; animal sacrifice	to herd, tend (animals)	thing; content, substance	special; particular; spy	animal sacrifice (literary)
110;93　7　(-)	110;93　9　(2)	110;93　8　(3)	110;93　8　(1)	110;93　10　(1)	110;93　10　(2)

车

轧	轨	轩	软	斩
軋 yà zhá gá	軌 guǐ	軒 xuān	軟 ruǎn	斬 zhǎn
grind, crush; squeeze out	rail, track, path, orbit	balcony; ancient carriage	soft, pliable; inferior; weak	chop, cut; behead
100;159　5　(4)	100;159　6　(3)	100;159　7　(-)	100;159　8　(2)	100;69　8　(4)

轴	辅	辆	转
軸 zhóu	輔 fǔ	輛 liàng	轉 zhuǎn zhuàn
axis, axle; spool, reel	assist	(measure word)	revolve; change; to forward; stroll
100;159　9　(-)	100;159　11　(1)	100;159　11　(1)	100;159　8　(2)

较	辖	轮	输
較 jiào	轄 xiá	輪 lún	輸 shū
compare; evident; dispute	linchpin; govern	wheel; take turns	to transport; be defeated
100;159　10　(1)	100;159　14　(4)	100;159　8　(2)	100;159　13　(1)

辐	轿	轻	辑	辙
輻 fú	轎 jiào	輕 qīng	輯 jí	轍 zhé
spoke (of wheel)	sedan chair	light, slight, minor; gently	collect, edit, precis	(wheel) track, rut; rhyme
100;159　13　(4)	100;159　10　(4)	100;159　9　(1)	100;159　13　(3)	100;159　16　(4)

片

版	牌	鼎
bǎn	pái	dǐng
printing; edition, page	card, tablet; brand (goods)	cauldron; tripod, tripartite
114;91　8　(2)	114;91　12　(2)	141;206　12　(-)

顶 頂 dǐng stand up to; top; utmost; & 170;181 8 (2)	**竹** zhú bamboo - 178;118 6 (2)

| **巧** qiǎo
skilful; cunning;
happily, luckily
48;48 5 (2) | **功** gōng
merit; achieve;
effect; skill
48;19 5 (2) | **攻** gōng
attack; accuse;
study
48;66 7 (2) | **巩** 鞏 gǒng
consolidate;
stable, strong
48;177 6 (2) | **项** 項 xiàng
item;
nape of neck
48;181 9 (2) | **式** shì
formula; format,
style; ceremony
56;56 6 (2) |

| **珠** zhū
pearl, bead,
(water) drop
88;96 10 (2) | **球** qiú
ball, sphere,
globe
88;96 11 (1) | **珑** 瓏 lóng
[exquisite, deft]
-
88;96 9 (4) | **环** 環 huán
ring, hoop;
surround
88;96 8 (2) | **琢** zhuó zuó
chisel,
carve
88;96 12 (4) | **玻** bō
[glass]
-
88;96 9 (2) |

| **玖** jiǔ
nine
-
88;96 7 (4) | **玫** méi
[rose]
-
88;96 8 (4) | **玛** 瑪 mǎ
[agate]
-
88;96 7 (-) | **现** 現 xiàn
present, now,
modern; appear
88;96 8 (1) | **珊** 珊 shān
[coral]
-
88;96 9 (4) | |

| **琼** 瓊 qióng
jade; palace
(literary)
88;96 12 (-) | **琦** qí
jade; admirable
(literary)
88;96 12 (-) | **璃** lí
[glass,
glaze]
88;96 14 (2) | **瑰** guī
marvelous
(literary)
88;96 13 (4) | **理** lǐ
reason, logic; science; texture;
manage; pay heed to; tidy up
88;96 11 (1) | |

| **玩** wán
play; trifle with;
enjoy; resort to
88;96 8 (1) | **瑞** ruì
auspicious,
lucky
88;96 13 (4) | **瑾** jǐn
fine jade;
lustrous
88;96 15 (-) | **珍** zhēn
treasure;
precious
88;96 9 (3) | **玲** líng
[tinkling of jade;
exquisite, deft]
88;96 9 (4) | **瑜** yú
fine jade;
luster; virtues
88;96 13 (-) |

| **班** bān
team; duty;
scheduled
88;96 10 (1) | **斑** bān
spots; stripes;
speckled
88;67 12 (4) | **瑚** hú
[coral]
-
88;96 13 (4) | **琳** lín
jade; valuables
(literary)
88;96 12 (-) | | |

| **刑** xíng
punishment;
torture
17;18 6 (4) | **形** xíng
appearance,
shape, form; &
63;59 7 (2) |

饣

饥 饑 jī
hunger, famine
68;184 5 (3)

饮 飲 yǐn yìn
drink
-
68;184 7 (3)

饪 飪 rèn
[cooking]
-
68;184 7 (4)

蚀 蝕 shí
lose; erode; eclipse
68;142 9 (3)

饿 餓 è
hunger, starve
68;184 10 (1)

饭 飯 fàn
food, meal, cooked rice
68;184 7 (1)

饲 飼 sì
fodder; to rear (animals)
68;184 8 (3)

饱 飽 bǎo
full, satisfied, eat one's fill
68;184 8 (1)

饺 餃 jiǎo
dumpling
-
68;184 9 (1)

馆 館 guǎn
hall, inn, shop, public building
68;184 11 (1)

饶 饒 ráo
plentiful; forgive; &
68;184 9 (3)

馈 饋 kuì
to present (a gift)
68;184 12 (4)

饼 餅 bǐng
cake
-
68;184 9 (2)

饰 飾 shì
adorn; cover up; play (role)
68;184 8 (3)

馒 饅 mán
steamed bread
68;184 14 (2)

馀 餘 yú
surplus; after (see Table 1)
68;184 10 (-)

馅 餡 xiàn
filling, stuffing (of food)
68;184 11 (4)

馋 饞 chán
greedy
-
68;184 12 (4)

矢

知 zhī
know; inform; administer
148;111 8 (1)

矩 jǔ
rules; square, rectangle
148;111 9 (3)

短 duǎn
brief; lacking; weak point
148;111 12 (1)

矫 矯 jiǎo jiáo
rectify; pretend; strong, brave
148;111 11 (-)

矮 ǎi
short; low rank
148;111 13 (1)

缶

缸 gāng
jar
-
175;121 9 (3)

缺 quē
to lack; absent; defect; vacancy
175;121 10 (2)

罐 guàn
tin, jar, pot
175;121 23 (2)

立

站 zhàn
station; (bus) stop; to stand
126;117 10 (1)

端 duān
tip, end; cause; carry; proper
126;117 14 (2)

靖 jìng
tranquillity; pacify
126;174 13 (-)

竭 jié
exhaust, use up
126;117 14 (3)

方 礻 衤

放 fàng
set free; expel;
put; adjust; &
85;66 8 (1)

旅 lǚ
travel;
brigade
85;70 10 (1)

族 zú
clan, race;
group, family
85;70 11 (1)

施 shī
carry out; use;
bestow; impose
85;70 9 (2)

旋 xuán xuàn
revolve; return;
whorl; lathe
85;70 11 (3)

旗 qí
flag,
banner
85;70 14 (2)

於 yú
in, to, at, of
(see Table 1)
85;70 8 (-)

礼 禮 lǐ
ceremony;
etiquette; gift
87;113 5 (1)

社 shè
society;
agency; &
87;113 7 (1)

祈 qí
worship,
pray, beg
87;113 8 (-)

祷 禱 dǎo
pray
-
87;113 11 (-)

祖 zǔ
ancestor;
grandparent
87;113 9 (1)

神 shén
gods; magical;
spirit; &
87;113 9 (1)

祥 xiáng
good luck,
auspicious
87;113 10 (4)

禅 禪 chán shàn
meditation;
Buddhist
87;113 12 (-)

祝 zhù
best wishes
-
87;113 9 (1)

视 視 shì
look at, regard,
inspect
87;147 8 (1)

祸 禍 huò
disaster;
bring misfortune
87;113 11 (4)

福 fú
good fortune,
blessing
87;113 13 (1)

禧 xǐ
blessings;
happy occasion
87;113 16 (-)

补 補 bǔ
mend; use; fill,
replace; nourish
129;145 7 (2)

初 chū
beginning;
first, original
129;18 7 (1)

袄 襖 ǎo
coat,
jacket
129;145 9 (4)

袜 襪 wà
socks,
stockings
129;145 10 (1)

衬 襯 chèn
lining; serve
as contrast
129;145 8 (2)

衫 shān
shirt,
vest
129;145 8 (2)

袖 xiù
sleeve
-
129;145 10 (2)

被 bèi
quilt; (particle:
passive verbs)
129;145 10 (1)

裤 褲 kù
pants,
trousers
129;145 12 (2)

袱 fú
[bundle
of cloth]
129;145 11 (3)

裙 qún
a skirt
-
129;145 12 (2)

袍 páo
robe,
gown
129;145 10 (3)

裕 yù
plentiful;
affluent
129;145 12 (3)

裸 luǒ
naked,
exposed
129;145 13 (-)

襟 jīn
brother in law;
front of garment
129;145 18 (-)

1	41
2	42
3	43
4	44
5	45
6	46
7	47
8	48
9	49
10	50
11	51
12	52
13	53
14	54
15	55
16	56
17	57
18	58
19	59
20	60
21	61
22	62
23	63
24	64
25	65
26	66
27	67
28	68
29	69
30	70
31	71
32	72
33	73
34	74
35	75
36	76
37	77
38	78
39	79
40	80

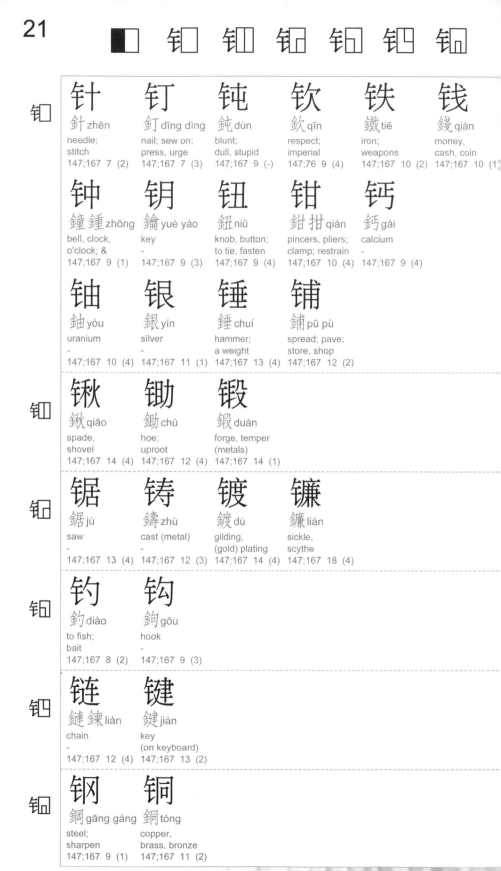

针	钉	钝	钦	铁	钱
針 zhēn	釘 dīng dìng	鈍 dùn	欽 qīn	鐵 tiě	錢 qián
needle; stitch	nail; sew on; press, urge	blunt; dull, stupid	respect; imperial	iron; weapons	money, cash, coin
147;167 7 (2)	147;167 7 (3)	147;167 9 (-)	147;76 9 (4)	147;167 10 (2)	147;167 10 (1)
钟	钥	钮	钳	钙	
鐘 鍾 zhōng	鑰 yuè yào	鈕 niǔ	鉗 拑 qián	鈣 gài	
bell, clock, o'clock; &	key -	knob, button; to tie, fasten	pincers, pliers; clamp; restrain	calcium -	
147;167 9 (1)	147;167 9 (3)	147;167 9 (4)	147;167 10 (4)	147;167 9 (4)	
铀	银	锤	铺		
鈾 yóu	銀 yín	錘 chuí	鋪 pū pù		
uranium -	silver -	hammer; a weight	spread; pave; store, shop		
147;167 10 (4)	147;167 11 (1)	147;167 13 (4)	147;167 12 (2)		
锹	锄	锻			
鍬 qiāo	鋤 chú	鍛 duàn			
spade, shovel	hoe; uproot	forge, temper (metals)			
147;167 14 (4)	147;167 12 (4)	147;167 14 (1)			
锯	铸	镀	镰		
鋸 jù	鑄 zhù	鍍 dù	鐮 lián		
saw -	cast (metal) -	gilding, (gold) plating	sickle, scythe		
147;167 13 (4)	147;167 12 (3)	147;167 14 (4)	147;167 18 (4)		
钓	钩				
釣 diào	鉤 gōu				
to fish; bait	hook -				
147;167 8 (2)	147;167 9 (3)				
链	键				
鏈 鍊 liàn	鍵 jiàn				
chain -	key (on keyboard)				
147;167 12 (4)	147;167 13 (2)				
钢	铜				
鋼 gāng gàng	銅 tóng				
steel; sharpen	copper, brass, bronze				
147;167 9 (1)	147;167 11 (2)				

钅 钷

钞
钞 chāo
banknote,
paper money
147;167 9 (3)

锦
锦 jǐn
brocade;
splendid
147;167 13 (4)

铺
铺 pū pù
spread; pave;
store, shop
147;167 12 (2)

镇
镇 zhèn
calm, quell;
iced; town; &
147;167 15 (3)

钻
鑽 zuān zuàn
penetrate, bore,
drill; diamond
147;167 10 (2)

钱
錢 qián
money,
cash, coin
147;167 10 (1)

铲
鏟 chǎn
shovel,
spade
147;167 11 (3)

锌
鋅 xīn
zinc
-
147;167 12 (4)

镜
鏡 jìng
mirror;
lens
147;167 16 (2)

镑
鎊 bàng
pound sterling
(UK money)
147;167 15 (-)

镶
鑲 xiāng
inlay;
edge
147;167 22 (4)

锐
銳 ruì
sharp;
vigor
147;167 12 (2)

销
銷 xiāo
to fuse; sell;
cancel; spend
147;167 12 (4)

锁
鎖 suǒ
lock,
padlock
147;167 12 (3)

镁
鎂 měi
magnesium
-
147;167 14 (4)

错
錯 cuò
mistake; fault;
alternating; &
147;167 13 (1)

铅
鉛 qiān
lead
(the metal)
147;167 10 (1)

铝
鋁 lǔ
aluminum
-
147;167 11 (3)

锅
鍋 guō
pot, pan,
cauldron
147;167 12 (2)

锡
錫 xī
tin
(the metal)
147;167 13 (3)

锣
鑼 luó
gong
-
147;167 13 (3)

镖
鏢 biāo
an old dart-like
weapon
147;167 16 (-)

锤
錘 chuí
hammer;
a weight
147;167 13 (4)

锈
銹 鏽 xiù
rust

147;167 12 (3)

铃
鈴 líng
bell
-
147;167 10 (2)

铭
銘 míng
inscription;
engrave
147;167 11 (4)

锋
鋒 fēng
point, edge
(of blade)
147;167 12 (4)

1	41
2	42
3	43
4	44
5	45
6	46
7	47
8	48
9	49
10	50
11	51
12	52
13	53
14	54
15	55
16	56
17	57
18	58
19	59
20	60
21	61
22	62
23	63
24	64
25	65
26	66
27	67
28	68
29	69
30	70
31	71
32	72
33	73
34	74
35	75
36	76
37	77
38	78
39	79
40	80

女

如□

奸	奴	妹	姓	好
*姦 jiān	nú	mèi	xìng	hǎo hào
evil; traitor; crafty; illicit	slave -	younger sister	surname, family name	good; be well; easy; so that; very; to like, love; be prone to
73;38 6 (4)	73;38 5 (3)	73;38 8 (1)	73;38 8 (1)	73;38 6 (1)

妇	妖	妊	她	姊	姨
婦 fù	yāo	*姙 rèn	tā	zǐ	yí
woman; wife	monster, devil; charming	conceive, be pregnant	she, her -	elder sister	aunt; sister in law
73;38 6 (2)	73;38 7 (4)	73;38 7 (-)	73;38 6 (1)	73;38 7 (-)	73;38 9 (2)

如	妞	姐	奶	妈	姆
rú	niū	jiě	*妳 嬭 nǎi	媽 mā	mǔ
such as; as if, if; as...as...; &	girl (colloq)	elder sister	breast; milk; suckle	mother, mum; aunt (colloq)	[nanny; housekeeper]
73;38 6 (1)	73;38 7 (-)	73;38 8 (1)	73;38 5 (↑)	73;38 6 (1)	73;38 8 (4)

如□

姚	娴	娜	嫩
yáo	嫻 嫺 xián	nuó	nèn
(surname) -	refined; adept (literary)	[fascinating; courteous]	tender; rookie; light (color)
73;38 9 (-)	73;38 10 (-)	73;38 9 (-)	73;38 14 (3)

妞□

妙	妨	娘	妒	姑	妓
miào	fáng fāng	孃 niáng	dù	gū	jì
wonderful; subtle	hinder, impede; harm	mother; aunt; young lady	jealous -	aunt; nun; sister in law	prostitute -
73;38 7 (2)	73;38 7 (3)	73;38 10 (1)	73;38 7 (4)	73;38 8 (1)	73;38 7 (-)

媳	嫁	婶	婉	娃	嫂
xí	jià	嬸 shěn	wǎn	wá	sǎo
daughter in law	marry (a man); transfer	aunt -	graceful; gracious	baby -	sister in law -
73;38 13 (3)	73;38 13 (3)	73;38 11 (3)	73;38 11 (-)	73;38 9 (3)	73;38 12 (2)

始	娱	娇	婚	嫌	媒
shǐ	娛 yú	嬌 jiāo	hūn	xián	méi
beginning -	joy; happy; amuse	lovely; delicate; pamper	marriage; to marry	suspicion; grudge; dislike	matchmaker, go-between
73;38 8 (1)	73;38 10 (4)	73;38 9 (4)	73;38 11 (2)	73;38 13 (3)	73;38 12 (4)

妞□
姻□

姥	嫉	妮	媚	姻
lǎo	jí	nī	mèi	yīn
[grandmother] -	jealousy; dislike	[girl] -	flatter; charming	marriage; in-laws
73;38 9 (3)	73;38 13 (4)	73;38 8 (-)	73;38 12 (-)	73;38 9 (2)

阝

队	阵	陈	陕
隊 duì	陣 zhèn	陳 chén	陝 shǎn
squad, team	formation, array; period	exhibit, explain; old, stale	Shaanxi -
33;170 4 (2)	33;170 6 (2)	33;170 7 (3)	33;170 8 (3)

阳	阻	限	阴
陽 yáng	zǔ	xiàn	陰 陰 yīn
yang, positive; sun; overt; &	hinder, block, obstruct	limit -	yin, negative; occult; shade; cloudy; moon; &
33;170 6 (1)	33;170 7 (3)	33;170 8 (2)	33;170 6 (1)

防	陪	障	陀	院
fáng	péi	zhàng	tuó	yuàn
dyke; defend; guard against	accompany -	obstruct, hinder; barrier	[(spinning) top] -	institute; courtyard
33;170 6 (2)	33;170 10 (2)	33;170 13 (3)	33;170 7 (-)	33;170 9 (1)

陆	陡	陵	隙	隘
陸 liù lù	dǒu	líng	*郤 隙 xì	ài
six; (dry) land	precipitous; abruptly	hill, mound; tomb	crevice, gap, rift; discord	narrow; mountain pass
33;170 7 (2)	33;170 9 (3)	33;170 10 (3)	33;170 12 (4)	33;170 12 (4)

际	陌	隔
際 jì	mò	gé
border; inter-; occasion; &	path, road	separate, apart; cut off
33;170 7 (2)	33;170 8 (3)	33;170 12 (2)

降	隆	陷	隐
jiàng xiáng	lóng lōng	xiàn	隱 yǐn
fall, drop, lower; give in; subdue	grand; thriving; intense; bulge	bogged down; pitfall; flaw; &	hidden, latent
33;170 8 (2)	33;170 11 (4)	33;170 10 (3)	33;170 11 (3)

阶	险	除
階 jiē	險 xiǎn	chú
steps, stairs; rank	danger; risky; sinister; almost	get rid of; divide by; except
33;170 6 (2)	33;170 9 (1)	33;170 9 (1)

附	阿	陶	随	隧	陋
fù	ā ē	táo	隨 suí	suì	lòu
append; agree; near to	('a' sound); pander to	earthenware; nurture; happy	follow; comply; allow; &	[tunnel] -	vulgar, humble; ugly; shallow
33;170 7 (1)	33;170 7 (2)	33;170 10 (4)	33;170 11 (2)	33;170 14 (4)	33;170 8 (4)

咱
咱
咱

咱 zán zan we (including you) 58;30 9 (1)	**嗅** xiù sniff - 58;30 13 (4)	**噢** ō (exclamation: Oh!) 58;30 15 (3)	**啤** pí [beer] - 58;30 11 (1)	**呜** wū hoot, toot 58;30 7 (4)	**鸣** míng chirp; to voice; make a sound 58;196 8 (3)
响 xiǎng sound, noise; loud 58;180 9 (1)	**咏** yǒng chant - 58;149 8 (4)	**哦** ó ò é (exclamation: What?, Oh!) 58;30 10 (3)	**喧** xuān noise, clamor 58;30 12 (4)		
吭 háng kēng throat; make a sound 58;30 7 (-)	**咬** yǎo bite; snap at; pronounce; & 58;30 9 (2)	**咳** hāi ké Doh!; cough 58;30 9 (1)	**哼** hēng hng moan; groan; hum; Humph! 58;30 10 (2)	**啼** tí weep, wail; to crow, caw 58;30 12 (-)	**嚷** rǎng rāng shout, make an uproar 58;30 20 (2)
咕 gū cluck, coo 58;30 8 (-)	**哇** wā wa cry, wail; (particle) 58;30 9 (2)	**嗦** suo [tremble; wordy] 58;30 13 (3)	**喷** pēn pèn squirt, spray; in season 58;30 12 (2)	**喃** nán [mutter, chatter] 58;30 12 (-)	**嘻** xī laugh, giggle 58;30 15 (-)
吵 chǎo chāo quarrel, make noise, disturb 58;30 7 (2)	**啃** kěn nibble, gnaw 58;30 11 (4)	**喘** chuǎn gasp, pant, breathe hard 58;30 12 (3)	**嗤** chī sneer 58;30 13 (-)	**啸** xiào whistle; roar (of animal) 58;30 11 (4)	

咱
咒

哨 shào sentry, guard; whistle; chirp 58;30 10 (3)	**咪** mī [mew, miaow; smiling] 58;30 9 (-)	**喽** lóu lou [underling]; (particle) 58;30 12 (3)	
哎 āi Ah!; Hey!; Look out! 58;30 8 (2)	**喵** miāo miaow - 58;30 11 (-)	**唠** láo [chatter] - 58;30 10 (4)	**哄** hǒng hōng hòng deceive; coax; hubbub 58;30 9 (4)

喝
hē hè
to drink;
to shout
58;30 12 (1)

唱
chàng
sing
–
58;30 11 (1)

噪
zào
chirp;
cacophony
58;30 16 (4)

喂
*餵 wèi
Hello?; Hey!;
to feed
58;184 12 (1)

哩
li lī
(particle)
–
58;30 10 (2)

嗯
ńg ňg ǹg
What?, Hey!,
Hmm.
58;30 13 (1)

嘿
hēi
Hey!
–
58;30 15 (2)

嗓
sǎng
throat;
voice
58;30 13 (2)

呼
hū
exhale; cry out;
'whoo' sound
58;30 8 (2)

唾
tuò
to spit;
saliva
58;30 11 (4)

嚼
jiáo jué
chew
–
58;30 20 (4)

哦
ó ò é
(exclamation:
What?, Oh!)
58;30 10 (3)

吩
fēn
[command,
order]
58;30 7 (2)

吟
yín
chant, recite;
(animal's) roar
58;30 7 (4)

哈
hā hǎ hà
exhale;
Aha!; laugh
58;30 9 (1)

啥
shà
what
–
58;30 11 (4)

喻
yù
explain; know;
analogy
58;30 12 (4)

吃
chī
eat; absorb; live
on; wipe out; &
58;30 6 (1)

哆
duō
[tremble,
shiver]
58;30 9 (3)

唤
唤 huàn
call,
rouse
58;30 10 (3)

唆
suō
incite
–
58;30 10 (4)

唉
āi ài
yes, all right;
Well!; Alas!
58;30 10 (3)

嘴
zuǐ
mouth;
spout
58;30 16 (1)

哗
嘩 譁 huā huá
clamor,
noise
58;30 9 (3)

口

叶
*葉 yè
leaf;
period, epoch
58;30 5 (2)

吐
tǔ tù
spit; vent;
vomit; disgorge
58;30 6 (2)

吨
噸 dūn
ton
-
58;30 7 (2)

味
wèi
taste; smell;
interest
58;30 8 (2)

咪
mī
[mew, miaow;
smiling]
58;30 9 (-)

呐
nà
[shout]
-
58;30 7 (1)

呻
shēn
[groan]
-
58;30 8 (4)

啸
嘯 xiào
whistle; roar
(of animal)
58;30 11 (4)

叫
*叫 jiào
cry, call; tell;
be called
58;30 5 (1)

吹
chuī
blow, puff;
brag; failure
58;30 7 (1)

咋
zǎ zhā zhà
Why?, How?;
[boast]; bite
58;30 8 (4)

吻
wěn
lips; kiss;
animal's mouth
58;30 7 (3)

呼
hū
exhale; cry out;
'whoo' sound
58;30 8 (2)

唾
tuò
to spit;
saliva
58;30 11 (4)

哦
ó ò é
(exclamation:
What?, Oh!)
58;30 10 (3)

叮
dīng
sting;
make sure
58;30 5 (4)

吓
嚇 hè xià
intimidate;
Pah! (annoyed)
58;30 6 (2)

吁
*籲 yù xū
plead;
groan; Oh!
58;30 7 (4)

呀
ya yā
(particle);
Oh!
58;30 7 (1)

啄
zhuó
peck at
-
58;30 11 (4)

吧
ba bā
(particle);
'crack' sound
58;30 7 (1)

叽
嘰 jī
chirp,
twitter
58;30 5 (-)

叨
tāo dāo
obliged;
[chatter]
58;30 5 (4)

叹
嘆 歎 tàn
sigh; admire;
acclaim
58;30 5 (3)

吸
xī
inhale, absorb;
attract
58;30 6 (2)

吗
嗎 ma má mǎ
(question
particle)
58;30 6 (1)

哩
lī lǐ
(particle)
-
58;30 10 (2)

叭
bā
'bang' sound
58;30 5 (3)

哑
哑 yǎ yā
dumb; hoarse; Oh!
58;30 9 (4)

啡
fēi
('fi' sound); [coffee]
58;30 11 (1)

啦
la lā
(particle) -
58;30 11 (1)

啪
pā
'bang' sound
58;30 11 (-)

咐
fu
[instruct; exhort]
58;30 8 (2)

唯
wéi wěi
solely; [yes-man]
58;30 11 (4)

喉
hóu
throat, larynx
58;30 12 (3)

咧
liě liē
[grin; careless]
58;30 9 (-)

喇
lǎ lá
trumpet, horn
58;30 12 (3)

嗽
sòu
cough -
58;30 14 (1)

吼
hǒu
roar, bellow
58;30 7 (3)

哟
哟 yo yō
(particle); Oh!
58;30 9 (3)

咖
kā gā
('ka' sound); [coffee]
58;30 8 (1)

啊
ā á ǎ à a
(exclamation: Eh?, Oh!, etc.)
58;30 11 (1)

嘲
cháo
to ridicule, mock
58;30 15 (4)

哪
na nǎ něi
(particle); Which?, What?
58;30 10 (1)

嘟
dū
toot, honk; pout
58;30 13 (-)

咙
咙 lóng
[throat] -
58;30 8 (3)

听
聽 tīng
listen; obey; allow
58;128 7 (1)

呢
ne ní
(particle); woollen
58;30 8 (1)

喔
wō ō
cock's crow; Oh!
58;30 12 (-)

嘱
囑 zhǔ
urge, advise
58;30 15 (3)

嘛
ma
(particle) -
58;30 14 (1)

叼
diāo
hold (in the mouth)
58;30 5 (4)

呵
hē
scold; exhale; Oh!
58;30 8 (3)

吗
嗎 ma má mǎ
(question particle)
58;30 6 (1)

呜
嗚 wū
hoot, toot
58;30 7 (4)

鸣
鳴 míng
chirp; to voice; make a sound
58;196 8 (3)

喊
hǎn
shout, cry, call
58;30 12 (1)

呕
嘔 ǒu
vomit; spit out
58;30 7 (4)

咽
嚥 yàn yān yè
swallow, gulp; throat
58;30 9 (2)

1 41
2 42
3 43
4 44
5 45
6 46
7 47
8 48
9 49
10 50
11 51
12 52
13 53
14 54
15 55
16 56
17 57
18 58
19 59
20 60
21 61
22 62
23 63
24 64
25 65
26 66
27 67
28 68
29 69
30 70
31 71
32 72
33 73
34 74
35 75
36 76
37 77
38 78
39 79
40 80

日

旷 曠 kuàng
spacious; carefree; &
103;72 7 (4)

昨 zuó
yesterday
-
103;72 9 (1)

昧 mèi
conceal; ignorant of
103;72 9 (4)

旺 wàng
flourishing; brisk
103;72 8 (4)

时 時 shí
time; hour; season; opportunity; present, current; now and then
103;72 7 (1)

明 míng
bright; clear; overt; next; &
103;72 8 (1)

映 yìng
reflect; shine
103;72 9 (2)

晒 曬 shài
to shine (sun); sunbathe
103;72 10 (2)

晌 shǎng
midday; part of the day
103;72 10 (4)

晖 暉 huī
sunshine
-
103;72 10 (-)

晾 liàng
to air, dry in the sun
103;72 12 (4)

暗 àn
dark; dim; hidden, secret
103;72 13 (2)

昭 zhāo
clear, evident
103;72 9 (-)

晤 wù
meet, interview
103;72 11 (4)

晓 曉 xiǎo
dawn; know; tell
103;72 10 (2)

晚 wǎn
evening, night; late; junior
103;72 11 (1)

晴 qíng
fine (weather)
103;72 12 (1)

暖 nuǎn
warm, genial
103;72 13 (1)

曝 pù bào
expose to the sun (literary)
103;72 19 (-)

晰 xī
clear, distinct
103;72 12 (3)

暇 xiá
leisure
-
103;72 13 (-)

白

的 de dí dì
(particle); bull's eye
150;106 8 (1)

魄 pò bó tuò
soul, spirit, vigor
150;194 14 (4)

酉

配 pèi
mix; match up; deserve; &
193;164 10 (2)

酌 zhuó
pour out (wine), drink; consider
193;164 10 (4)

酗 xù
[get drunk]
-
193;164 11 (4)

酬 chóu
reward; fulfil; entertain friends
193;164 13 (3)

醉 zuì
be drunk
-
193;164 15 (2)

醇 chún
alcohol; good wine
193;164 15 (-)

酵 jiào
ferment, leaven
193;164 14 (-)

酷 kù
cruel, harsh; extremely
193;164 14 (3)

酿 釀 niàng niáng
brew, ferment; lead to; wine
193;164 14 (4)

酝 醞 yùn
[brew]
-
193;164 11 (4)

酶 méi
ferment, yeast; enzyme
193;164 14 (4)

醋 cù
vinegar; jealousy
193;164 15 (2)

酸 suān
acid; sour; ache; grief; &
193;164 14 (1)

醒 xǐng
revive, wake up; awake; &
193;164 16 (2)

盯	眯	眼	眠	助
dīng	瞇 mī mǐ	yǎn	mián	zhù
observe, gaze at	squint; get (dust) in eyes	eye; key point	sleep -	help, assist
141;109 7 (3)	141;109 11 (3)	141;109 11 (1)	141;109 10 (3)	28;19 7 (1)

睦	睹	瞎	睛	瞒
mù	dǔ	xiā	jīng	瞞 mán
harmonious -	see -	blind; senseless	eyeball -	deceive
141;109 13 (4)	141;109 13 (4)	141;109 15 (3)	141;109 13 (1)	141;109 15 (3)

眨	睬	睡	瞬
zhǎ	cǎi	shuì	shùn
wink, blink	take note -	sleep -	blink, wink
141;109 9 (4)	141;109 13 (4)	141;109 13 (1)	141;109 17 (-)

盼	睁	瞻	瞧	瞪
pàn	睜 zhēng	zhān	qiáo	dèng
hope for; look	open (eyes)	look ahead, look up	look, see (colloq)	stare, glare
141;109 9 (2)	141;109 11 (2)	141;109 18 (4)	141;109 17 (2)	141;109 17 (3)

瞩	眶
矚 zhǔ	kuàng
gaze, look at	eyesocket
141;109 17 (4)	141;109 11 (4)

耻	取	耶	耽	耿	聊
*恥 chǐ	qǔ	yē yé	dān	gěng	liáo
shame, disgrace	take; obtain; choose; &	('je' sound) -	delay; indulge in	honest, just; dedicated	merely; slightly; chat
163;128 10 (4)	163;29 8 (1)	34;128 8 (-)	163;128 10 (3)	163;128 10 (4)	163;128 11 (2)

聘	联	聪	职	敢
pìn	聯 lián	聰 cōng	職 zhí	gǎn
employ, engage	unite, join, link up	acute hearing; intelligent	duty, job, post	bold; dare; be sure
163;128 13 (4)	163;128 12 (1)	163;128 15 (2)	163;128 11 (2)	113;66 11 (1)

畔	略	畴	邮
pàn	lüè	疇 chóu	郵 yóu
side, border, (river) bank	slightly; omit; plan; seize; &	category; farmland	post, mail
142;102 10 (3)	142;102 11 (2)	142;102 12 (4)	143;163 7 (1)

1	41
2	42
3	43
4	44
5	45
6	46
7	47
8	48
9	49
10	50
11	51
12	52
13	53
14	54
15	55
16	56
17	57
18	58
19	59
20	60
21	61
22	62
23	63
24	64
25	65
26	66
27	67
28	68
29	69
30	70
31	71
32	72
33	73
34	74
35	75
36	76
37	77
38	78
39	79
40	80

■ 石 歹

石

矿 礦 kuàng
ore, mine
136;112 8 (2)

砍 kǎn
chop, hack
136;112 9 (2)

矽 xī
silicon
-
136;112 8 (-)

破 pò
destroy; split; broken; torn; &
136;112 10 (1)

砖 磚 zhuān
brick
-
136;112 9 (3)

础 礎 chǔ
plinth, base
136;112 10 (1

砰 pēng
bang, thump
136;112 10 (-)

研 yán
grind; study, research
136;112 9 (1)

硬 yìng
hard, tough; with difficulty; &
136;112 12 (2)

硕 碩 shuò
huge
-
136;112 11 (-)

码 碼 mǎ
numeral; wharf; yard (3 ft)
136;112 8 (2)

砂 shā
sand, grit
136;112 9 (4)

碎 suì
smash; broken; garrulous
136;112 13 (2)

硫 liú
sulfur
-
136;112 12 (4)

磅 bàng páng
weigh; scales; pound (16 oz)
136;112 15 (3)

碗 wǎn
a bowl
-
136;112 13 (1)

辟 *闢 pì bì
open up (land); incisive; refute
186;160 13 (2

碑 bēi
stele (upright stone tablet)
136;112 13 (2)

硅 guī
silicon
-
136;112 11 (4)

磕 kē
knock against
-
136;112 15 (4)

碳 tàn
carbon
136;112 14 (4)

碟 dié
small dish, small plate
136;112 14 (4)

确 確 què
true, real; firmly (believe)
136;112 12 (

碰 pèng
bump; meet; try one's luck
136;112 13 (1)

磁 cí
magnet; porcelain
136;112 14 (1)

磋 cuō
to polish; consult
136;112 14 (4)

磷 lín
phosphorus
-
136;112 17 (4)

碌 碌 lù liù
busy; ordinary
136;112 13 (4)

碍 礙 ài
obstruct, impede
136;112 13 (3

砌 qì
lay (bricks); steps
136;112 9 (4)

砸 zá
break, smash, pound, crush
136;112 10 (3)

破 pò
destroy; split; broken; torn; &
136;112 10 (1)

碱 jiǎn
alkali, (caustic) soda
136;112 14 (3)

歹

列 liè
arrange, line up; rank, file; list; &
97;18 6 (2)

歼 殲 jiān
annihilate
-
97;78 7 (3)

殊 shū
different; special; very
97;78 10 (2)

殃 yāng
disaster; bring misfortune
97;78 9 (4)

残 殘 cán
incomplete; injure; savage
97;78 9 (3)

殖 zhí
breed, reproduce
97;78 12 (3)

死 sǐ
die; death; rigid
97;78 6 (1)

外 wài
outside; foreign; besides; &
64;36 5 (1)

邪	鴉 鸦	雅
xié	yā	yǎ
evil; heretical	a crow -	proper; elegant; your (polite)
34;163 6 (4)	99;196 9 (4)	99;172 12 (4)

乱	敌	辞	甜	刮
亂 luàn	敵 dí	辭 cí	tián	guā
confused; riot; random; &	foe; oppose	depart; decline; dismiss; &	sweet; (sleep) soundly	scrape; extort; to blow; &
177;5 7 (1)	177;66 10 (2)	177;160 13 (3)	177;99 11 (2)	177;18 8 (1)

跃	跌	践	跟	距
躍 yuè	diē	踐 jiàn	gēn	jù
leap, jump	fall, decline	trample; carry out	heel; follow; with	distance (from, apart)
196;157 11 (2)	196;157 12 (2)	196;157 12 (1)	196;157 13 (1)	196;157 11 (2)

趴	跳	躊	跑
pā	tiào	躊 chóu	pǎo
bend over; lie prone	jump, leap; omit; throb	[hesitate] -	run; flee; away
196;157 9 (3)	196;157 13 (1)	196;157 14 (4)	196;157 12 (1)

踪	蹄	踏	跨	蹦
蹤 zōng	tí	tà tā	kuà	bèng
tracks, footprint	hoof -	tread, trample; on the spot	stride; bestride, straddle	jump, leap, hop
196;157 15 (4)	196;157 16 (3)	196;157 15 (3)	196;157 13 (2)	196;157 18 (4)

蹲	蹭	蹰
dūn	cèng	chú
crouch, squat	rub; loiter	[hesitate] -
196;157 19 (2)	196;157 19 (4)	196;157 18 (4)

跺	蹋	踢	躁	踊
duò	tà	tī	zào	踴 yǒng
stamp (foot) -	[trample on] -	kick -	impetuous; restless	jump up, leap up
196;157 13 (4)	196;157 17 (4)	196;157 15 (1)	196;157 20 (3)	196;157 14 (3)

蹈	踩	跪	路	蹬
dǎo	cǎi	guì	lù	dēng dèng
skip; tread, trample	step on, tread	kneel -	road, route; way; region; &	step on, trample
196;157 17 (3)	196;157 15 (2)	196;157 13 (2)	196;157 13 (1)	196;157 19 (3)

1	41
2	42
3	43
4	44
5	45
6	46
7	47
8	48
9	49
10	50
11	51
12	52
13	53
14	54
15	55
16	56
17	57
18	58
19	59
20	60
21	61
22	62
23	63
24	64
25	65
26	66
27	67
28	68
29	69
30	70
31	71
32	72
33	73
34	74
35	75
36	76
37	77
38	78
39	79
40	80

肚	胜	肤	胖	胀	肿
dù dǔ	勝 shèng	膚 fū	pàng pán	脹 zhàng	腫 zhǒng
belly, abdomen; tripe	victory; superb; surpass; &	skin; [superficial]	fat, plump; contented	expand, swell; bloated	swollen -
118;130 7 (2)	118;19 9 (1)	118;130 8 (2)	118;130 9 (2)	118;130 8 (3)	118;130 8 (3)

肝	肌	肠	豚
gān	jī	腸 cháng	tún
liver -	muscle -	intestines -	pig, piglet
118;130 7 (2)	118;130 6 (3)	118;130 7 (2)	118;152 11 (-)

肥	朋	服	那
féi	péng	fú	nà nèi nè nā
fat; baggy; fertile; fertilizer	friend -	clothes; serve; obey; &	that; in that case
118;130 8 (2)	118;74 8 (1)	118;74 8 (1)	34;163 6 (1)

胁	膨	脚	鹏
脅 xié	péng	腳 jiǎo	鵬 péng
upper body, ribs; coerce	[inflate, expand; swollen]	foot, base; leg	roc (fabled giant bird)
118;130 8 (3)	118;130 16 (3)	118;130 11 (1)	152;196 13 (-)

脏
臟 髒 zàng zāng
viscera; dirty
118;130 10 (1)

肘	胸	胞	腻
zhǒu	xiōng	bāo	膩 nì
elbow -	chest, thorax; at heart	placenta; siblings	greasy; tired of; dirt; meticulous
118;130 7 (-)	118;130 10 (2)	118;130 9 (3)	118;130 13 (-)

腿
tuǐ
leg; thigh; ham
118;130 13 (1)

■□　肛

脉	腺	脾	膊	彤

脉 脈 mài mò
vein; pulse;
lovingly
118;130 9 (2)

腺 xiàn
gland
-
118;130 13 (-)

脾 pí
spleen
-
118;130 12 (2)

膊 bó
arm
-
118;130 14 (2)

彤 tóng
red
(literary)
63;59 7 (-)

肺 fèi
lungs
-
118;130 8 (2)

肪 fáng
[animal fat]
-
118;130 8 (4)

胶 膠 jiāo
glue; sticky;
rubber
118;130 10 (3)

脑 腦 nǎo
brain
-
118;130 10 (2)

膀 bǎng pāng páng
upper arm;
swell; bladder
118;130 14 (2)

腔 qiāng
cavity;
tune; accent
118;130 12 (3)

腕 wàn
wrist
-
118;130 12 (-)

肢 zhī
limb
-
118;130 8 (4)

脖 bó
neck
-
118;130 11 (2)

膝 xī
knee
-
118;130 15 (4)

脂 zhī
grease, fat;
rouge
118;130 10 (4)

脱 tuō
cast off, shed;
omit; escape
118;130 11 (1)

腾 騰 téng tēng
jump, ascend;
make room
118;187 13 (3)

膛 táng
chest, thorax;
hollow chamber
118;130 15 (4)

腊 臘 là xī
cured (meat);
December
118;130 12 (4)

膜 mó
membrane
-
118;130 14 (4)

朦 méng
[dim,
hazy]
118;74 17 (-)

股 gǔ
thigh; section;
strand; a share
118;130 8 (3)

胆 膽 dǎn
courage, guts;
gall bladder
118;130 9 (2)

腥 xīng
raw meat, fish;
fishy
118;130 13 (4)

腰 yāo
waist; pocket;
halfway up
118;130 13 (2)

腮 sāi
cheeks
-
118;130 13 (4)

腹 fù
belly,
abdomen
118;130 13 (4)

胳 gē gé
[arm]
-
118;130 10 (2)

脆 cuì
crisp;
brittle
118;130 10 (2)

脸 臉 liǎn
face,
countenance
118;130 11 (1)

胎 tāi
embryo; birth;
a tire; padding
118;130 9 (-)

舟

舶	航	舵	舱	彤
bó	háng	duò	艙 cāng	tóng
(sea-going) ship	boat, ship; to sail, fly	rudder, helm	cabin, hold (on ship)	red (literary)
182;137 11 (4)	182;137 10 (2)	182;137 11 (4)	182;137 10 (3)	63;59 7 (-)

舰	船	般	艘	艇
艦 jiàn	chuán	bān	sōu	tǐng
warship	boat, ship	sort, kind; manner	(measure word)	boat
-			-	
182;137 10 (3)	182;137 11 (1)	182;137 10 (1)	182;137 15 (3)	182;137 12 (4)

身

躬	射	躯	躲	躺
gōng	shè	軀 qū	duǒ	tǎng
to bend, bow; in person	shoot (gun); radiate; allude	human body	hide oneself; avoid	lie down, recline
200;158 10 (4)	200;41 10 (2)	200;158 11 (-)	200;158 13 (2)	200;158 15 (1)

良

朗	郎
lǎng	láng
bright; loud and clear	man, person; darling
118;74 10 (2)	34;163 8 (2)

艮

即	既
jí	jì
right away; approach; i.e.	already; since; as well as
184;26 7 (2)	184;71 9 (2)

欧
歐 ōu
Europe;
(surname)
120;76 8 (3)

殴
毆 ōu
beat,
strike
119;79 8 (4)

鸥
鷗 ōu
gull
152;196 9 (-)

财
財 cái
wealth,
property
106;154 7 (3)

败
敗 bài
defeated; fail;
defeat; spoil; &
106;66 8 (2)

账
賬 zhàng
accounts,
credit
106;154 8 (-)

贱
賤 jiàn
cheap; lowly;
my (humble)
106;154 9 (3)

则
則 zé
rules; norm,
model; then; &
106;18 6 (2)

贴
貼 tiē
paste; nestle;
subsidize
106;154 9 (2)

赔
賠 péi
compensate;
suffer a loss
106;154 12 (2)

赎
贖 shú
redeem,
ransom, atone
106;154 12 (-)

赠
贈 zèng
give (as gift)
-
106;154 16 (3)

赚
賺 zhuàn zuàn
make a profit
-
106;154 14 (3)

贬
貶 biǎn
demote;
censure
106;154 8 (4)

赐
賜 cì
bestow,
grant
106;154 12 (-)

赂
賂 lù
[bribe]
-
106;154 10 (4)

贩
販 fàn
buy and sell;
dealer
106;154 8 (4)

贿
賄 huì
bribe
-
106;154 10 (4)

赌
賭 dǔ
gamble,
bet
106;154 12 (4)

购
購 gòu
buy
-
106;154 8 (2)

贼
賊 zéi
thief; traitor;
furtive; cunning
106;154 10 (4)

赋
賦 fù
bestow;
compose poem
106;154 12 (4)

驮
馱 tuó duò
carry (on back,
of animals)
75;187 6 (3)

驰
馳 chí
gallop, go fast;
far and wide
75;187 6 (4)

驶
駛 shǐ
(of a vehicle)
to go; to speed
75;187 8 (3)

驱
驅 qū
drive (vehicle);
expel; run fast
75;187 7 (4)

驴
驢 lú
donkey
-
75;187 7 (3)

驻
駐 zhù
stay; halt;
be stationed
75;187 8 (3)

驼
駝 tuó
camel;
hump-backed
75;187 8 (3)

骇
駭 hài
startled,
astonished
75;187 9 (-)

骗
騙 piàn
deceive,
swindle
75;187 12 (2)

骑
騎 qí
ride (animal,
bicycle)
75;187 11 (1)

驳
駁 bó
refute;
a barge
75;187 7 (4)

骏
駿 jùn
fine horse,
steed
75;187 10 (-)

验
驗 yàn
examine;
effective
75;187 10 (1)

骄
驕 jiāo
arrogant
-
75;187 9 (2)

骆
駱 luò
[camel]
-
75;187 9 (3)

骚
騷 sāo
disturb, upset;
literary; &
75;187 12 (3)

骡
騾 luó
mule
-
75;187 14 (4)

骤
驟 zhòu
sudden;
trot (horse)
75;187 17 (3)

虫 鱼 角

虫

虹	虾	蚁	蛛	蚂	蛾
hóng	蝦 xiā	蟻 yǐ	zhū	螞 mǎ mà	é
rainbow	shrimp	ant	spider	[ant; locust]	moth
-	-	-			
174;142 9 (4)	174;142 9 (3)	174;142 9 (4)	174;142 12 (4)	174;142 9 (4)	174;142 13 (4)

蜘	蝴	螂
zhī	hú	láng
[spider]	[butterfly]	[mantis, cockroach]
-	-	
174;142 14 (4)	174;142 15 (3)	174;142 14 (-)

蚊	蛇	蟑	螃	蝗	蝉
wén	shé yí	zhāng	páng	huáng	蟬 chán
mosquito	snake	[cockroach]	[crab]	locust	cicada
		-	-		
174;142 10 (3)	174;142 11 (2)	174;142 17 (-)	174;142 16 (-)	174;142 15 (4)	174;142 14 (4)

蛙	蜻	蜡	蝶
wā	qīng	蠟 là	dié
frog	[dragonfly]	wax, polish; candle	butterfly
174;142 12 (3)	174;142 14 (4)	174;142 14 (3)	174;142 15 (3)

蝇	螺	蜂
蠅 yíng	luó	fēng
a fly	snail, conch; spiral	bee, wasp; swarm
-		
174;142 14 (3)	174;142 17 (4)	174;142 13 (2)

蜓
tíng
[dragonfly]
174;142 12 (4)

鱼

稣	鲜	鲸	鲍
穌 sū	鮮 xiān xiǎn	鯨 jīng	鮑 bào
revive	fresh; colorful; tasty; seafood	whale	[abalone]; (surname)
-		-	
210;115 13 (-)	210;195 14 (2)	210;195 16 (3)	210;195 13 (-)

角

触	解
觸 chù	jiě jiè xiè
touch	untie; explain; solve; dispel; &
-	
201;148 13 (2)	201;148 13 (1)

卓 辛 革 其

韩	朝	乾	翰
韓 hán	cháo zhāo	qián	hàn
(surname)	facing; dynasty;	male (archaic)	writing brush;
-	morning; day; &	(see Table 1)	writing (literary)
203;178 12 (-)	203;74 12 (1)	203;5 11 (-)	203;124 16 (-)

辣	辨	辩	辫	瓣
là	biàn	辯 biàn	辮 biàn	bàn
spicy, acrid;	differentiate,	dispute,	plait, braid;	petal, segment,
vicious	distinguish	debate	pigtail	piece; valve
186;160 14 (3)	186;160 16 (4)	186;160 16 (3)	186;120 17 (4)	186;97 19 (3)

勒	鞋	鞠	靴	鞭
lēi lè	xié	jū	xuē	biān
tighten, rein in;	shoe	to rear, bring	boot	whip
compel	-	up; nourish	-	-
212;19 11 (4)	212;177 15 (1)	212;177 17 (4)	212;177 13 (4)	212;177 18 (4)

欺	斯	期
qī	sī	qī jī
deceive;	this; thus;	expect; period;
bully	('si' sound)	appointed time
120;76 12 (2)	115;69 12 (3)	118;74 12 (1)

1	41
2	42
3	43
4	44
5	45
6	46
7	47
8	48
9	49
10	50
11	51
12	52
13	53
14	54
15	55
16	56
17	57
18	58
19	59
20	60
21	61
22	62
23	63
24	64
25	65
26	66
27	67
28	68
29	69
30	70
31	71
32	72
33	73
34	74
35	75
36	76
37	77
38	78
39	79
40	80

丨一	以 yǐ using; so as to; according to; & 23;9 4 (1)	北 běi north - 39;21 5 (1)	乖 guāi obedient; quick-witted 4;4 8 (3)	乘 chéng shèng ride; multiply; make use of 149;4 10 (2)	剩 shèng surplus, residue 17;18 12 (1)
束 求 来 屯 皮	赖 賴 lài rely; linger; deny; shirk 192;154 13 (4)	救 jiù rescue, aid 113;66 11 (2)	颊 頰 jiá cheeks - 170;181 12 (4)	顿 頓 dùn pause; arrange; suddenly; & 170;181 10 (1)	颇 頗 pō quite, rather 153;181 11 (
崔 求 髟 与	鹤 鶴 hè crane (bird) - 152;196 15 (-)	叔 shū uncle; brother in law 35;29 8 (2)	疑 yí doubt - 39;103 14 (2)	鼎 dǐng cauldron; tripod, tripartite 141;206 12 (-)	
血 由 申 亡 文	衅 釁 xìn quarrel - 181;164 11 (4)	邮 郵 yóu post, mail 143;163 7 (1)	畅 暢 chàng smooth, fluent; uninhibited 144;72 8 (3)	氓 méng máng the common people 43;83 8 (3)	刘 劉 liú (surname) 84;18 6 (3)
丰 韦 丰	邦 bāng nation, state 34;163 6 (4)	韧 韌 rèn tough; pliable yet strong 91;178 7 (4)	艳 艷 豔 豐 yàn gorgeous; romantic 27;139 10 (3)		
音 亲 冢 京	韵 *韻 yùn rhyme; melodic tone; charming 211;180 13 (4)	新 xīn new - 115;69 13 (1)	毅 yì firm, resolute 119;79 15 (3)	就 jiù right away; only, just; even if; then; precisely; concerning; & 9;43 12 (1)	
占 古 圭 壴	战 戰 zhàn war, battle; tremble 101;62 9 (2)	故 gù former; to die; on purpose; & 113;66 9 (1)	胡 *鬍 hú reckless; beard; & 118;130 9 (2)	封 fēng seal up; bestow 54;41 9 (1)	鼓 gǔ drum; rouse; bellows; bulge 224;207 13 (2
赤 克 青 害	赫 hè impressive - 190;155 14 (4)	兢 jīng [conscientious] - 12;10 14 (4)	静 靜 jìng still, calm, quiet 202;174 14 (1)	豁 huō huò crack; forsake; open; exempt 199;150 17 (4)	

幺 ㄠ 夫

加	幻	幼	雄	規
jiā	huàn	yòu	xióng	規 guī
plus; add, augment	unreal; changeable	young; child	male; mighty, grand; hero	rule, law; plan; admonish
28;19 5 (1)	76;52 4 (3)	76;52 5 (3)	208;172 12 (2)	107;147 8 (2)

肖

从	巫	能
從 cóng cōng	wū	néng
from; to follow; secondary; &	witch, wizard	able to; energy; capability
23;60 4 (1)	48;48 7 (4)	37;130 10 (1)

齿 昔

收	龄	鹊
shōu	齡 líng	鵲 què
receive; collect up; cease; &	age, years, duration	magpie -
113;66 6 (1)	206;211 13 (2)	152;196 13 (4)

并

翔	瓶
xiáng	píng
soar, hover	bottle, vase, jug
157;124 12 (4)	98;98 10 (1)

彳 刍

外	竹	皱
wài	zhú	皺 zhòu
outside; foreign; besides; &	bamboo -	crease, wrinkle
64;36 5 (1)	178;118 6 (2)	153;107 10 (3)

1	41
2	42
3	43
4	44
5	45
6	46
7	47
8	48
9	49
10	50
11	51
12	52
13	53
14	54
15	55
16	56
17	57
18	58
19	59
20	60
21	61
22	62
23	63
24	64
25	65
26	66
27	67
28	68
29	69
30	70
31	71
32	72
33	73
34	74
35	75
36	76
37	77
38	78
39	79
40	80

丁 干 正 而	顶 頂 dǐng — stand up to; top; utmost; & 170;181 8 (2)	刊 kān — print; publication 17;18 5 (3)	政 zhèng — politics; administration 113;66 9 (1)	耐 nài — endure, bear 169;126 9 (2)

艮 甲 里 果	既 jì — already; since; as well as 184;71 9 (2)	即 jí — right away; approach; i.e. 184;26 7 (2)	鸭 鴨 yā — a duck 152;196 10 (3)	野 yě — countryside; wild; limit; & 195;166 11 (2)	夥 huǒ — many (literary) (see Table 1) 142;36 15 (-)

厉 厄 镸 臣 臣	励 勵 lì — encourage — 28;19 7 (2)	顾 顧 gù — look around; look after; visit 170;181 10 (1)	肆 sì — reckless; unbridled; four 124;129 13 (4)	颐 頤 yí — cheeks; keep fit (literary) 170;181 13 (-)	卧 臥 wò — lie down; berth, sleeper 164;131 8 (3)

习 予 至 正	羽 yǔ — feather — 183;124 6 (2)	预 預 yù — in advance — 170;181 10 (1)	豫 yù — pleased; Henan (literary) 31;152 15 (3)	颈 頸 jīng gěng — neck 170;181 11 (4)	疏 shū — sparse; neglec unfamiliar; & 31;103 12 (4)

己 弓 弜 君	改 gǎi — change, alter, rectify 113;66 7 (1)	弱 ruò — weak; inferior; a bit less 71;57 10 (2)	疆 jiāng — boundary, frontier 71;102 19 (3)	群 qún — crowd, group, herd 157;123 13 (2)

云 元 豆	动 動 dòng — move, act; use; alter; arouse 28;19 6 (1)	魂 hún — soul, spirit 216;194 13 (3)	顽 頑 wán — stupid; naughty; stubborn 170;181 10 (3)	豌 wān — [pea] — 191;151 15 (4)

后 周 骨	辟 *闢 pì bì — open up (land); incisive; refute 186;160 13 (2)	雕 diāo — carve, engrave; vulture, eagle 208;172 16 (3)	髓 suǐ — (bone) marrow; pith 214;188 21 (-)

⬛◻

手

拜
bài
pay a visit;
bow to
111;64 9 (2)

掰
bāi
break (with the
fingers)
111;64 12 (4)

我
wǒ
I, me, my,
we, our
101;62 7 (1)

鹅
鵝 é
goose
-
152;196 12 (2)

斤戶委

卯
mǎo
EB;
mortise
32;26 5 (-)

卿
qīng
minister
(archaic)
32;26 10 (-)

欣
xīn
happy,
joyful
115;76 8 (3)

所
suǒ
place; building;
(particle)
115;63 8 (1)

魏
wèi
(old kingdom;
surname)
216;194 18 (4)

王耳月

卵
luǎn
egg
-
227;26 7 (3)

印
yìn
print, stamp,
seal; tally with
32;26 6 (2)

段
duàn
section,
segment
119;79 9 (1)

殷
yīn yān
ardent; cordial;
rich; & (literary)
119;79 10 (4)

令

斜
xié
slanting,
oblique
82;68 11 (2)

叙
*敍 敘 xù
chat; narrate;
assess; &
35;29 9 (3)

邻
鄰 lín
neighbor
-
34;163 7 (2)

领
領 lǐng
neck, collar; to lead, guide;
get (award); outline; &
170;181 11 (1)

舍分公

鸽
鴿 gē
dove,
pigeon
152;196 11 (3)

舒
shū
stretch, unfold;
leisurely
23;135 12 (1)

颁
頒 bān
publish; to
issue, send out
170;181 10 (4)

颂
頌 sòng
praise;
song, eulogy
170;181 10 (3)

計里

删
*刪 shān
delete,
omit
17;18 7 (3)

毁
huǐ
destroy;
defame
119;79 13 (3)

1	41
2	42
3	43
4	44
5	45
6	46
7	47
8	48
9	49
10	50
11	51
12	52
13	53
14	54
15	55
16	56
17	57
18	58
19	59
20	60
21	61
22	62
23	63
24	64
25	65
26	66
27	67
28	68
29	69
30	70
31	71
32	72
33	73
34	74
35	75
36	76
37	77
38	78
39	79
40	80

厂

厅 廳 tīng
hall; office; department
13;53 4 (2)

厉 厲 lì
stern, strict; sharpen
13;27 5 (2)

历 曆歷 lì
undergo; all of; chronicle
13;72 4 (1)

厌 厭 yàn
detest, dislike; fed up; sated
13;27 6 (2)

压 壓 yā yà
press, crush; suppress; &
13;32 6 (2)

厂 廠 chǎng
factory, depot
13;53 2 (1)

厄 è
adversity; nub (literary)
13;27 4 (-)

辰 chén
stars; EB; time, occasion
187;161 7 (4)

厘 釐 lí
fraction, centi-, %; li (Chin unit)
13;166 9 (2)

石 shí dàn
stone, rock; inscription
136;112 5 (2)

雁 yàn
wild goose
-
13;172 12 (4)

厢 廂 xiāng
side; side room; (house) wing; &
13;53 11 (3)

厕 廁 cè si
toilet, washroom
13;53 8 (2)

厨 廚 chú
kitchen
-
13;53 12 (2)

厚 hòu
thick; generous; deep; to stress
13;27 9 (2)

原 yuán
original, raw; a plain; excuse
13;27 10 (1)

愿 *願 yuàn
willing; wish, desire; vow
81;61 14 (1)

厦 廈 shà xià
tall building; mansion
13;53 12 (4)

唇 *脣 chún
lips
-
187;30 10 (3)

辱 rǔ
disgrace; to insult
187;161 10 (3

厂

斤 jīn
(unit of weight: 1/2 kilogram)
115;69 4 (1)

斥 chì
denounce; exclude
115;69 5 (3)

反 fǎn
contrary; anti-, counter-
22;29 4 (1)

后 *後 hòu
back, behind, after; empress
22;30 6 (1)

爪 zhǎo zhuǎ
claw, talon
116;87 4 (4)

瓜 guā
melon; gourd
151;97 5 (2)

盾 dùn
shield
-
22;109 9 (2)

质 質 zhì
quality, nature; simple; query
22;154 8 (2)

ナ

右 yòu
right (hand)
-
14;30 5 (1)

左 zuǒ
left (hand); different; wrong
14;48 5 (1)

友 yǒu
friend
-
14;29 4 (1)

灰 huī
ash, dust; gray; disheartened
14;86 6 (2)

布 *佈 bù
cloth; spread; deploy; declare
14;50 5 (1)

有 yǒu yòu
have, possess; there is / are; &
14;74 6 (1)

在 zài
exist; be -ing; at; depends; &
14;32 6 (1)

存 cún
exist; preserve; deposit; &
14;39 6 (2)

龙 龍 lóng
dragon; imperial
137;212 5 (2)

尤 yóu
especially; blame, fault
53;43 4 (1)

寿 壽 shòu
longevity; age; birthday; funeral
54;33 7 (3)

尹 尸 户

老	考	孝	者	煮
lǎo	kǎo	xiào	zhě	zhǔ
old; longtime; always; &	inspect, test; examine	filial piety; mourning	person, -er, -ist; this	to cook, boil
92;125 6 (1)	92;125 6 (1)	92;39 7 (4)	92;125 8 (1)	80;86 12 (2)

尼	屎	尿	屈	尾	屏
ní	shǐ	niào suī	qū	wěi	bǐng píng
Buddhist nun; ('ni' sound)	excrement; secretion	urine; urinate	bend; yield, submit; wrong	tail, end	reject; screen; hold (breath); &
67;44 5 (4)	67;44 9 (4)	67;44 7 (4)	67;44 8 (3)	67;44 7 (2)	67;44 9 (4)

屉	届	居	屑
* tì	jiè	jū	xiè
drawer; food steamer	appointed time	reside; house; to claim; &	fragments, scraps; trivial
67;44 8 (4)	67;44 8 (2)	67;44 8 (2)	67;44 10 (4)

展	屋	屠	层	属	屡
zhǎn	wū	tú	céng	shǔ zhǔ	lǚ
unfold; display; postpone	a room; house	massacre; to butcher	layer, tier; story, floor	category; belong to	repeatedly -
67;44 10 (1)	67;44 9 (1)	67;44 11 (4)	67;44 7 (1)	67;44 12 (2)	67;44 12 (4)

屁	履	局	尺	尽
pì	lǚ	jú	chǐ	jìn jǐn
break wind, fart	shoe; tread, footstep; fulfil	office; situation; trap; part; &	ruler, foot (12 inches)	used up; entire; utmost; &
67;44 7 (3)	67;44 15 (4)	67;44 7 (1)	117;44 4 (2)	117;108 6 (2)

尸	昼	民	眉
shī	zhòu	mín	méi
corpse -	daytime	the people; folk, popular; civilian	eyebrow
67;44 3 (4)	117;72 9 (4)	227;83 5 (1)	141;109 9 (3)

启	肩	房	扁	雇	扇
qǐ	jiān	fáng	biǎn piān	gù	shàn shān
open, begin; enlighten	shoulder -	house; building; a room	flat, flatten	hire, employ	fan -
86;30 7 (2)	86;130 8 (2)	86;63 8 (1)	86;63 9 (2)	86;172 12 (3)	86;63 10 (2)

户
hù
door; family; bank account
86;63 4 (1)

广

庄
莊 zhuāng
village; solemn;
premises
44;140 6 (2)

庆
慶 qìng
celebration;
congratulate
44;53 6 (2)

床
chuáng
bed
-
44;53 7 (1)

应
應 yīng yìng
should; agree;
respond; cope
44;61 7 (2)

皮
pí
skin, leather;
outer layer; &
153;107 5 (2)

广
廣 guǎng
wide, broad;
spread; many
44;53 3 (1)

庙
廟 miào
temple
-
44;53 8 (2)

库
庫 kù
warehouse
-
44;53 7 (3)

座
zuò
seat, place;
pedestal
44;53 10 (1)

庐
廬 lú
hut,
cottage
44;53 7 (-)

序
xù
sequence;
preface
44;53 7 (2)

底
dǐ
bottom, base;
end; rough cop
44;53 8 (2)

店
diàn
shop, store;
inn
44;53 8 (1)

庚
gēng
age;
7th; HS
44;53 8 (-)

康
kāng
health
-
44;53 11 (1)

唐
táng
Tang
(dynasty)
44;30 10 (4)

庸
yōng
ordinary;
inferior
44;53 11 (4)

廉
lián
cheap;
honest
44;53 13 (4)

度
dù duó
degrees; times;
spend (time); &
44;53 9 (1)

席
xí
seat, place;
mat; banquet
44;50 10 (2)

鹿
lù
deer
-
222;198 11 (4)

腐
fǔ
bean curd;
rotten, decayed
44;130 14 (2)

鹰
鷹 yīng
eagle,
hawk
152;196 18 (4)

座
zuò
seat, place;
pedestal
44;53 10 (1)

麼
mó
[petty, clown]
(see Table 1)
221;200 14 (-)

摩
mó mā
rub; scrape;
contemplate
221;64 15 (3)

魔
mó
demon;
magical
221;194 20 (4)

磨
mó mò
rub, grind; sharpen; wear down;
pester; dawdle, kill time; mill; &
221;112 16 (2)

府
fǔ
government;
mansion; &
44;53 8 (1)

麻
má mā
rough, coarse;
hemp; &
221;200 11 (1)

廊
láng
veranda, porch,
corridor
44;53 11 (3)

廓
kuò
wide;
outline
44;53 13 (3)

庞
龐 páng
huge; a face;
disorderly
44;53 8 (4)

废
廢 fèi
abandon; junk,
waste; disabled
44;53 8 (3)

庭
tíng
courtyard;
law court
44;53 9 (1)

座
zuò
seat, place;
pedestal
44;53 10 (1)

虍

虎
hǔ
tiger
-
173;141 8 (2)

虐
nüè
tyrannical,
cruel
173;141 9 (-)

虏
虜 lǔ
captive,
capture
173;141 8 (2)

虑
慮 lǜ
ponder;
anxiety
173;61 10 (2)

虚
xū
empty; modest;
feeble; sham; &
173;141 11 (2)

疗	疾	疲	症	病	疤
療 liáo	jí	pí	zhèng zhēng	bìng	bā
cure, heal	illness; to hate; hardship; quick	weary, tired out	disease, illness	disease; ill; fault, defect	scar -
127;104 7 (3)	127;104 10 (3)	127;104 10 (2)	127;104 10 (3)	127;104 10 (1)	127;104 9 (4)
疟	痕	疯	痴	瘫	瘾
瘧 nüè yào	hén	瘋 fēng	*癡 chī	癱 tān	癮 yǐn
malaria -	scar; mark, stain	mad, insane	stupid, silly; crazy about	paralysis -	addiction; mad about (pastime)
127;104 8 (-)	127;104 11 (3)	127;104 9 (3)	127;104 13 (4)	127;104 15 (4)	127;104 16 (-)
瘦	痰	痒	瘩	痛	
shòu	tán	癢 yǎng	dá da	tòng	
thin, lean, weak, meager	phlegm, spit	itch -	[pimple; tangle]	pain, ache; sorrow; deeply	
127;104 14 (2)	127;104 13 (4)	127;104 11 (4)	127;104 14 (4)	127;104 12 (1)	
疮	疹	疫	癌	瘟	痹
瘡 chuāng	zhěn	yì	ái	wēn	痺 bì
a sore; a wound	rash (on skin)	epidemic, plague	cancer -	(contagious, acute) disease	numb; rheumatism
127;104 9 (4)	127;104 10 (-)	127;104 9 (4)	127;104 17 (3)	127;104 14 (4)	127;104 13 (4)
疙	疼	痪	瘤	瘸	
gē	téng	瘓 huàn	liú	qué	
swelling, pimple; knot	ache, pain; to love	[paralysis] -	tumor -	lame; limp (colloq)	
127;104 8 (4)	127;104 10 (1)	127;104 12 (4)	127;104 15 (4)	127;104 16 (4)	

在	存	彦	危	眉
zài	cún	彥 yàn	wēi	méi
exist; be -ing; at; depends; &	exist; preserve; deposit; &	a good man (literary)	danger; near death	eyebrow -
14;32 6 (1)	14;39 6 (2)	63;59 9 (-)	27;26 6 (1)	141;109 9 (3)
龙	发	寿	皮	看
龍 lóng	發 髮 fā fà	壽 shòu	pí	kàn kān
dragon; imperial	emit; become; develop; hair; &	longevity; age; birthday; funeral	skin, leather; outer layer; &	watch; look at; look after; &
137;212 5 (2)	35;105 5 (1)	54;33 7 (3)	153;107 5 (2)	141;109 9 (1)
无	死	石	名	君
無 wú	sǐ	shí dàn	míng	jūn
without; not; nothing; &	die; death; rigid	stone, rock; inscription	name; renown; famous	monarch; gentleman; Mr.
53;86 4 (2)	97;78 6 (1)	136;112 5 (2)	64;30 6 (1)	58;30 7 (4)

差 → 58
旃 → 20

差 → 58
旃 → 20

1	41
2	42
3	43
4	44
5	45
6	46
7	47
8	48
9	49
10	50
11	51
12	52
13	53
14	54
15	55
16	56
17	57
18	58
19	59
20	60
21	61
22	62
23	63
24	64
25	65
26	66
27	67
28	68
29	69
30	70
31	71
32	72
33	73
34	74
35	75
36	76
37	77
38	78
39	79
40	80

辽	迈	还	迁	达	边
遼 liáo	邁 mài	還 hái huán	遷 qiān	達 dá	邊 biān bian
distant	stride;	still, yet; fairly;	move;	reach, attain;	side; rim; limit;
-	old (in years)	also; return	change	notify; &	border; close to
47;162 5 (4)	47;162 6 (2)	47;162 7 (1)	47;162 6 (4)	47;162 6 (2)	47;162 5 (1)

违	连	进	述	迷	逮
違 wéi	連 lián	進 jìn	shù	mí	dǎi dài
disobey;	in succession;	proceed; enter;	narrate,	lost, confused;	catch, arrest;
be separated	link; include; &	take in; into	tell	fascinated by	reach
47;162 7 (2)	47;162 7 (1)	47;162 7 (1)	47;162 8 (2)	47;162 9 (2)	47;162 11 (3)

迭	逐	迟	退	迪	速
dié	zhú	遲 chí	tuì	dí	sù
repeatedly;	chase; expel;	late,	retreat; wane;	initiate; to	fast, rapid;
to alternate	bit by bit	delayed	quit; give back	guide (literary)	speed
47;162 8 (-)	47;162 10 (2)	47;162 7 (1)	47;162 9 (1)	47;162 8 (-)	47;162 10 (2)

迎	逃	巡	避
yíng	táo	xún	bì
meet; greet,	flee; evade,	patrol; round	avoid, evade;
welcome	escape	(of drinks)	repel
47;162 7 (1)	47;162 9 (2)	47;47 6 (4)	47;162 16 (2)

逛	逝	逊	邀
guàng	shì	遜 xùn	yāo
stroll,	pass away,	abdicate;	invite; ask for;
wander, roam	die	modest	intercept
47;162 10 (2)	47;162 10 (3)	47;162 9 (4)	47;162 16 (2)

近	返	遮
jìn	fǎn	zhē
near, close;	to return	cover, conceal;
intimate; recent	-	block, impede
47;162 7 (1)	47;162 7 (3)	47;162 14 (3)

迅	过
xùn	過 guò guo guō
swift,	to cross; exceed; after, over;
fast	very, too (much); (particle)
47;162 6 (2)	47;162 6 (1)

辶

迫	追	述	这	迹	遍
pò pǎi	zhuī	shù	zhè zhèi	*迹 蹟 jī	biàn
compel; urgent; approach	pursue; recall; look into; &	narrate, tell	this; here; now	tracks, traces, vestige; a sign	everywhere; (no. of) times
47;162 8 (2)	47;162 9 (2)	47;162 8 (2)	47;162 7 (1)	47;162 9 (2)	47;162 12 (1)

递	送	逆	遂	道	遵
dì	sòng	nì	suì suí	dào	zūn
hand over; successively	carry; escort; deliver; give	disobey; rebel; inverse, contra-	succeed, fulfil	road, way; line; Taoist; say; &	abide by, obey
47;162 10 (2)	47;162 9 (1)	47;162 9 (4)	47;162 12 (-)	47;162 12 (1)	47;162 15 (2)

逍	迷
xiāo	mí
[unrestrained]	lost, confused; fascinated by
-	
47;162 10 (-)	47;162 9 (2)

选	造	逮	遗	遣	遭
xuǎn	zào	dǎi dài	yí wèi	qiǎn	zāo
select, elect	make, build; to train; concoct	catch, arrest; reach	lose; omit; bequeath	send; dispel	suffer mishap
47;162 9 (2)	47;162 10 (2)	47;162 11 (3)	47;162 12 (3)	47;162 13 (4)	47;162 14 (2)

远	运	逗	逼	通
yuǎn	yùn	dòu	bī	tōng tòng
distant	move, transport; luck; to use	stay; amusing; tease	compel; press for; close in on	go through, passable; connect; know; expert; common; whole
-				
47;162 7 (1)	47;162 7 (1)	47;162 10 (2)	47;162 12 (2)	47;162 10 (1)

适	透	遥	逻	遇
shì	tòu	yáo	luó	yù
suitable; proceed	penetrate; thoroughly; &	distant (literary)	patrol	meet; chance; behave towards
			-	
47;162 9 (1)	47;162 10 (2)	47;162 13 (3)	47;162 11 (3)	47;162 12 (1)

迄	逸	逢	途	逾
qì	yì	féng	tú	yú
up to, until; up to now	leisure; flee; gone; excel	meet, encounter	way, route	exceed
				-
47;162 6 (-)	47;162 11 (-)	47;162 10 (2)	47;162 10 (2)	47;162 12 (-)

莲	蓬
lián	péng
lotus	disheveled; fluffy
-	
50;140 10 (4)	50;140 13 (3)

1	41
2	42
3	43
4	44
5	45
6	46
7	47
8	48
9	49
10	50
11	51
12	52
13	53
14	54
15	55
16	56
17	57
18	58
19	59
20	60
21	61
22	62
23	63
24	64
25	65
26	66
27	67
28	68
29	69
30	70
31	71
32	72
33	73
34	74
35	75
36	76
37	77
38	78
39	79
40	80

走 爻 是 鬼

走

赴
fù
go to; attend
189;156 9 (4)

赵
趙 zhào
(surname)
-
189;156 9 (3)

赶
趕 gǎn
hurry; catch up; catch (bus); &
189;156 10 (2)

起
qǐ qi
raise, rise; up; begin; able to
189;156 10 (1)

趋
趨 qū
hurry; tendency
189;156 12 (4)

趁
chèn
take advantage of; whilst
189;156 12 (2)

越
yuè
surmount; overstep; &
189;156 12 (2)

趟
tàng
(measure word)
-
189;156 15 (2)

超
chāo
exceed, ultra-, super-
189;156 12 (2)

趣
qù
interest, liking, delight
189;156 15 (2)

爻

廷
tíng
(imperial or feudal) court
36;54 6 (-)

延
yán
prolong, extend; delay; send for
36;54 7 (2)

建
jiàn
build; establish; suggest
36;54 8 (1)

是

匙
chí shi
spoon
-
213;21 11 (3)

题
題 tí
topic, subject; inscribe
213;181 15 (1)

鬼

魁
kuí
head, chief; outstanding
216;194 13 (-)

魅
mèi
demon
-
216;194 15 (-)

鬼
guǐ
ghost; stealthy; sinister; &
216;194 9 (2)

处
處 chǔ chù
manage; deal
with; place; &
65;141　5　(1)

翅
chì
wing,
fin
183;124　10　(2)

爬
pá
crawl;
climb
116;87　8　(1)

毯
tǎn
blanket;
carpet, rug
112;82　12　(2)

勉
miǎn
strive;
encourage
28;19　9　(3)

翘
翹 qiào qiáo
lift up, raise;
bend upwards
183;124　12　(3)

彪
biāo
young tiger
(literary)
63;59　11　(-)

1	41
2	42
3	43
4	44
5	45
6	46
7	47
8	48
9	49
10	50
11	51
12	52
13	53
14	54
15	55
16	56
17	57
18	58
19	59
20	60
21	61
22	62
23	63
24	64
25	65
26	66
27	67
28	68
29	69
30	70
31	71
32	72
33	73
34	74
35	75
36	76
37	77
38	78
39	79
40	80

斗
* 鬥 dòu dǒu
fight; dovetail;
dipper; &
82;68 4 (2)

头
頭 tóu tou
head; top; first,
chief; end; &
52;181 5 (1)

少
shǎo shào
few; lacking;
Stop!; young; &
79;42 4 (1)

以
yǐ
using; so as to;
according to; &
23;9 4 (1)

□少 → 44

寸
cùn
very small;
inch
54;41 3 (2)

刁
diāo
cunning
-
6;18 2 (4)

习
習 xí
practice; be
used to; habit
6;124 3 (1)

可
kě
approve; indeed;
can, may; &
58;30 5 (1)

司
sī
attend to;
department
6;30 5 (2)

飞
飛 fēi
to fly;
swiftly; &
7;183 3 (1)

勺
sháo
spoon,
ladle
26;20 3 (2)

匀
yún
evenly;
to spare
26;20 4 (3)

勾
gōu gòu
cancel; collude;
sketch; &
26;20 4 (3)

句
jù
sentence,
line of verse
26;30 5 (1)

旬
xún
10-day period;
decade (of life)
26;72 6 (3)

包
bāo
wrap; package;
hire; assure; &
26;20 5 (1)

匈
xiōng
('hun' sound)
-
26;20 6 (4)

与
與 yǔ yù yú
and; with; to;
help; give; &
2;134 3 (2)

马
馬 mǎ
horse
-
75;187 3 (1)

乌
烏 wū
crow;
black, dark
4;86 4 (4)

鸟
鳥 niǎo
bird
-
152;196 5 (2)

式
shì
formula; format,
style; ceremony
56;56 6 (2)

武
wǔ
military,
martial; brave
102;77 8 (2)

戒
jiè
on guard; warn;
quit (habit); &
101;62 7 (4)

或
huò
or; either;
perhaps
101;62 8 (1)

贰
貳 èr
two
-
56;154 9 (4)

戊
wù
5th;
HS
138;62 5 (-)

戌
xū
EB
-
138;62 6 (-)

咸
* 鹹 xián
salty
-
138;30 9 (3)

成
chéng
to become;
succeed; &
138;62 6 (1)

威
wēi
strength, might;
coerce
138;38 9 (3)

戚
qī
relatives;
sorrow
138;62 11 (2)

哉
zāi
Alas!; Why?
(literary)
165;30 9 (-)

栽
zāi
to plant; insert;
impose; to fall
165;75 10 (3)

裁
cái
cut out; reduce;
to judge; &
165;145 12 (3)

载
載 zǎi zài
year; to record;
carry
165;159 10 (3)

截
jié
cut, sever;
intercept; up to
165;62 14 (3)

戴
dài
wear (hat etc.);
honor
165;62 17 (1)

同 tóng tòng same, equal; together, with 19;30 6 (1)	向 *嚮 xiàng facing; towards; direction; & 4;30 6 (1)	网 網 wǎng net; catch with a net; network 19;120 6 (2)	冈 岡 gāng ridge (of hill) 19;46 4 (4)	内 nèi inside, inner; one's wife 19;11 4 (1)	肉 ròu meat, flesh; pulp 19;130 6 (1)

尚 shàng esteem, respect; yet 79;42 8 (3)	周 *週 zhōu circuit; week; thoughtful; & 19;30 8 (1)	丹 dān red, cinnabar 19;3 4 (4)	舟 zhōu boat (literary) 182;137 6 (4)	为 為 wéi wèi do, act, act as; become; be equal to; for the sake of 1;86 4 (1)

贝 貝 bèi sea shell - 106;154 4 (4)	见 見 jiàn see; meet, visit; evident; opinion 107;147 4 (1)	尽 盡 儘 jìn jǐn used up; entire; utmost; & 117;108 6 (2)	冒 mào emit; take risk; bold; fraud 104;13 9 (1)	参 參 can cēn shēn join in; consult, refer; ginseng 37;28 8 (1)

凡 fán common, ordinary; every 30;16 3 (2)	风 風 fēng wind; scenery; habits; news 121;182 4 (1)	凤 鳳 fèng phoenix - 30;196 4 (4)	凰 huáng [phoenix] - 30;16 11 (4)	爪 zhǎo zhuǎ claw, talon 116;87 4 (4)	瓜 guā melon, gourd 151;97 5 (2)

闪 閃 shǎn flash; lightning; dodge; sprain 46;169 5 (2)	闭 閉 bì shut; close 46;169 6 (2)	闲 閑 閒 xián unused, idle; leisure 46;169 7 (2)	闺 閨 guī small door; boudoir 46;169 9 (4)	闰 閏 rùn leap (year) - 46;169 7 (-)	闹 鬧 nào noisy; to vent; suffer from; & 46;191 8 (2)

问 問 wèn ask; ask after; interrogate 46;30 6 (1)	间 間 jiān jiàn between; room; to separate; & 46;169 7 (1)	闻 聞 wén hear; smell; news; fame 46;128 9 (1)	闯 闖 chuǎng rush; break through 46;169 6 (2)	闸 閘 zhá brake; sluice 46;169 8 (4)	阐 闡 chǎn explain, enlighten 46;169 11 (4)

闷 悶 mēn mèn stuffy; sealed, airtight; bored 46;61 7 (3)	阀 閥 fá valve; powerful person 46;169 9 (4)	阂 閡 hé barrier; cut off from 46;169 9 (3)	阅 閱 yuè read; review; to experience 46;169 10 (2)	阔 闊 kuò wide, vast; wealthy 46;169 12 (2)	阁 閣 gé pavilion; Excellency; & 46;169 9 (4)

门 門 mén gate, door; family; sect; & 46;169 3 (1)

1	41
2	42
3	43
4	44
5	45
6	46
7	47
8	48
9	49
10	50
11	51
12	52
13	53
14	54
15	55
16	56
17	57
18	58
19	59
20	60
21	61
22	62
23	63
24	64
25	65
26	66
27	67
28	68
29	69
30	70
31	71
32	72
33	73
34	74
35	75
36	76
37	77
38	78
39	79
40	80

凶 *兇 xiōng
ominous; ferocious; &
38;17 4 (3)

画 畫 huà
picture; (of Ch char) stroke
38;102 8 (1)

函 hán
letter, mail
38;17 8 (4)

齿 齒 chǐ
tooth
-
206;211 8 (3)

凿 鑿 záo zuò
chisel; mortise; make a hole
140;167 12 (3)

鼎 dǐng
cauldron; tripod, tripartite
141;206 12 (-)

幽 yōu
secluded; quiet; gloomy; Hades
60;52 9 (4)

凹 āo
concave, hollow
227;17 5 (4)

凸 tū
protruding, raised; convex
227;17 5 (4)

义 義 yì
justice; meaning; &
25;123 3 (1)

以 yǐ
using; so as to; according to; &
23;9 4 (1)

区 區 qū ōu
area, district; classify
15;23 4 (2)

巨 jù
huge, gigantic
15;48 4 (2)

臣 chén
vassal; courtier, minister
164;131 6 (4)

匠 jiàng
craftsman
-
15;22 6 (4)

医 醫 yī
doctor; heal; medical
15;164 7 (1)

匹 pǐ
equal to; a match for
15;23 4 (2)

匪 fěi
bandit, robber
15;22 10 (4)

匣 xiá
small box, casket
15;22 7 (-)

囚 qiú
prisoner, imprison
59;31 5 (-)

四 sì
four
-
59;31 5 (1)

因 yīn
cause, reason; because of
59;31 6 (1)

困 kùn
surround; hard pressed; weary
59;31 7 (1)

团 團 糰 tuán
group; unite; ball; dumpling
59;31 6 (1)

围 圍 wéi
surround, enclose; around
59;31 7 (1)

回 *迴 huí
return; reply; re-; times
59;31 6 (1)

国 國 guó
nation; national; Chinese
59;31 8 (1)

元 園 yuán
garden, park
59;31 7 (1)

圆 圓 yuán
circle; tactful; yuan; justify; &
59;31 10 (1)

圈 quān juān juàn
circle, ring; encircle, pen in
59;31 11 (2)

固 gù
solid, sturdy, firm; strengthen
59;31 8 (2)

图 圖 tú
picture, map; plan; seek
59;31 8 (1)

囱 cōng
[chimney]
-
4;31 7 (3)

田 tián
field, farmland
142;102 5 (2)

曰 yuē
say
(literary)
104;73 4 (4)

日 rì
sun; day, daily; time
103;72 4 (1)

目 mù
eye; item; catalog
141;109 5 (1)

叉 chā chǎ chá
fork; cross ('x' mark)
35;29 3 (2)

丹 dān
red, cinnabar
19;3 4 (4)

瓦 wǎ wà
(roof) tile; earthenware
98;98 4 (3)

母 mǔ
mother; female (animal)
2;80 5 (1)

衍
yǎn
redundant;
spread (literary)
62;144 9 (4)

衔 xián
hold (in mouth);
rank, title
62;167 11 (4)

街
jiē
street
-
62;144 12 (1)

衡
héng
scales; weigh,
measure
62;144 16 (3)

行
xíng háng
go; do, perform; capable; OK;
for now; line; (business) firm
62;144 6 (1)

辨
biàn
differentiate,
distinguish
186;160 16 (4)

辩 biàn
dispute,
debate
186;160 16 (3)

瓣
bàn
petal, segment,
piece; valve
186;97 19 (3)

辫 biàn
plait, braid;
pigtail
186;120 17 (4)

班
bān
team; duty;
scheduled
88;96 10 (1)

斑
bān
spots; stripes;
speckled
88;67 12 (4)

承
chéng
undertake;
indebted; &
5;64 8 (2)

鼎
dǐng
cauldron;
tripod, tripartite
141;206 12 (-)

掰
bāi
break (with the
fingers)
111;64 12 (4)

能
néng
able to; energy;
capability
37;130 10 (1)

疑
yí
doubt
-
39;103 14 (2)

毁
huǐ
destroy;
defame
119;79 13 (3)

毅
yì
firm,
resolute
119;79 15 (3)

赫
hè
impressive
-
190;155 14 (4)

兢
jīng
[conscientious]
-
12;10 14 (4)

鼓
gǔ
drum; rouse;
bellows; bulge
224;207 13 (2)

豁
huō huò
crack; forsake;
open; exempt
199;150 17 (4)

舒
shū
stretch, unfold;
leisurely
23;135 12 (1)

静
靜 jìng
still, calm,
quiet
202;174 14 (1)

龄
齡 líng
age, years,
duration
206;211 13 (2)

聚
jù
assemble,
get together
163;128 14 (3)

1	41
2	42
3	43
4	44
5	45
6	46
7	47
8	48
9	49
10	50
11	51
12	52
13	53
14	54
15	55
16	56
17	57
18	58
19	59
20	60
21	61
22	62
23	63
24	64
25	65
26	66
27	67
28	68
29	69
30	70
31	71
32	72
33	73
34	74
35	75
36	76
37	77
38	78
39	79
40	80

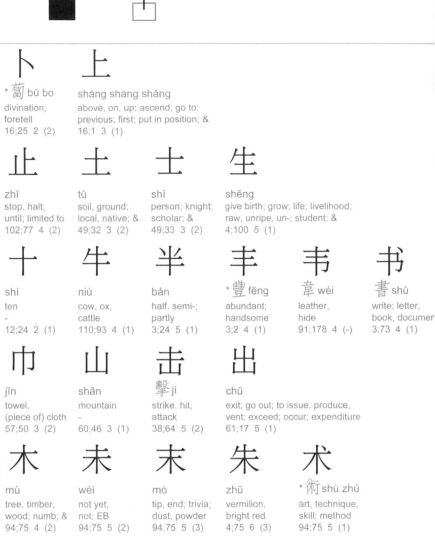

卜
*蔔 bū bo
divination;
foretell
16;25 2 (2)

上
shàng shang shǎng
above, on, up; ascend; go to;
previous; first; put in position; &
16;1 3 (1)

止
zhǐ
stop, halt;
until; limited to
102;77 4 (2)

土
tǔ
soil, ground;
local, native; &
49;32 3 (2)

士
shì
person; knight;
scholar; &
49;33 3 (2)

生
shēng
give birth; grow; life; livelihood;
raw, unripe, un-; student; &
4;100 5 (1)

十
shí
ten
-
12;24 2 (1)

牛
niú
cow, ox,
cattle
110;93 4 (1)

半
bàn
half, semi-;
partly
3;24 5 (1)

丰
*豐 fēng
abundant;
handsome
3;2 4 (1)

韦
韋 wéi
leather,
hide
91;178 4 (-)

书
書 shū
write; letter;
book, documer
3;73 4 (1)

巾
jīn
towel,
(piece of) cloth
57;50 3 (2)

山
shān
mountain
-
60;46 3 (1)

击
擊 jí
strike, hit,
attack
38;64 5 (2)

出
chū
exit; go out; to issue, produce,
vent; exceed; occur; expenditure
61;17 5 (1)

木
mù
tree, timber,
wood; numb; &
94;75 4 (2)

未
wèi
not yet,
not; EB
94;75 5 (2)

末
mò
tip, end; trivia;
dust, powder
94;75 5 (3)

朱
zhū
vermilion,
bright red
4;75 6 (3)

术
*術 shù zhú
art, technique,
skill; method
94;75 5 (1)

本
běn
root, base; this;
book, edition; &
94;75 5 (1)

米
mǐ
rice;
meter (length)
159;119 6 (1)

来
來 lái lai
come, arrive; do; bring;
future; during; approx.; &
94;9 7 (1)

虫
*蟲 chóng
insect;
worm
174;142 6 (2)

東 jiǎn
card, note,
letter
192;75 9 (4)

束 shù
bind, tie;
bundle; restrain
192;75 7 (1)

串
chuàn
get mixed up;
gang up; &
3;2 7 (3)

中
zhōng zhòng
middle, mid-; among; Chinese;
in progress; fit for; hit, be hit by
105;2 4 (1)

申
shēn
explain, state;
EB; Shanghai
144;102 5 (3)

电
電 diàn
electric,
electricity
104;173 5 (1)

由
yóu
by; from; allow;
due to; obey; &
143;102 5 (2)

事
shì
affair, matter;
do; job; &
2;6 8 (1)

甫
fǔ
just now
(literary)
1;101 7 (-)

七
qī qí
seven
-
2;1 2 (1)

屯
tún
village; collect;
station (troops)
227;45 4 (4)

长 cháng zhǎng
long; long-term; steadily; forte;
grow; senior, chief; get, acquire
4;168 4 (1)

才
*纔 cái
ability, talent;
only, just
2;64 3 (1)

水
shuǐ
water; liquid;
river, lake
125;85 4 (1)

求
qiú
beg, request;
seek
1;85 7 (1)

隶
隸 lì
subordinate,
servant, slave
124;171 8 (3)

人
rén
person, people;
others; &
23;9 2 (1)

入
rù
enter; income;
conform
23;11 2 (2)

火
huǒ
fire
-
83;86 4 (1)

尤
yóu
especially;
blame, fault
53;43 4 (1)

内
nèi
inside, inner;
one's wife
19;11 4 (1)

肉
ròu
meat, flesh;
pulp
19;130 6 (1)

大
dà dài
big; great;
strong; fully; &
52;37 3 (1)

犬
quǎn
dog
-
96;94 4 (4)

太
tài
excessive, too,
over-; utmost
52;37 4 (1)

夫
fū fú
husband;
man
52;37 4 (1)

失
shī
lose; fail to;
error; deviate
4;37 5 (2)

央
yāng
center;
implore
52;37 5 (2)

丈
zhàng
(unit of length:
10 feet); &
2;1 3 (2)

史
shǐ
history
-
58;30 5 (1)

头
頭 tóu tou
head; top; first;
chief; end; &
52;181 5 (1)

夹
夾 jiā jiá gā
squeeze; mix;
pincers; clip; &
52;37 6 (2)

爽
shuǎng
clear; forthright;
be well; deviate
52;89 11 (4)

夷
yí
safety; wipe out
(literary)
52;37 6 (-)

专
專 zhuān
specialized;
expert
11;41 4 (2)

车
車 chē jū
car, vehicle,
machine
100;159 4 (1)

东
東 dōng
east;
master, host
227;75 5 (1)

幺
yāo
one (on dice);
when speaking)
76;52 3 (-)

乡
鄉 xiāng
country, rural;
hometown
227;163 3 (2)

片
piàn piān
sheet, slice;
fragment; film
114;91 4 (1)

九
jiǔ
nine;
many
7;5 2 (1)

丸
wán
ball;
pellet, pill
66;3 3 (3)

方
fāng
direction; place;
square; &
85;70 4 (1)

力
lì
strength, force,
power; strive
28;19 2 (1)

为
為 wéi wèi
do, act, act as; become;
be equal to; for the sake of
1;86 4 (1)

女
nǚ
woman; female;
daughter, girl
73;38 3 (1)

广
廣 guǎng
wide, broad;
spread; many
44;53 3 (1)

皮
pí
skin, leather;
outer layer; &
153;107 5 (2)

戈
gē
lance, spear,
(an old weapon)
101;62 4 (4)

戊
wù
5th;
HS
138;62 5 (-)

农
農 nóng
agriculture;
peasant
18;161 6 (1)

1	41
2	42
3	43
4	44
5	45
6	46
7	47
8	48
9	49
10	50
11	51
12	52
13	53
14	54
15	55
16	56
17	57
18	58
19	59
20	60
21	61
22	62
23	63
24	64
25	65
26	66
27	67
28	68
29	69
30	70
31	71
32	72
33	73
34	74
35	75
36	76
37	77
38	78
39	79
40	80

一 yī yí yì
one; a; once; each; whole; &
2;1 1 (1)

厂 廠 chǎng
factory, depot
13;53 2 (1)

丁 dīng zhēng
4th; HS; man, population
2;1 2 (3)

下 xià xia
below, down; descend; unload; next; inferior; send; decide; &
16;1 3 (1)

不 bù bú
no, not, un-; can't
95;1 4 (1)

平 píng
flat, even, level; calm; average
2;51 5 (1)

于 *於 yú
in, at, to; from, than
11;7 3 (2)

干 *乾 幹 gān gàn
dry; futile; adopt (child); main part, trunk; do, work; fight
11;51 3 (1)

开 開 kāi kai
open; start; operate; &
51;169 4 (1)

牙 yá
tooth; ivory
99;92 4 (2)

无 無 wú
without; not; nothing; &
53;86 4 (2)

天 tiān
sky, Heaven; God; day; season; weather; nature, natural
90;37 4 (1)

工 gōng
to work, worker; industry; skill
48;48 3 (1)

王 wáng
king
-
88;96 4 (2)

玉 yù
jade; your (polite)
131;96 5 (2)

丐 gài
beg; beggar (literary)
2;1 4 (-)

正 zhèng zhēng
correct, straight, upright, proper; exactly; main, chief; January; &
102;77 5 (1)

万 *萬 wàn mò
ten thousand; many; utterly
2;1 3 (1)

歹 dǎi
bad, evil
-
97;78 4 (4)

互 hù
mutual
-
2;7 4 (1)

五 wǔ
five
-
2;7 4 (1)

瓦 wǎ wà
(roof) tile; earthenware
98;98 4 (3)

巫 wū
witch, wizard
48;48 7 (4)

雨 yǔ
rain
-
204;173 8 (1)

而 ér
and; due to; but; (from …) to
169;126 6 (1)

丙 bǐng
3rd; HS
2;1 5 (3)

两 兩 liǎng
two, a couple; both; a few; &
2;11 7 (1)

百 bǎi
a hundred; numerous
150;106 6 (1)

面 *麵 麪 miàn
face; surface; extent; flour; &
2;176 9 (1)

再 zài
again; further; more; before; &
2;13 6 (1)

更 gèng gēng
even more; to change
2;73 7 (1)

西 xī
west
-
166;146 6 (1)

酉 yǒu
EB
-
193;164 7 (-)

耳 ěr
ear; on each side
163;128 6 (2)

亚 亞 yà
inferior; Asia
168;7 6 (3)

严 嚴 yán
tight; strict, severe
168;30 7 (2)

	几 *幾 jǐ jī	又 yòu	叉 chā chǎ chá	shī	尺 chǐ	民 mín

几
*幾 jǐ jī
a few, several; how many
30;16 2 (1)

又
yòu
again; further, and, but; &
35;29 2 (1)

叉
chā chǎ chá
fork;
cross ('x' mark)
35;29 3 (2)

shī
corpse
-
67;44 3 (4)

尺
chǐ
ruler, foot
(12 inches)
117;44 4 (2)

民
mín
the people; folk, popular; civilian
227;83 5 (1)

己
jǐ
self;
6th; HS
72;49 3 (1)

已
yǐ
already;
to end, cease
72;49 3 (1)

巳
sì
EB
-
72;49 3 (-)

巴
bā
hope for; stick to; next to
227;49 4 (2)

弓
gōng
(stringed) bow;
arch, bend
71;57 3 (3)

了
* le liǎo liào
(particle); finish;
know; observe
5;6 2 (1)

乙
yǐ
2nd;
HS
7;5 1 (3)

fēi
to fly;
swiftly; &
7;183 3 (1)

子
zǐ zi
child; son; egg, seed;
person; thing; EB
74;39 3 (1)

刀
dāo
knife; razor;
sword
27;18 2 (1)

刃
rèn
blade; sword,
knife; kill
27;18 3 (4)

乃
nǎi
be; then; your
(literary)
4;4 2 (4)

及
jí
attain; timely,
on time; and
4;29 3 (2)

卫
wèi
protect,
defend, guard
32;144 3 (2)

口
kǒu
mouth;
opening; &
58;30 3 (1)

日
rì
sun;
day, daily; time
103;72 4 (1)

曰
yuē
say
(literary)
104;73 4 (4)

丑
*chǒu
ugly;
disgraceful; EB
2;1 4 (3)

且
qiě
as well as;
for a while
2;1 5 (1)

目
mù
eye;
item; catalog
141;109 5 (1)

凸
tū
protruding,
raised; convex
227;17 5 (4)

凹
āo
concave,
hollow
227;17 5 (4)

田
tián
field,
farmland
142;102 5 (2)

甲
jiǎ
1st; HS;
shell, armor
104;102 5 (3)

果
guǒ
fruit; result;
sure enough; &
94;75 8 (1)

里
*裡 li lǐ
in, inside;
mile, 1/2 km; &
195;166 7 (1)

月
yuè
moon;
month
118;74 4 (1)

用
yòng
use, using;
(don't) need; &
19;101 5 (1)

甩
shuǎi
cast off; toss;
swing to and fro
19;101 5 (2)

毋
wú
Don't!
(literary)
2;80 4 (-)

丹
dān
red,
cinnabar
19;3 4 (4)

母
mǔ
mother;
female (animal)
2;80 5 (1)

册
*cè
copy, volume
(books)
2;13 5 (2)

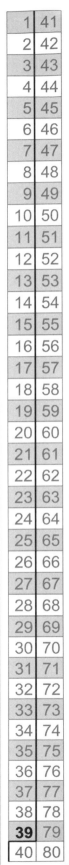

甘	甘	井	弗	曲	革
niàn	gān	jǐng	fú	qū qǔ	gé
twenty	sweet;	a well, pit;	not	a bend; bent;	leather, hide; t
-	willing	neat, orderly	(literary)	wrong; melody	change; expel
93;55 3 (-)	135;99 5 (3)	11;7 4 (2)	71;57 5 (-)	104;73 6 (3)	212;177 9 (2)

业 業 yè	止 zhǐ	也 yě	世 shì	片 piàn piān
business;	stop, halt;	also;	life; generation;	sheet, slice;
already	until; limited to	still, even so	era; world	fragment; film
140;75 5 (1)	102;77 4 (2)	5;5 3 (1)	2;1 5 (1)	114;91 4 (1)

千	币 幣 bì	禾	手	毛
qiān	money	hé	shǒu	máo
thousand;	-	grain, cereal;	hand; by hand;	fur, hair, wool; scared; rough;
numerous		rice	hold; person	gross (profit); 1/10 yuan; &
12;24 3 (1)	57;50 4 (2)	149;115 5 (4)	111;64 4 (1)	112;82 4 (1)

壬	乎	*昇 shēng	我
rén	hū	rise, raise;	wǒ
9th;	(suffix;	promote; liter	I, me, my,
HS	particle)		we, our
49;33 4 (-)	2;4 5 (2)	4;24 4 (2)	101;62 7 (1)

斤	斥	丘	氏	乐 樂 yuè lè	爪
jīn	chì	qiū	shì	music;	zhǎo zhuǎ
(unit of weight;	denounce;	mound,	family name;	enjoy; happy	claw,
1/2 kilogram)	exclude	grave	surname; née		talon
115;69 4 (1)	115;69 5 (3)	4;1 5 (3)	122;83 4 (3)	4;75 5 (1)	116;87 4 (4)

系 *係 繫 xì	乖	乘	秉	垂	重
fasten; system;	guāi	chéng shèng	bǐng	chuí	chóng zhòng
department; &	obedient;	ride; multiply;	grasp; control	droop;	repeat; heavy;
77;120 7 (1)	quick-witted	make use of	(literary)	hang down	to stress; &
	4;4 8 (3)	149;4 10 (2)	149;115 8 (4)	4;32 8 (3)	4;166 9 (1)

夕	久	欠	矢	尔 爾 ěr
xī	jiǔ	qiàn	shǐ	
dusk, sunset, evening	long time; lasting	lacking; owe; yawn; &	arrow; vow	you; like that, that (literary)
64;36 3 (4)	4;4 3 (1)	120;76 4 (2)	148;111 5 (-)	79;89 5 (3)

午	乍	年
wǔ	zhà	nián
noon; EB	suddenly; at first; extend	year; annual; age; New Year
20;24 4 (1)	20;4 5 (-)	20;51 6 (1)

勿	匆	争 争 zhēng
wù	* 忽 cōng	
must not, Don't!	hasty	compete (for), argue (about)
26;20 4 (4)	26;20 5 (3)	27;87 6 (2)

丫

yā
fork (in tree), bifurcation
24;2 3 (-)

〇

líng
zero
-
227;0 1 (-)

1	41
2	42
3	43
4	44
5	45
6	46
7	47
8	48
9	49
10	50
11	51
12	52
13	53
14	54
15	55
16	56
17	57
18	58
19	59
20	60
21	61
22	62
23	63
24	64
25	65
26	66
27	67
28	68
29	69
30	70
31	71
32	72
33	73
34	74
35	75
36	76
37	77
38	78
39	79
40	80

丶

卜
*蔔 bǔ bo
divination; foretell
16;25 2 (2)

小
xiǎo
small; young; petty
79;42 3 (1)

尔
爾 ěr
you; like that, that (literary)
79;89 5 (3)

不
bù bú
no, not, un-; can't
95;1 4 (1)

下
xià xia
below, down; descend; unload; next; inferior; send; decide; &
16;1 3 (1)

心
xīn
heart; core; feelings
81;61 4 (1)

必
bì
necessarily; certainly
1;61 5 (1)

办
辦 bàn
manage; set up; punish
28;160 4 (1)

亦
yì
also, too (literary)
162;8 6 (4)

玉
yù
jade; your (polite)
131;96 5 (2)

犬
quǎn
dog
-
96;94 4 (4)

尤
yóu
especially; blame, fault
53;43 4 (1)

术
*術 shù zhú
art, technique, skill; method
94;75 5 (1)

书
書 shū
write; letter, book, document
3;73 4 (1)

甫
fǔ
just now (literary)
1;101 7 (-)

戈
gē
lance, spear, (an old weapon)
101;62 4 (4)

戊
wù
5th; HS
138;62 5 (-)

求
qiú
beg, request; seek
1;85 7 (1)

球
qiú
ball, sphere, globe
88;96 11 (1)

我
wǒ
I, me, my, we, our
101;62 7 (1)

发
發 髮 fā fà
emit; become; develop; hair; &
35;105 5 (1)

泼
潑 pō
sprinkle; stir, poke; unreasonable
40;85 8 (2)

拨
撥 bō
stir, poke; allocate; batch
55;64 8 (3)

拔
bá
root out; select; seize; &
55;64 8 (2)

孙
孫 sūn
grandchild
-
74;39 6 (3)

秘
*祕 mì bì
secret
149;115 10 (2)

泌
mì
secrete
40;85 8 (3)

协
協 xié
together, jointly; assist
12;24 6 (3)

胁
脅 xié
upper body, ribs; coerce
118;130 8 (3)

苏
蘇 囌 sū
revive; ('su' sound)
50;140 7 (4)

□代 → 4
□戈 → 4
□戋 → 4
□少 → 4
□尤 → 4
□龙 → 4
□人 → 4
□犬 → 4
□下 → 4
□不 → 4
□尔 → 5
□甫 → 5

卜

外
wài
outside; foreign; besides; &
64;36 5 (1)

扑
撲 pū
rush at, attack; to flap, flutter
55;64 5 (2)

补
補 bǔ
mend; use; fill, replace; nourish
129;145 7 (2)

卦
guà
divination
-
16;25 8 (-)

朴
*樸 pǔ pō pò piáo
plain, simple
94;75 6 (2)

卧
臥 wò
lie down; berth, sleeper
164;131 8 (3)

处
處 chǔ chù
manage; deal with; place; &
65;141 5 (1)

赴
fù
go to; attend
189;156 9 (4)

火 huǒ fire - 83;86 4 (1)	业 業 yè business; already 140;75 5 (1)	亚 亞 yà inferior; Asia 168;7 6 (3)	哑 啞 yǎ yā dumb; hoarse; Oh! 58;30 9 (4)	碰 pèng bump; meet; try one's luck 136;112 13 (1)

□比 → 42
□长 → 43
□火 → 46
□平 → 47

水 shuǐ water; liquid; river, lake 125;85 4 (1)	冰 *冰 bīng ice - 8;15 6 (2)	承 chéng undertake; indebted; & 5;64 8 (2)	火 huǒ fire - 83;86 4 (1)	求 qiú beg, request; seek 1;85 7 (1)	飞 飛 fēi to fly; swiftly; & 7;183 3 (1)

八 bā eight - 24;12 2 (1)	扒 bā pá cling; to dig up, rake; to stew; & 55;64 5 (3)	叭 bā 'bang' sound 58;30 5 (3)	趴 pā bend over; lie prone 196;157 9 (3)

引 yǐn to guide, lead; lure; cite; & 71;57 4 (2)	川 chuān river; a plain 4;47 3 (4)	训 訓 xùn teach, instruct; model, example 10;149 5 (2)	圳 zhèn irrigation ditch; [Shenzhen] 49;32 6 (-)	渊 淵 yuān deep; profound 40;85 11 (-)
州 zhōu state, prefecture 1;47 6 (4)	洲 zhōu continent; shoals, islet 40;85 9 (4)	酬 chóu reward; fulfil; entertain friends 193;164 13 (3)	叫 *呌 jiào cry, call; tell; be called 58;30 5 (1)	纠 糾 jiū entangle; rectify 77;120 5 (2)

形 xíng appearance, shape, form; & 63;59 7 (2)	杉 shān shā China fir tree 94;75 7 (-)	衫 shān shirt, vest 129;145 8 (2)	彤 tóng red (literary) 63;59 7 (-)	彩 cǎi color; variety; acclaim; prize 63;59 11 (1)	彭 péng (surname) - 63;59 12 (4)
彰 zhāng apparent, evident 63;59 14 (4)	影 yǐng shadow; image, photo, movie 63;59 15 (1)	澎 pēng péng splash; sound of waves 40;85 15 (-)	膨 péng [inflate, expand; swollen] 118;130 16 (3)	彬 bīn [urbane, refined] 94;59 11 (-)	彪 biāo young tiger (literary) 63;59 11 (-)

非 fēi not, no, non-; wrong; evil 205;175 8 (1)	诽 誹 fēi slander - 10;149 10 (4)	啡 fēi ('fi' sound); [coffee] 58;30 11 (1)	徘 pái [hesitate, waver, linger] 62;60 11 (4)	排 pái pǎi line up; row, line; platoon; rehearse; raft; eject; push; pie 55;64 11 (1)

1	**41**
2	42
3	43
4	44
5	45
6	46
7	47
8	48
9	49
10	50
11	51
12	52
13	53
14	54
15	55
16	56
17	57
18	58
19	59
20	60
21	61
22	62
23	63
24	64
25	65
26	66
27	67
28	68
29	69
30	70
31	71
32	72
33	73
34	74
35	75
36	76
37	77
38	78
39	79
40	80

刊 kān print; publication 17;18 5 (3)	**刑** xíng punishment; torture 17;18 6 (4)	**列** liè arrange, line up; rank, file; list; & 97;18 6 (2)	**利** lì profit, benefit; sharp 149;18 7 (1)	**判** pàn distinguish; to judge; & 17;18 7 (2)	**划** *劃 huà huá delimit; assign; scratch; & 101;18 6 (1)
刺 cì thorn; prick; assassinate; & 17;18 8 (2)	**制** *製 zhì make; draw up; control; system 17;18 8 (2)	**则** 則 zé rules; norm, model; then; & 106;18 6 (2)	**删** *刪 shān delete, omit 17;18 7 (3)	**剩** shèng surplus, residue 17;18 12 (1)	

俐 lì [clever] - 21;9 9 (4)	**例** lì example; rules; precedent 21;9 8 (1)	**侧** 側 cè side; to lean, incline 21;9 8 (3)	**测** 測 cè to measure; predict, infer 40;85 9 (2)	**倒** dǎo dào topple, collapse; exchange; pour; invert; go back; & 21;9 10 (1)	
捌 bā eight - 55;64 10 (4)	**喇** lǎ lá trumpet, horn 58;30 12 (3)	**咧** liě liē [grin; careless] 58;30 9 (-)	**剩** shèng surplus, residue 17;18 12 (1)		

刘 劉 liú (surname) - 84;18 6 (3)	**剖** pōu cut open; analyze 17;18 10 (3)	**刻** kè quarter (hour); engrave; & 17;18 8 (1)	**割** gē cut, sever 17;18 12 (2)	**剂** 劑 jì prescription, dose 160;18 8 (4)	
剃 tì shave - 17;18 9 (4)	**削** xiāo xuē to peel, pare, whittle, sharpen 17;18 9 (3)	**刹** shā chà brake, stop; temple 17;18 8 (4)	**剑** 劍 jiàn sword - 17;18 9 (4)	**创** 創 chuàng chuāng do for first time; wound 17;18 6 (2)	
到 dào arrive; up to, until; thoughtful 171;18 8 (1)	**副** fù deputy, vice-; to fit, match up 17;18 11 (2)	**别** 別 bié biè other; Don't!, to leave; & 17;18 7 (1)	**剥** 剝 bāo bō peel off 17;18 10 (3)	**刮** guā scrape; extort; to blow; & 177;18 8 (1)	**剩** shèng surplus, residue 17;18 12 (1)

剧 劇 jù play, drama; acute, severe 17;18 10 (2)	**刷** shuā shuō brush - 17;18 8 (2)	**刚** 剛 gāng firm, solid; just, barely; just now 17;18 6 (1)	**则** 則 zé rules; norm, model; then; & 106;18 6 (2)	**刨** *鉋 bào páo (carpenter's) plane; dig 17;18 7 (4)

亿
億 yì
a hundred million
21;9 3 (1)

忆
憶 yì
recollect
-
41;61 4 (2)

儿
兒 ér
child, youth; son; ('r' suffix)
29;10 2 (1)

礼
禮 lǐ
ceremony; etiquette; gift
87;113 5 (1)

孔
kǒng
hole, aperture
74;39 4 (2)

轧
軋 yà zhá gá
grind, crush; squeeze out
100;159 5 (4)

扎
* 紮 紥 zhā zhá zā
prick, stab; encamp; tie up
55;64 4 (2)

乱
亂 luàn
confused; riot; random; &
177;5 7 (1)

吼
hǒu
roar, bellow
58;30 7 (3)

乳
rǔ
breast; milk; give birth to; &
116;5 8 (4)

无
無 wú
without; not; nothing; &
53;86 4 (2)

抚
撫 fǔ
pacify; caress; nurture
55;64 7 (4)

▢尤 → 45
▢尤 → 45

北
běi
north
-
39;21 5 (1)

比
bǐ
compare; than; to gesture; &
123;81 4 (1)

此
cǐ
this
-
102;77 6 (2)

批
pī
slap; criticize; batch
55;64 7 (1)

乖
guāi
obedient; quick-witted
4;4 8 (3)

乘
chéng shèng
ride; multiply; make use of
149;4 10 (2)

死
sǐ
die; death; rigid
97;78 6 (1)

尼
ní
Buddhist nun; ('ni' sound)
67;44 5 (4)

匙
chí shi
spoon
-
213;21 11 (3)

能
néng
able to; energy; capability
37;130 10 (1)

化
huà huā
alter; -ise; -ify; melt; spend; &
21;21 4 (1)

讹
訛 é
error; extort; blackmail
10;149 6 (4)

靴
xuē
boot
-
212;177 13 (4)

龙
龍 lóng
dragon; imperial
137;212 5 (2)

▢龙 → 45

兆
zhào
omen; portend; million, mega-
29;10 6 (4)

挑
tiāo tiǎo
choose; carry; poke; stir up
55;64 9 (2)

桃
táo
peach
-
94;75 10 (3)

跳
tiào
jump, leap; omit; throb
196;157 13 (1)

姚
yáo
(surname)
-
73;38 9 (-)

飞
飛 fēi
to fly; swiftly; &
7;183 3 (1)

吨
噸 dūn
ton
-
58;30 7 (2)

纯
純 chún
pure, simple; skilful
77;120 7 (3)

钝
鈍 dùn
blunt; dull, stupid
147;167 9 (-)

1	41
2	**42**
3	43
4	44
5	45
6	46
7	47
8	48
9	49
10	50
11	51
12	52
13	53
14	54
15	55
16	56
17	57
18	58
19	59
20	60
21	61
22	62
23	63
24	64
25	65
26	66
27	67
28	68
29	69
30	70
31	71
32	72
33	73
34	74
35	75
36	76
37	77
38	78
39	79
40	80

十　寸　扌　斗　半　羊

十

汁 zhī
juice
-
40;85 5 (4)

计 計 jì
compute; plan;
meter, gauge
10;149 4 (1)

什 *甚 shén shí
[what?];
sundry; ten
21;9 4 (1)

叶 *葉 yè
leaf;
period, epoch
58;30 5 (2)

针 針 zhēn
needle;
stitch
147;167 7 (2)

寸

讨 討 tǎo
discuss; incur;
demand; &
10;149 5 (1)

付 fù
pay,
hand over
21;9 5 (2)

村 cūn
village
-
94;75 7 (1)

衬 襯 chèn
lining; serve
as contrast
129;145 8 (2)

对 對 duì
correct, yes; regarding; versus;
to face; towards; deal with; &
35;41 5 (1)

肘 zhǒu
elbow
-
118;130 7 (-)

射 shè
shoot (gun);
radiate; allude
200;41 10 (2)

时 時 shí
time; hour; season; opportunity;
present, current; now and then
103;72 7 (1)

耐 nài
endure,
bear
169;126 9 (2)

封 fēng
seal up;
bestow
54;41 9 (1)

咐 fu
[instruct;
exhort]
58;30 8 (2)

附 fù
append; agree;
near to
33;170 7 (1)

谢 謝 xiè
thanks; politely
decline; wither
10;149 12 (1)

树 樹 shù
tree; to plant,
set up; uphold
94;75 9 (1)

扌

材 cái
materials;
timber; ability
94;75 7 (2)

财 財 cái
wealth,
property
106;154 7 (3)

斗

料 liào
raw materials;
grain; expect
159;68 10 (2)

科 kē
area of study;
section; branch
149;115 9 (1)

斜 xié
slanting,
oblique
82;68 11 (2)

抖 dǒu
tremble, shake;
rouse
55;64 7 (2)

魁 kuí
head, chief;
outstanding
216;194 13 (-)

半

畔 pàn
side, border,
(river) bank
142;102 10 (3)

伴 bàn
partner;
accompany
21;9 7 (3)

拌 bàn
mix
-
55;64 8 (4)

衅 釁 xìn
quarrel
-
181;164 11 (4)

胖 pàng pán
fat, plump;
contented
118;130 9 (2)

羊

详 詳 xiáng
detailed;
fully known
10;149 8 (2)

群 qún
crowd, group,
herd
157;123 13 (2)

鲜 鮮 xiān xiǎn
fresh; colorful;
tasty; seafood
210;195 14 (2)

洋 yáng
ocean; foreign,
Western; vast
40;85 9 (2)

样 樣 yàng
sample; shape;
appearance; &
94;75 10 (1)

祥 xiáng
good luck,
auspicious
87;113 10 (4)

长 弋 戈 戋

胀
胀 zhàng
expand, swell;
bloated
118;130 8 (3)

张
張 zhāng
open; expand;
display; look
71;57 7 (1)

帐
帳賬 zhàng
canopy, curtain;
accounts
57;50 7 (3)

账
賬 zhàng
accounts,
credit
106;154 8 (-)

涨
漲 zhǎng zhàng
rise, go up;
swell
40;85 10 (2)

代
dài
substitute for;
era, generation
21;9 5 (1)

试
試 shì
try, attempt;
trial, test
10;149 8 (1)

赋
賦 fù
bestow;
compose poem
106;154 12 (4)

腻
膩 nì
greasy; tired of;
dirt; meticulous
118;130 13 (-)

伐
fá
cut down (tree);
attack
21;9 6 (4)

找
zhǎo
seek; call on;
give change
55;64 7 (1)

戏
戲 xì
to play; make
fun of; a show
35;62 6 (2)

战
戰 zhàn
war, battle;
tremble
101;62 9 (2)

戊
wù
5th;
HS
138;62 5 (-)

戌
xū
EB
-
138;62 6 (-)

诫
誡 jiè
warn,
admonish
10;149 9 (4)

械
xiè
tool, weapon,
instrument
94;75 11 (2)

绒
絨 róng
soft cloth,
velvet, flannel
77;120 9 (4)

贼
賊 zéi
thief; traitor;
furtive; cunning
106;154 10 (4)

诚
誠 chéng
sincere
-
10;149 8 (2)

城
chéng
(city) wall;
city
49;32 9 (1)

域
yù
region,
territory
49;32 11 (3)

减
*减 jiǎn
subtract,
deduct, reduce
8;15 11 (2)

喊
hǎn
shout, cry,
call
58;30 12 (1)

饿
餓 è
hunger,
starve
68;184 10 (1)

哦
ó ò é
(exclamation:
What?, Oh!)
58;30 10 (3)

蛾
é
moth
-
174;142 13 (4)

浅
淺 qiǎn
shallow; simple;
light (color) &
40;85 8 (1)

栈
棧 zhàn
storehouse;
stable; inn
94;75 9 (-)

钱
錢 qián
money,
cash, coin
147;167 10 (1)

线
綫線 xiàn
thread; route,
line; brink; clue
77;120 8 (2)

残
殘 cán
incomplete;
injure; savage
97;78 9 (3)

践
踐 jiàn
trample;
carry out
196;157 12 (1)

贱
賤 jiàn
cheap; lowly;
my (humble)
106;154 9 (3)

溅
濺 jiàn
splash
-
40;85 12 (3)

1	41
2	42
3	**43**
4	44
5	45
6	46
7	47
8	48
9	49
10	50
11	51
12	52
13	53
14	54
15	55
16	56
17	57
18	58
19	59
20	60
21	61
22	62
23	63
24	64
25	65
26	66
27	67
28	68
29	69
30	70
31	71
32	72
33	73
34	74
35	75
36	76
37	77
38	78
39	79
40	80

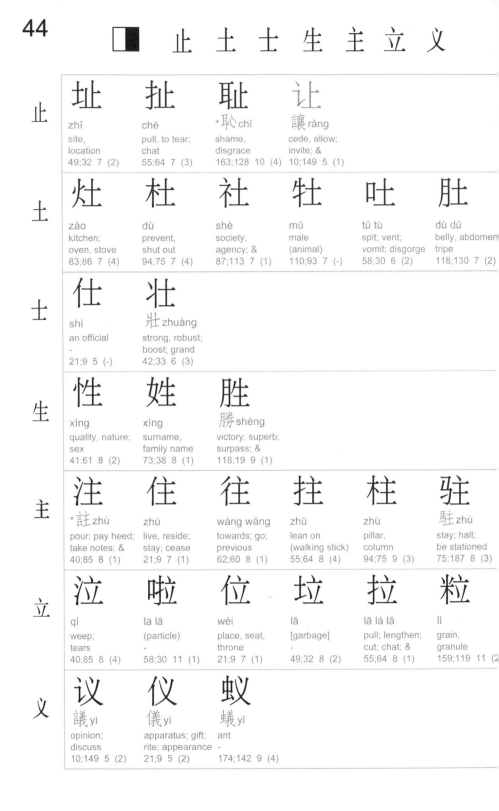

止

址 zhǐ site, location 49;32 7 (2)

扯 chě pull, to tear; chat 55;64 7 (3)

耻 *恥 chǐ shame, disgrace 163;128 10 (4)

让 讓 ràng cede, allow; invite; & 10;149 5 (1)

土

灶 zào kitchen; oven, stove 83;86 7 (4)

杜 dù prevent, shut out 94;75 7 (4)

社 shè society; agency; & 87;113 7 (1)

牡 mǔ male (animal) 110;93 7 (-)

吐 tǔ tù spit; vent; vomit; disgorge 58;30 6 (2)

肚 dù dǔ belly, abdomen tripe 118;130 7 (2)

士

仕 shì an official - 21;9 5 (-)

壮 壯 zhuàng strong, robust; boost; grand 42;33 6 (3)

生

性 xìng quality, nature; sex 41;61 8 (2)

姓 xìng surname, family name 73;38 8 (1)

胜 勝 shèng victory; superb; surpass; & 118;19 9 (1)

主

注 *註 zhù pour; pay heed; take notes; & 40;85 8 (1)

住 zhù live, reside; stay; cease 21;9 7 (1)

往 wàng wǎng towards; go; previous 62;60 8 (1)

拄 zhǔ lean on (walking stick) 55;64 8 (4)

柱 zhù pillar, column 94;75 9 (3)

驻 駐 zhù stay; halt; be stationed 75;187 8 (3)

立

泣 qì weep; tears 40;85 8 (4)

啦 la lā (particle) - 58;30 11 (1)

位 wèi place, seat, throne 21;9 7 (1)

垃 lā [garbage] - 49;32 8 (2)

拉 lā lá lǎ pull; lengthen; cut; chat; & 55;64 8 (1)

粒 lì grain, granule 159;119 11 (2

义

议 議 yì opinion; discuss 10;149 5 (2)

仪 儀 yí apparatus; gift; rite; appearance 21;9 5 (2)

蚁 蟻 yǐ ant - 174;142 9 (4)

坟
墳 fén
grave, tomb
49;32　7　(3)

纹
紋 wén
wrinkles; grain (of wood)
77;120　7　(3)

蚊
wén
mosquito
-
174;142　10　(3)

坑
kēng
hole, pit; tunnel; entrap
49;32　7　(3)

抗
kàng
resist, defy, anti-
55;64　7　(2)

杭
háng
Hangzhou
-
94;75　8　(-)

炕
kàng
to dry; kang, heated bricks
83;86　8　(4)

航
háng
boat, ship; to sail, fly
182;137　10　(2)

吭
háng kēng
throat; make a sound
58;30　7　(-)

访
訪 fǎng
visit; inquire, search for
10;149　6　(1)

坊
fáng fāng
workshop, mill; lane, alley
49;32　7　(4)

彷
páng
[hesitate, waver]
62;60　7　(-)

仿
倣 fǎng
imitate; resemble
21;9　6　(2)

伤
傷 shāng
wound; harm, hurt; get sick of
21;9　6　(2)

纺
紡 fǎng
spin (cotton); reel
77;120　7　(2)

防
fáng
dyke; defend; guard against
33;170　6　(2)

肪
fáng
[animal fat]
-
118;130　8　(4)

妨
fáng fāng
hinder, impede; harm
73;38　7　(3)

扩
擴 kuò
expand, extend
55;64　6　(2)

矿
礦 kuàng
ore, mine
136;112　8　(2)

旷
曠 kuàng
spacious; carefree; &
103;72　7　(4)

沪
滬 hù
Shanghai
-
40;85　7　(4)

护
護 hù
protect, guard
55;149　7　(2)

妒
dù
jealous
73;38　7　(4)

驴
驢 lú
donkey
75;187　7　(3)

沙
shā
sand; granules; hoarse
40;85　7　(2)

炒
chǎo
fry, stir-fry; heat up
83;86　8　(3)

砂
shā
sand, grit
136;112　9　(4)

妙
miào
wonderful; subtle
73;38　7　(2)

抄
chāo
copy; shortcut; confiscate; &
55;64　7　(2)

吵
chǎo chǎo
quarrel, make noise, disturb
58;30　7　(2)

纱
紗 shā
yarn, gauze
77;120　7　(3)

钞
鈔 chāo
banknote, paper money
147;167　9　(3)

秒
miǎo
second (of time, arc)
149;115　9　(2)

渺
miǎo
vast (lake, sea); hazy; negligible
40;85　12　(4)

1	41
2	42
3	43
4	**44**
5	45
6	46
7	47
8	48
9	49
10	50
11	51
12	52
13	53
14	54
15	55
16	56
17	57
18	58
19	59
20	60
21	61
22	62
23	63
24	64
25	65
26	66
27	67
28	68
29	69
30	70
31	71
32	72
33	73
34	74
35	75
36	76
37	77
38	78
39	79
40	80

尤

优	扰	犹	就
優 yōu	擾 rǎo	猶 yóu	jiù
excellent	harass, disturb; trouble	still, yet	right away; only, just; even if; then; precisely; concerning; &
-			
21;9 6 (2)	55;64 7 (2)	69;94 7 (3)	9;43 12 (1)

龙

咙	拢	珑
嚨 lóng	攏 lǒng	瓏 lóng
[throat]	approach; sum; tie up; comb	[exquisite, deft]
-		
58;30 8 (3)	55;64 8 (3)	88;96 9 (4)

尤

沈	枕	耽
shěn	zhěn	dān
(surname)	pillow; block	delay; indulge in
-		
40;85 7 (3)	94;75 8 (3)	163;128 10 (3)

也

他	池	地	她	驰
tā	chí	dì de	tā	馳 chí
he, him; other, another	pond; sunken area	earth, soil; place; &	she, her	gallop, go fast; far and wide
21;9 5 (1)	40;85 6 (2)	49;32 6 (1)	73;38 6 (1)	75;187 6 (4)

沐	休	林	淋	琳
mù	xiū	lín	lín lìn	lín
wash (hair), [bathe]	to stop; to rest; Don't!	forest, grove; group	drenched; filter	jade; valuables (literary)
40;85 7 (-)	21;9 6 (1)	94;75 8 (2)	40;85 11 (3)	88;96 12 (-)
味	昧	妹	魅	
wèi	mèi	mèi	mèi	
taste; smell; interest	conceal; ignorant of	younger sister	demon -	
58;30 8 (2)	103;72 9 (4)	73;38 8 (1)	216;194 15 (-)	
沫	抹	袜		
mò	mā mǒ mò	襪 wà		
foam	to plaster; wipe, erase; to skirt	socks, stockings		
40;85 8 (4)	55;64 8 (3)	129;145 10 (1)		
株	珠	殊	蛛	
zhū	zhū	shū	zhū	
tree trunk; a plant	pearl, bead, (water) drop	different; special; vcry	spider -	
94;75 10 (2)	88;96 10 (2)	97;78 10 (2)	174;142 12 (4)	
冻	栋	陈	阵	
凍 dòng	棟 dòng	陳 chén	陣 zhèn	
freeze -	supporting beam, ridgepole	exhibit, explain; old, stale	formation, array; period	
8;15 7 (2)	94;75 9 (4)	33;170 7 (3)	33;170 6 (2)	
伟	纬	韩		
偉 wěi	緯 wěi	韓 hán		
great -	latitude, weft	(surname)		
21;9 6 (1)	77;120 7 (-)	203;178 12 (-)		
津	律	肆		
jīn	lǜ	sì		
ferry; moist; sweat; saliva	law, rule	reckless; unbridled; four		
40;85 9 (4)	62;60 9 (2)	124;129 13 (4)		

人				
认 認 rèn	从 從 cóng cōng	队 隊 duì	纵 縱 zòng	巫 wū
recognize, admit; adopt 10;149 4 (1)	from; to follow; secondary; & 23;60 4 (1)	squad, team 33;170 4 (2)	leap; vertical; indulge; release 77;120 7 (3)	witch, wizard 48;48 7 (4)

亻			
以 yǐ	似 sì shì	拟 擬 nǐ	玖 jiū
using; so as to; according to; & 23;9 4 (1)	similar; seem; than 21;9 6 (2)	draft; intend; imitate 55;64 7 (4)	nine - 88;96 7 (4)

火					
伙 *夥 huǒ	狄 dí	秋 qiū	耿 gěng	揪 jiū	锹 鍬 qiāo
partner; group; provisions 21;9 6 (2)	(surname) - 69;94 7 (-)	fall, autumn; period, year 149;115 9 (1)	honest, just; dedicated 163;128 10 (4)	hold tight; seize; pull 55;64 12 (3)	spade, shovel 147;167 14 (

犬			
伏 fú	状 狀 zhuàng	汰 tài	驮 馱 tuó duò
prostrate; hide; confess; & 21;9 6 (4)	form, condition; certificate; & 42;94 7 (2)	clean out; discard 40;85 7 (4)	carry (on back, of animals) 75;187 6 (3)
狱 獄 yù	袱 fú	默 mò	献 獻 xiàn
prison, jail; lawsuit 69;94 9 (3)	[bundle of cloth] 129;145 11 (3)	silent; tacit 223;203 16 (2)	offer, proffer; display 96;94 13 (2)

丈	
仗 zhàng	杖 zhàng
hold (weapon); rely on; battle 21;9 5 (3)	cane, crutch, walking stick 94;75 7 (-)

失		
秩 zhì	铁 鐵 tiě	跌 diē
decade; in good order (literary) 149;115 10 (2)	iron; weapons 147;167 10 (2)	fall, decline 196;157 12 (2)

夹		
狭 狹 xiá	峡 峽 xiá	陕 陝 shǎn
narrow - 69;94 9 (4)	gorge, ravine 60;46 9 (3)	Shaanxi - 33;170 8 (3)

功
gōng
merit; achieve;
effect; skill
48;19 5 (2)

劝
勸 quàn
advise; urge,
encourage
35;19 4 (2)

幼
yòu
young;
child
76;52 5 (3)

助
zhù
help,
assist
28;19 7 (1)

伪
偽 僞 wěi
fake,
bogus
21;9 6 (4)

动
動 dòng
move, act; use;
alter; arouse
28;19 6 (1)

劲
勁 jìn jìng
strength, vigor;
mood; sturdy
28;19 7 (2)

励
勵 lì
encourage
-
28;19 7 (2)

锄
鋤 chú
hoe;
uproot
147;167 12 (4)

劫
jié
disaster; rob,
raid (literary)
133;19 7 (4)

勃
bó
suddenly;
[thriving]
28;19 9 (3)

勘
kān
collate, edit;
survey
28;19 11 (4)

勒
lēi lè
tighten, rein in;
compel
212;19 11 (4)

勤
qín
diligent; duties;
frequently
28;19 13 (3)

仇
chóu
hatred;
enemy
21;9 4 (3)

轨
軌 guǐ
rail, track,
path, orbit
100;159 6 (3)

执
執 zhí
hold; manage; persist;
abide by; capture; receipt
55;32 6 (2)

决
*決 jué
decide, resolve;
definitely; &
8;15 6 (1)

诀
訣 jué
farewell;
know-how
10;149 6 (-)

快
kuài
quick; soon;
sharp; happy; &
41;61 7 (1)

块
塊 kuài
clod, lump;
yuan (colloq)
49;32 7 (1)

抉
jué
pick, single out
(literary)
55;64 7 (-)

缺
quē
to lack; absent;
defect; vacancy
175;121 10 (2)

秧
yāng
seedling;
small fry; vine
149;115 10 (3)

殃
yāng
disaster; bring
misfortune
97;78 9 (4)

映
yìng
reflect;
shine
103;72 9 (2)

传
傳 chuán zhuàn
pass on,
transmit; &
21;9 6 (2)

砖
磚 zhuān
brick
-
136;112 9 (3)

转
轉 zhuǎn zhuàn
revolve; change;
to forward; stroll
100;159 8 (2)

丁

灯 燈 dēng
lamp, light, lantern
83;86 6 (1)

叮 dīng
sting; make sure
58;30 5 (4)

钉 釘 dīng dìng
nail; sew on; press, urge
147;167 7 (3)

盯 dīng
observe, gaze at
141;109 7 (3)

打 dǎ dá
hit; make; tie up; send; fetch; buy; shoot; calculate; dozen; &
55;64 5 (1)

订 訂 dìng
fix; agree on; book (seats); &
10;149 4 (2)

竹 zhú
bamboo
-
178;118 6 (2)

下

吓 嚇 hè xià
intimidate; Pah! (annoyed)
58;30 6 (2)

虾 蝦 xiā
shrimp
-
174;142 9 (3)

不

环 環 huán
ring, hoop; surround
88;96 8 (2)

怀 懷 huái
bosom; cherish; yearn; pregnant
41;61 7 (3)

杯 bēi
cup
-
94;75 8 (1)

坏 壞 huài
bad, evil; spoil, ruin
49;32 7 (1)

坯 pī
semi-finished product
49;32 8 (4)

干

汗 hàn hán
sweat
-
40;85 6 (2)

杆 桿 gān gǎn
pole, shaft
94;75 7 (2)

秆 稈 gǎn
stalk, stem
149;115 8 (4)

奸 *姦 jiān
evil; traitor; crafty; illicit
73;38 6 (4)

肝 gān
liver
-
118;130 7 (2)

轩 軒 xuān
balcony; ancient carriage
100;159 7 (-)

吁 *籲 yù xū
plead; groan; Oh!
58;30 6 (4)

许 許 xǔ
allow; promise; praise; maybe
10;149 6 (1)

赶 趕 gǎn
hurry; catch up; catch (bus); &
189;156 10 (2)

平

评 評 píng
comment on, appraise, judge
10;149 7 (1)

坪 píng
level ground
49;32 8 (-)

秤 chèng
steelyard, weighing scales
149;115 10 (4)

砰 pēng
bang, thump
136;112 10 (-)

呼 hū
exhale; cry out; 'whoo' sound
58;30 8 (2)

□ 丁 丂 工 王

衍	衔	街	衡	行
yǎn	銜 xián	jiē	héng	xíng háng
redundant; spread (literary)	hold (in mouth); rank, title	street -	scales; weigh; measure	go; do, perform; capable; OK; for now; line; (business) firm
62;144 9 (4)	62,167 11 (4)	62;144 12 (1)	62;144 16 (3)	62;144 6 (1)

朽	巧
xiǔ	qiǎo
decayed, rotten; senile	skilful; cunning; happily, luckily
94;75 6 (3)	48;48 5 (2)

江	扛	杠	红	缸	虹
jiāng	káng gāng	gàng	紅 hóng gong	gāng	hóng
river -	to shoulder, lift, carry	bar, pole; delete	red; bonus	jar	rainbow -
40;85 6 (1)	55;64 6 (2)	94;75 7 (4)	77;120 6 (1)	175;121 9 (3)	174;142 9 (4)

汪	狂	枉	旺	班	斑
wāng	kuáng	wǎng	wàng	bān	bān
form puddles; (dog's) bark	crazy; violent; wild; arrogant	crooked; to wrong; in vain	flourishing; brisk	team; duty; scheduled	spots; stripes; speckled
40;85 7 (4)	69;94 7 (3)	94;75 8 (3)	103;72 8 (4)	88;96 10 (1)	88;67 12 (4)

1	41
2	42
3	43
4	44
5	45
6	46
7	**47**
8	48
9	49
10	50
11	51
12	52
13	53
14	54
15	55
16	56
17	57
18	58
19	59
20	60
21	61
22	62
23	63
24	64
25	65
26	66
27	67
28	68
29	69
30	70
31	71
32	72
33	73
34	74
35	75
36	76
37	77
38	78
39	79
40	80

瓦

瓶 píng
瓶
bottle, vase, jug
98;98　10　(1)

甄 zhēn
甄
examine, sift (literary)
98;98　13　(-)

页

顷 qǐng
頃
just now; (unit of land area)
39;181　8　(3)

顶 dǐng
頂
stand up to; top; utmost; &
170;181　8　(2)

项 xiàng
項
item; nape of neck
48;181　9　(2)

顿 dùn
頓
pause; arrange; suddenly; &
170;181　10　(1)

侦 zhēn
偵
spy; scout; detect
21;9　8　(4)

颗 kē
顆
(measure word)
-
170;181　14　(2)

颊 jiá
頰
cheeks
-
170;181　12　(4)

颇 pō
頗
quite, rather
153;181　11　(4)

赖 lài
賴
rely; linger; deny; shirk
192;154　13　(4)

锁 suǒ
鎖
lock, padlock
147;167　12　(3)

烦 fán
煩
vexed; tired of; bother, trouble
83;86　10　(1)

顺 shùn
順
obey; suitable; along; in order
170;181　9　(2)

倾 qīng
傾
collapse; lean, incline; pour out
21;9　10　(3)

懒 lǎn
懶
lazy; sluggish
41;61　16　(2)

顾 gù
顧
look around; look after; visit
170;181　10　(1)

硕 shuò
碩
huge
-
136;112　11　(-)

颐 yí
頤
cheeks; keep fit (literary)
170;181　13　(-)

额 é
額
forehead; specific amount
170;181　15　(3)

频 pín
頻
frequently
-
170;181　13　(4)

颠 diān
顛
summit; jolt; topple, fall over
170;181　16　(4)

颜 yán
顏
face; prestige; color
170;181　15　(1)

颖 yǐng
穎
tip, point; clever (literary)
170;115　13　(4)

颤 zhàn chàn
顫
shiver, tremble
170;181　19　(3)

须 xū
須鬚
have to, must; beard
63;181　9　(1)

颂 sòng
頌
praise; song, eulogy
170;181　10　(3)

颁 bān
頒
publish; to issue, send out
170;181　10　(4)

领 lǐng
領
neck, collar; to lead, guide; get (award); outline; &
170;181　11　(1)

预 yù
預
in advance
-
170;181　10　(1)

颈 jǐng gěng
頸
neck
-
170;181　11　(4)

顽 wán
頑
stupid; naughty; stubborn
170;181　10　(3)

颓 tuí
頹
decadent; ruined; dejected
170;181　13　(-)

题 tí
題
topic, subject; inscribe
213;181　15　(1)

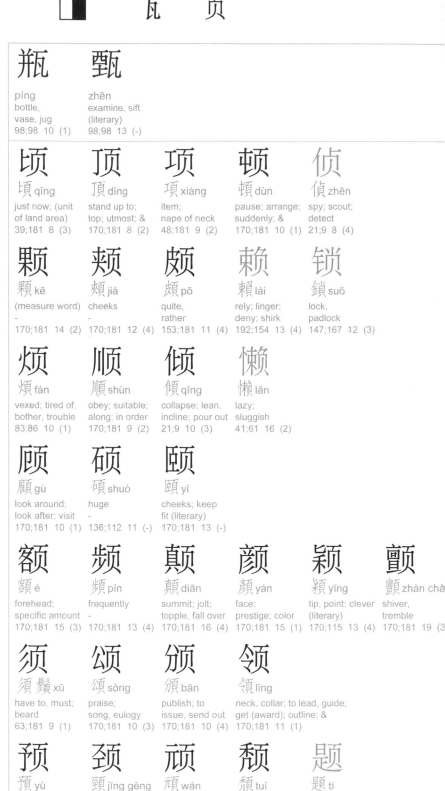

仟	**歼**	**纤**			
qiān	殲 jiān	纖 繾 xiān qiàn			
thousand	annihilate	tiny, slender; tow-rope			
-	-				
21;9 5 (-)	97;78 7 (3)	77;120 6 (2)			

任	**妊**	**饪**			
rèn rén	*姙 rèn	飪 rèn			
appoint; allow; despite; &	conceive, be pregnant	[cooking]			
21;9 6 (1)	73;38 7 (-)	68;184 7 (4)			

沃	**妖**	**袄**	**跃**		
wò	yāo	襖 ǎo	躍 yuè		
irrigate; fertile	monster, devil; charming	coat, jacket	leap, jump		
40;85 7 (4)	73;38 7 (4)	129;145 9 (4)	196;157 11 (2)		

泛	**贬**	**眨**			
*氾 汎 fàn	貶 biǎn	zhǎ			
general, vague; to flood	demote; censure	wink, blink			
40;85 7 (2)	106;154 8 (4)	141;109 9 (4)			

讥	**机**	**饥**	**肌**	**凯**	**叽**
譏 jī	機 jī	饑 jī	jī	凱 kǎi	嘰 jī
ridicule	machine; opportunity; &	hunger, famine	muscle	triumphant	chirp, twitter
-			-	-	
10;149 4 (4)	94;75 6 (1)	68;184 5 (3)	118;130 6 (3)	30;16 8 (4)	58;30 5 (-)

巩	**帆**
鞏 gǒng	fān
consolidate; stable, strong	a sail; canvas
48;177 6 (2)	57;50 6 (4)

观	**规**	**现**	**视**	**舰**
觀 guān guàn	規 guī	現 xiàn	視 shì	艦 jiàn
observe; view; Taoist temple	rule, law; plan; admonish	present, now, modern; appear	look at, regard, inspect	warship
35;147 6 (1)	107;147 8 (2)	88;96 8 (1)	87;147 8 (1)	-
				182;137 10 (3)

坝	**狈**
壩 bà	狽 bèi
dyke, dam, embankment	[legendary wolf; dire straits]
49;32 7 (3)	69;94 7 (4)

1 41
2 42
3 43
4 44
5 45
6 46
7 47
8 **48**
9 49
10 50
11 51
12 52
13 53
14 54
15 55
16 56
17 57
18 58
19 59
20 60
21 61
22 62
23 63
24 64
25 65
26 66
27 67
28 68
29 69
30 70
31 71
32 72
33 73
34 74
35 75
36 76
37 77
38 78
39 79
40 80

幻 huàn unreal; changeable 76;52 4 (3)	**刁** diāo cunning - 6;18 2 (4)	**习** 習 xí practice; be used to; habit 6;124 3 (1)	**叼** diāo hold (in the mouth) 58;30 5 (4)		
门 門 mén gate, door; family; sect; & 46;169 3 (1)	**们** 們 men (plural suffix) 21;9 5 (1)	**润** 潤 rùn moist; lubricate; adorn; profit 40;85 10 (3)	**搁** 擱 gē gé put; put aside; endure 55;64 12 (2)	**悯** 憫 mǐn pity, sympathize 41;61 10 (-)	**娴** 嫻嫻 xián refined; adept (literary) 73;38 10 (-)

羽 yǔ feather - 183;124 6 (2)	**翔** xiáng soar, hover 157;124 12 (4)	**翻** fān turn over; to cross; & 183;124 18 (1)

切 qiē qiè slice; eager to; accord with; & 27;18 4 (1)	**叨** tāo dāo obliged; [chatter] 58;30 5 (4)	**韧** 韌韌 rèn tough; pliable yet strong 91;178 7 (4)	**初** chū beginning; first, original 129;18 7 (1)
沏 qī infuse - 40;85 7 (4)	**彻** 徹 chè thorough; penetrate 62;60 7 (2)	**砌** qì lay (bricks); steps 136;112 9 (4)	

河 hé river - 40;85 8 (1)	**何** hé What?, Who? etc. (literary) 21;9 7 (1)	**柯** kē stalk; handle (literary) 94;75 9 (-)	**呵** hē scold; exhale; Oh! 58;30 8 (3)	**阿** ā ē ('a' sound); pander to 33;170 7 (2)	**啊** ā á ǎ à (exclamation: Eh?, Oh!, etc. 58;30 11 (1)

词 詞 cí words, speech 10;149 7 (1)	**伺** sì cì to watch; await; serve 21;9 7 (3)	**饲** 飼 sì fodder; to rear (animals) 68;184 8 (3)

奶	仍	扔
*妳 嬭 nǎi	réng	rēng
breast;	still,	hurl;
milk; suckle	yet	throw away
73;38 5 (1)	21;9 4 (2)	55;64 5 (2)

吸	圾	级	极
xī	jī	級 jí	極 jí
inhale, absorb;	[garbage]	rank, grade;	extreme,
attract	-	step	pole, polar
58;30 6 (2)	49;32 6 (2)	77;120 6 (1)	94;75 7 (1)

汤	扬	杨	场
湯 tāng	揚 yáng	楊 yáng	場 chǎng cháng
hot water;	raise; winnow;	poplar	site, spot,
soup	publicize	-	field; &
40;85 6 (1)	55;64 6 (1)	94;75 7 (4)	49;32 6 (1)

肠	畅
腸 cháng	暢 chàng
intestines	smooth, fluent;
-	uninhibited
118;130 7 (2)	144;72 8 (3)

记	纪	配
記 jì	紀 jì	pèi
recall; a mark;	discipline; age,	mix; match up;
note down	era; chronicle	deserve; &
10;149 5 (1)	77;120 6 (1)	193;164 10 (2)

躬	粥	弱
gōng	zhōu	ruò
to bend, bow;	gruel,	weak; inferior;
in person	porridge	a bit less
200;158 10 (4)	71;119 12 (3)	71;57 10 (2)

冯	玛	吗	妈	码	蚂
馮 féng	瑪 mǎ	嗎 ma má mǎ	媽 mā	碼 mǎ	螞 mǎ mà
(surname)	[agate]	(question	mother, mum;	numeral; wharf;	[ant;
		particle)	aunt (colloq)	yard (3 ft)	locust]
-	-				
8;187 5 (4)	88;96 7 (-)	58;30 6 (1)	73;38 6 (1)	136;112 8 (2)	174;142 9 (4)

欠

次 cì
sequence; 2nd;
next; inferior
8;76 6 (1)

炊 chuī
to cook
-
83;86 8 (4)

軟 软 ruǎn
soft, pliable;
inferior; weak
100;159 8 (2)

飲 饮 yǐn yìn
drink
-
68;184 7 (3)

玖 jiǔ
nine
-
88;96 7 (4)

吹 chuī
blow, puff;
brag; failure
58;30 7 (1)

歡 欢 huān
pleased,
happy, joyful
35;76 6 (1)

欣 xīn
happy,
joyful
115;76 8 (3)

砍 kǎn
chop,
hack
136;112 9 (2)

欺 qī
deceive;
bully
120;76 12 (2)

欽 钦 qīn
respect;
imperial
147;76 9 (4)

歐 欧 ōu
Europe;
(surname)
120;76 8 (3)

掀 xiān
lift
(lid or cover)
55;64 11 (2)

嗽 sòu
cough
-
58;30 14 (1)

欲 *慾 yù
desire, wish;
about to
199;76 11 (4)

欸 誒 ēi éi ěi èi ǎ
(exclamation:
Hey!, etc.)
120;149 11 (-)

款 *欵 kuǎn
funds; clause;
sincere; &
120;76 12 (2)

歇 xiē
stop work,
take a rest
120;76 13 (2)

歌 gē
song;
sing
120;76 14 (1)

歉 qiàn
apology;
crop failure
120;76 14 (2)

尔

你 *妳 nǐ
you,
your
21;9 7 (1)

彌 瀰 弥 mí
full; more;
redeem
71;57 8 (4)

稱 称 chēng chèn
call, name;
weigh; suitable
149;115 10 (2)

乍

詐 诈 zhà
cheat, swindle;
feign; bluff
10;149 7 (4)

炸 zhà zhá
explode; to
bomb; deep-fry
83;86 9 (3)

咋 zǎ zhā zhà
Why?, How?;
[boast]; bite
58;30 8 (4)

昨 zuó
yesterday
-
103;72 9 (1)

作 zuò zuō zuó
do, make, write; act as; pretend;
regard as; get up (from bed); &
21;9 7 (1)

的
de dí dì
(particle);
bull's eye
150;106 8 (1)

钓 釣 diào
to fish;
bait
147;167 8 (2)

约 約 yuē yāo
make appointment; agreement;
restrict; approx; brief; frugal; &
77;120 6 (2)

酌
zhuó
pour out (wine),
drink; consider
193;164 10 (4)

豹
bào
leopard,
panther
198;153 10 (-)

哟 喲 yo yō
(particle);
Oh!
58;30 9 (3)

均
jūn
equal, even,
balanced; all
49;32 7 (2)

韵 *韻 yùn
rhyme; melodic
tone; charming
211;180 13 (4)

胞
bāo
placenta;
siblings
118;130 9 (3)

炮
pào páo bāo
artillery; to dry;
quick-fry
83;86 9 (2)

抱
bào
cherish; adopt;
embrace; &
55;64 8 (1)

饱 飽 bāo
full, satisfied,
eat one's fill
68;184 8 (1)

跑
pǎo
run; flee;
away
196;157 12 (1)

泡
pào pāo
bubble; soak;
dawdle; spongy
40;85 8 (3)

袍
páo
robe,
gown
129;145 10 (3)

鲍 鮑 bào
[abalone];
(surname)
210;195 13 (-)

仔
zǐ zī zǎi
young animal;
[careful]
21;9 5 (2)

籽
zǐ
seed
-
159;119 9 (4)

好
hǎo hào
good; be well; easy; so that;
very; to like, love; be prone to
73;38 6 (1)

野
yě
countryside;
wild; limit; &
195;166 11 (2)

舒
shū
stretch, unfold;
leisurely
23;135 12 (1)

1	41
2	42
3	43
4	44
5	45
6	46
7	47
8	48
9	49
10	**50**
11	51
12	52
13	53
14	54
15	55
16	56
17	57
18	58
19	59
20	60
21	61
22	62
23	63
24	64
25	65
26	66
27	67
28	68
29	69
30	70
31	71
32	72
33	73
34	74
35	75
36	76
37	77
38	78
39	79
40	80

攵

收 shōu
receive; collect up; cease; &
113;66 6 (1)

改 gǎi
change, alter, rectify
113;66 7 (1)

攻 gōng
attack; accuse; study
48;66 7 (2)

枚 méi
(measure word) -
94;75 8 (4)

牧 mù
to herd, tend (animals)
110;93 8 (3)

拔 bá
root out; select seize; &
55;64 8 (2)

玫 méi
[rose] -
88;96 8 (4)

政 zhèng
politics; administration
113;66 9 (1)

救 jiù
rescue, aid
113;66 11 (2)

败 bài
defeated; fail; defeat; spoil; &
106;66 8 (2)

放 fàng
set free; expel; put; adjust; &
85;66 8 (1)

效 xiào
effect; work for; imitate
113;66 10 (2)

敦 dūn duì
sincere; ancient pot
113;66 12 (-)

故 gù
former; to die; on purpose; &
113;66 9 (1)

教 jiāo jiào
teach; tell; religion
113;66 11 (1)

敷 fū
lay out; apply (lotion); suffice
113;66 15 (4)

散 sàn sǎn
disperse; fall apart; dispel; &
113;66 12 (1)

敬 jìng
respect; offer politely
113;66 12 (2)

敞 chǎng
spacious; open, uncovered
113;66 12 (4)

敝 bì
shabby; my, our (humble)
113;66 11 (-)

数 shù shǔ shuò
number; a few; to count; often
113;66 13 (1)

致 *缀 zhì
send; result in; fine, delicate; &
171;133 10 (2)

敢 gǎn
bold; dare; be sure
113;66 11 (1)

败 bài
defeated; fail; defeat; spoil; &
106;154 8 (2)

敌 dí
foe; oppose
177;66 10 (2)

敏 mǐn
nimble, agile, adroit
113;66 11 (3)

敲 qiāo
knock, strike, hit
218;66 14 (2)

做 zuò
make, do, write; be, become; &
21;9 11 (1)

傲 ào
defy; proud, arrogant
21;9 13 (2)

微 wēi
micro-, tiny; wane; subtle
62;60 13 (2)

徽 huī
emblem -
62;60 17 (4)

撤 chè
remove, withdraw
55;64 15 (3)

撒 sā sǎ
let go; scatter, spill, drop
55;64 15 (2)

撇 piē piě
abandon, cast off; fling; skim
55;64 14 (4)

激 jī
violent; arouse; annoy; chill
40;85 16 (2)

缴 jiǎo
pay, hand over; capture
77;120 16 (4)

辙 zhé
(wheel) track, rut; rhyme
100;159 16 (4)

嫩 nèn
tender; rookie; light (color)
73;38 14 (3)

墩 dūn
mound; block
49;32 15 (-)

汉	**仅**	**权**	**叹**	**双**	**奴**
漢 hàn	僅 jǐn	權 quán	嘆歎 tàn	雙 shuāng	nú
Chinese (lang); Han; man	merely; barely	rights; power, authority; &	sigh; admire; acclaim	two, twin, dual, bi-, double	slave -
40;85 5 (1)	21;9 4 (2)	94;75 6 (3)	58;30 5 (3)	35;172 4 (1)	73;38 5 (3)
取	**叔**	**叙**	**淑**	**椒**	**趣**
qǔ	shū	*敍敘 xù	shū	jiāo	qù
take; obtain; choose; &	uncle; brother in law	chat; narrate; assess; &	virtuous (literary)	spice plant, pepper, chili	interest, liking, delight
163;29 8 (1)	35;29 8 (2)	35;29 9 (3)	40;85 11 (-)	94;75 12 (3)	189;156 15 (2)
扳	**版**	**板**	**叛**	**饭**	**贩**
bān	bǎn	*闆 bǎn	pàn	飯 fàn	販 fàn
pull; to turn	printing; edition, page	board, plank; hard, stiff	betray -	food, meal, cooked rice	buy and sell; dealer
55;64 7 (4)	114;91 8 (2)	94;75 8 (1)	227;29 9 (4)	68;184 7 (1)	106;154 8 (4)
波	**彼**	**坡**	**披**	**破**	**被**
bō	bǐ	pō	pī	pò	bèi
a wave -	that; the other; he, she	slope	drape over; unroll; split	destroy; split; broken; torn; &	quilt; (particle: passive verbs)
40;85 8 (3)	62;60 8 (3)	49;32 8 (2)	55;64 8 (2)	136;112 10 (1)	129;145 10 (1)
皱					
皺 zhòu					
crease, wrinkle					
153;107 10 (3)					
听	**析**	**祈**	**斩**	**折**	
聽 tīng	xī	qí	斬 zhǎn	摺 zhé zhē shé	
listen; obey; allow	divide, dissect, discriminate	worship, pray, beg	chop, cut; behead	bend; fold; break; lose; rebate; be convinced; amount to; &	
58;128 7 (1)	94;75 8 (2)	87;113 8 (-)	100;69 8 (4)	55;64 7 (2)	
所	**新**	**斯**	**断**	**拆**	**诉**
suǒ	xīn	sī	斷 duàn	chāi cā	訴 sù
place; building; (particle)	new -	this; thus; ('si' sound)	break off, snap; quit; decide	tear apart, dismantle	inform; accuse; complain
115;63 8 (1)	115;69 13 (1)	115;69 12 (3)	115;69 11 (2)	55;64 8 (2)	10;149 7 (1)
浙	**渐**	**惭**	**撕**	**晰**	
zhè	漸 jiàn jiān	慚 cán	sī	xī	
Zhejiang -	gradually -	ashamed -	rip, tear	clear, distinct	
40;85 10 (3)	40;85 11 (2)	41;61 11 (3)	55;64 15 (2)	103;72 12 (3)	

1	41
2	42
3	43
4	44
5	45
6	46
7	47
8	48
9	49
10	50
11	**51**
12	52
13	53
14	54
15	55
16	56
17	57
18	58
19	59
20	60
21	61
22	62
23	63
24	64
25	65
26	66
27	67
28	68
29	69
30	70
31	71
32	72
33	73
34	74
35	75
36	76
37	77
38	78
39	79
40	80

口

加	如	扣	和	知
jiā	rú	kòu	hé hè huó huò	zhī
plus; add, augment	such as; as if, if; as...as...; &	arrest; fasten; knot; deduct; &	harmony; mild; with; sum; mix	know; inform; administer
28;19 5 (1)	73;38 6 (1)	55;64 6 (2)	149;30 8 (1)	148;111 8 (1)

咖	蜘
kā gā	zhī
('ka' sound); [coffee]	[spider] -
58;30 8 (1)	174;142 14 (4)

中

仲	冲
zhòng	*冲 衝 chōng chòng
go-between; middle (of 3)	add water, rinse, flush; rush; clash; vigorous; &
21;9 6 (-)	8;15 6 (2)

肿	钟	种
腫 zhǒng	鐘 鍾 zhōng	種 zhǒng zhòng
swollen -	bell, clock, o'clock; &	seed; species; type; cultivate
118;130 8 (3)	147;167 9 (1)	149;115 9 (1)

虫

浊	蚀	独	烛	融	触
濁 zhuó	蝕 shí	獨 dú	燭 zhú	róng	觸 chù
turbid, muddy; chaotic	lose; erode; eclipse	single, alone, only	candle; watt	melt, thaw; blend	touch -
40;85 9 (4)	68;142 9 (3)	69;94 9 (2)	83;86 10 (3)	174;142 16 (4)	201;148 13 (2)

曲

油	抽	轴	袖	铀	细
yóu	chōu	軸 zhóu	xiù	鈾 yóu	細 xì
oil, grease, fat; to paint	to extract; to smoke; whip; &	axis, axle; spool, reel	sleeve -	uranium	tiny, slender; delicate; careful
40;85 8 (2)	55;64 8 (1)	100;159 9 (-)	129;145 10 (2)	147;167 10 (4)	77;120 8 (1)

申

伸	呻	绅	坤	神	押
shēn	shēn	紳 shēn	kūn	shén	yā
stretch, extend	[groan]	gentry -	feminine -	gods; magical; spirit; &	detain; escort; mortgage; &
21;9 7 (2)	58;30 8 (4)	77;120 8 (4)	49;32 8 (-)	87;113 9 (1)	55;64 8 (3)

拒 **jù**	1 41

拒
jù
resist, reject,
refuse
55;64 7 (2)

柜
*櫃 guì jù
cupboard;
(shop) counter
94;75 8 (3)

矩
jǔ
rules; square,
rectangle
148;111 9 (3)

距
jù
distance
(from, apart)
196;157 11 (2)

呕
嘔 ǒu
vomit;
spit out
58;30 7 (4)

枢
樞 shū
axis, pivot,
hub
94;75 8 (-)

驱
驅 qū
drive (vehicle);
expel; run fast
75;187 7 (4)

躯
軀 qū
human
body
200;158 11 (-)

汹
洶 xiōng
[turbulent]
-
40;85 7 (4)

酗
xù
[get drunk]
-
193;164 11 (4)

洒
灑 sǎ
sprinkle;
spill
40;85 9 (2)

栖
棲 qī
stay;
perch (birds)
94;75 10 (-)

牺
犧 xī
animal sacrifice
(literary)
110;93 10 (2)

晒
曬 shài
to shine (sun);
sunbathe
103;72 10 (2)

酒
jiǔ
wine,
liquor
40;164 10 (1)

扫
掃 sǎo sào
clear away,
sweep
55;64 6 (2)

妇
婦 fù
woman;
wife
73;38 6 (2)

归
歸 guī
return;
converge; &
70;77 5 (3)

日 白 丑 艮 良

日

旧
舊 jiù
old, former,
outdated; worn
103;134 5 (1)

阳
陽 yáng
yang, positive;
sun; overt; &
33;170 6 (1)

白

伯
bó bǎi
uncle;
earl
21;9 7 (2)

怕
pà
afraid; worried;
possibly
41;61 8 (1)

泊
bó pō
anchor, moor;
lake, pool
40;85 8 (4)

帕
pà
handkerchief;
turban
57;50 8 (-)

拍
pāi
clap, beat time;
bat, racquet; &
55;64 8 (1)

柏
bǎi bò
cypress,
cedar
94;75 9 (3)

舶
bó
(sea-going)
ship
182;137 11 (4)

啪
pā
'bang'
sound
58;30 11 (-)

丑

扭
niǔ
turn round; roll;
wrench; grapple
55;64 7 (2)

纽
紐 niǔ
handle, button,
knob; fasten
77;120 7 (4)

钮
鈕 niǔ
knob, button;
to tie, fasten
147;167 9 (4)

妞
niǔ
girl
(colloq)
73;38 7 (-)

艮

艰
艱 jiān
difficult
-
35;138 8 (2)

狠
hěn
ruthless;
resolute
69;94 9 (3)

恨
hèn
hate;
regret
41;61 9 (2)

根
gēn
root; basis;
thoroughly
94;75 10 (1)

很
hěn
very
-
62;60 9 (1)

限
xiàn
limit
-
33;170 8 (2)

银
銀 yín
silver
-
147;167 11 (1)

跟
gēn
heel; follow;
with
196;157 13 (1)

眼
yǎn
eye;
key point
141;109 11 (1)

良

浪
làng
wave, billow;
dissolute
40;85 10 (2)

狼
láng
wolf
-
69;94 10 (2)

娘
孃 niáng
mother; aunt;
young lady
73;38 10 (1)

粮
糧 liáng
grain,
provisions
159;119 13 (2)

酿
釀 niàng niáng
brew, ferment;
lead to; wine
193;164 14 (4)

沮
jǔ
dispirited;
prevent
40;85 8 (-)

诅
詛 zǔ
[to curse]
-
10;149 7 (-)

姐
jiě
elder
sister
73;38 8 (1)

租
zū
rent, hire,
lease
149;115 10 (1)

泪
淚 lèi
teardrop
-
40;85 8 (2)

相
xiāng xiàng
mutual; looks;
photo; &
94;109 9 (1)

祖
zǔ
ancestor;
grandparent
87;113 9 (1)

组
組 zǔ
organize;
group
77;120 8 (1)

阻
zǔ
hinder, block,
obstruct
33;170 7 (3)

粗
cū
thick, coarse,
rough; careless
159;119 11 (2)

明
míng
bright; clear;
overt; next; &
103;72 8 (1)

朋
péng
friend
-
118;74 8 (1)

阴
陰 yīn
yin, negative; occult;
shade; cloudy; moon; &
33;170 6 (1)

胡
* 鬍 hú
reckless;
beard; &
118;130 9 (2)

钥
鑰 yuè yào
key
-
147;167 9 (3)

朝
cháo zhāo
facing; dynasty;
morning; day; &
203;74 12 (1)

朗
lǎng
bright;
loud and clear
118;74 10 (2)

期
qī jī
expect; period;
appointed time
118;74 12 (1)

溯
sù
go against flow;
trace back
40;85 13 (-)

湖
hú
lake
-
40;85 12 (3)

瑚
hú
[coral]
-
88;96 13 (4)

蝴
hú
[butterfly]
-
174;142 15 (3)

糊
hú hū hù
paste, gum;
plaster
159;119 15 (2)

潮
cháo
tide, upsurge;
damp
40;85 15 (1)

嘲
cháo
to ridicule,
mock
58;30 15 (4)

棚
péng
shed, shack;
awning
94;75 12 (3)

绷
繃 bēng bèng běng
stretch taut;
rebound; crack
77;120 11 (4)

悄
qiāo qiǎo
quiet;
softly
41;61 10 (2)

消
xiāo
vanish; dispel;
leisurely
40;85 10 (1)

俏
qiào
handsome;
in demand
21;9 9 (3)

捎
shāo shào
take,
bring; &
55;64 10 (4)

梢
shāo
tip (of twig,
branch)
94;75 11 (4)

稍
shāo
slightly
-
149;115 12 (2)

哨
shào
sentry, guard;
whistle; chirp
58;30 10 (3)

销
銷 xiāo
to fuse; sell;
cancel; spend
147;167 12 (4)

1	41
2	42
3	43
4	44
5	45
6	46
7	47
8	48
9	49
10	50
11	51
12	52
13	**53**
14	54
15	55
16	56
17	57
18	58
19	59
20	60
21	61
22	62
23	63
24	64
25	65
26	66
27	67
28	68
29	69
30	70
31	71
32	72
33	73
34	74
35	75
36	76
37	77
38	78
39	79
40	80

卩　卩　阝

卩

卯	印	即	却	卸	卵
mǎo	yìn	jí	*卻 què	xiè	luǎn
EB; mortise	print, stamp, seal; tally with	right away; approach; i.e.	but, however; retreat; refuse	unload; remove; get rid of	egg -
32;26 5 (-)	32;26 6 (2)	184;26 7 (2)	133;26 7 (2)	32;26 8 (3)	227;26 7 (3)

仰	抑	柳	聊
yǎng	yì	liǔ	liáo
face up; admire; rely on	repress; restrain	willow -	merely; slightly; chat
21;9 6 (2)	55;64 7 (3)	94;75 9 (3)	163;128 11 (2)

脚	御	卿	犯	起
腳 jiǎo	*禦 yù	qīng	fàn	qǐ qi
foot, base; leg	drive (vehicle); resist; imperial	minister (archaic)	offense; attack; criminal	raise, rise; up; begin; able to
118;130 11 (1)	62;60 12 (3)	32;26 10 (-)	69;94 5 (2)	189;156 10 (1)

阝

邦	邮	邢	邪	那	耶
bāng	郵 yóu	xíng	xié	nà nèi nè nā	yē yé
nation, state	post, mail	(surname) -	evil; heretical	that; in that case	('je' sound)
34;163 6 (4)	143;163 7 (1)	34;163 6 (4)	34;163 6 (4)	34;163 6 (1)	34;128 8 (-)

邓	郎	郁	郑	邻
鄧 dèng	láng	*鬱 yù	鄭 zhèng	鄰 lín
(surname) -	man, person; darling	fragrant; lush; despondent	(surname) -	neighbor
34;163 4 (4)	34;163 8 (2)	34;163 8 (4)	34;163 8 (4)	34;163 7 (2)

郊	部	郭	都	鄙
jiāo	bù	guō	dōu dū	bǐ
suburbs, outskirts	part, section, unit; troops	outer wall (of city)	all; capital, metropolis	low, vulgar; my (humble)
34;163 8 (2)	34;163 10 (1)	34;163 10 (4)	34;163 10 (1)	34;163 13 (4)

掷	绑	椰	嘟	螂
擲 zhì zhī	綁 bǎng	yē	dū	láng
throw -	bind, tie	coconut -	toot, honk; pout	[mantis, cockroach]
55;64 11 (4)	77;120 9 (3)	94;75 12 (-)	58;30 13 (-)	174;142 14 (-)

挪	娜	哪	郎	郑	郁
nuó	nuó	na nǎ něi	láng	鄭 zhèng	*鬱 yù
move	[fascinating; courteous]	(particle); Which?, What?	man, person; darling	(surname)	fragrant; lush; despondent
55;64 9 (4)	73;38 9 (-)	58;30 10 (1)	34;163 8 (2)	34;163 8 (4)	34;163 8 (4)

鸣	鸡	鸭	鸦	鸥	鹅
鳴 míng	雞 鷄 jī	鴨 yā	鴉 yā	鷗 ōu	鵝 é
chirp; to voice; make a sound	chicken, cock, hen	a duck	a crow	gull	goose
58;196 8 (3)	35;172 7 (1)	152;196 10 (3)	99;196 9 (4)	152;196 9 (-)	152;196 12 (2)

鸽	鹊	鹤
鴿 gē	鵲 què	鶴 hè
dove, pigeon	magpie	crane (bird)
152;196 11 (3)	152;196 13 (4)	152;196 15 (-)

鸿	鹏	捣	呜
鴻 hóng	鵬 péng	搗 dǎo	嗚 wū
swan, goose; grand	roc (fabled giant bird)	to pound, beat; harass	hoot, toot
40;196 11 (-)	152;196 13 (-)	55;64 10 (4)	58;30 7 (4)

愧	槐	瑰	魄	魂	魏
kuì	huái	guī	pò bó tuò	hún	wèi
ashamed	acacia, locust tree	marvelous (literary)	soul, spirit, vigor	soul, spirit	(old kingdom; surname)
41;61 12 (3)	94;75 13 (4)	88;96 13 (4)	150;194 14 (4)	216;194 13 (3)	216;194 18 (4)

辟	辞	锌	僻
*闢 pì bì	辭 cí	鋅 xīn	pì
open up (land); incisive; refute	depart; decline; dismiss; &	zinc	secluded, eccentric
186;160 13 (2)	177;160 13 (3)	147;167 12 (4)	21;9 15 (4)

辨	辩	辫	瓣
biàn	辯 biàn	辮 biàn	bàn
differentiate, distinguish	dispute, debate	plait, braid; pigtail	petal, segment, piece; valve
186;160 16 (4)	186;160 16 (3)	186;120 17 (4)	186;97 19 (3)

凉	谅	惊	掠
*涼 liáng liàng	諒 liàng	驚 jīng	lüè
cool, cold; disappointed	forgive; guess, suppose	startled, alarmed	plunder; sweep past
8;15 10 (1)	10;149 10 (1)	41;187 11 (2)	55;64 11 (3)

琼	晾	鲸
瓊 qióng	liàng	鯨 jīng
jade; palace (literary)	to air, dry in the sun	whale
88;96 12 (-)	103;72 12 (4)	210;195 16 (3)

1	41
2	42
3	43
4	44
5	45
6	46
7	47
8	48
9	49
10	50
11	51
12	52
13	53
14	**54**
15	55
16	56
17	57
18	58
19	59
20	60
21	61
22	62
23	63
24	64
25	65
26	66
27	67
28	68
29	69
30	70
31	71
32	72
33	73
34	74
35	75
36	76
37	77
38	78
39	79
40	80

只

识	积	帜	职	况	祝
識 shí zhì	積 jī	幟 zhì	職 zhí	* 況 kuàng	zhù
knowledge; know; opinion	amass, store; long-standing	flag, banner (literary)	duty, job, post	situation; compare	best wishes -
10;149 7 (1)	149;115 10 (2)	57;50 8 (3)	163;128 11 (2)	8;15 7 (1)	87;113 9 (1)

支

枝	技	歧	妓	肢	鼓
zhī	jì	qí	jì	zhī	gǔ
branch, twig	skill, ability, talent	fork (in road); diverge	prostitute -	limb -	drum; rouse; bellows; bulge
94;75 8 (3)	55;64 7 (1)	102;77 8 (4)	73;38 7 (-)	118;130 8 (4)	224;207 13 (2

殳

设	没	役	投	股	般
設 shè	沒 méi mò	yì	tóu	gǔ	bān
to found, establish; &	[not]; sink, submerge	compel; battle; service; servant	fling; leap into; send; deliver; &	thigh; section; strand; a share	sort, kind; manner
10;149 6 (1)	40;85 7 (1)	62;60 7 (4)	55;64 7 (2)	118;130 8 (3)	182;137 10 (1

段	殷	毅	毁	殿	殴
duàn	yīn yān	yì	huǐ	diàn	毆 ōu
section, segment	ardent; cordial; rich; & (literary)	firm, resolute	destroy; defame	hall, palace; at the rear	beat, strike
119;79 9 (1)	119;79 10 (4)	119;79 15 (3)	119;79 13 (3)	119;79 13 (3)	119;79 8 (4)

搬	缎	锻			
bān	緞 duàn	鍛 duàn			
move (house); remove; &	satin -	forge, temper (metals)			
55;64 13 (1)	77;120 12 (4)	147;167 14 (1)			

叚

假	暇				
jiǎ jià	xiá				
fake; borrow; vacation; &	leisure -				
21;9 11 (1)	103;72 13 (-)				

青

请	清	情	靖	猜	精
請 qǐng	qīng	qíng	jìng	cāi	jīng
please; ask, invite	clear; settle up; quiet; fully; &	emotion; love; favor; situation	tranquillity; pacify	guess, suspect	splendid; spirit fine; clever; &
10;149 10 (1)	40;85 11 (1)	41;61 11 (1)	126;174 13 (-)	69;94 11 (2)	159;119 14 (1

蜻	晴	睛			
qīng	qíng	jīng			
[dragonfly] -	fine (weather)	eyeball			
174;142 14 (4)	103;72 12 (1)	141;109 13 (1)			

泽
澤 zé
pond, marsh;
damp; luster
40;85　8 (3)

择
擇 zé zhái
pick,
choose
55;64　8 (2)

释
釋 shì
explain; resolve;
release
197;165　12 (2)

佳
jiā
beautiful,
fine
21;9　8 (3)

挂
掛 guà
hang; to phone;
worry; register
55;64　9 (1)

桂
guì
laurel, cassia,
cinnamon tree
94;75　10 (4)

娃
wá
baby

73;38　9 (3)

哇
wā wa
cry, wail;
(particle)
58;30　9 (2)

蛙
wā
frog
-
174;142　12 (3)

鞋
xié
shoe
-
212;177　15 (1)

准
*準 zhǔn
allow; quasi-;
definitely; &
8;15　10 (1)

淮
huái
[Huaihe river]
-
40;85　11 (4)

谁
誰 shuí shéi
Who?;
anyone
10;149　10 (1)

惟
wéi
solely;
thought
41;61　11 (4)

稚
zhì
young,
infantile
149;115　13 (3)

榷
què
discuss
-
94;75　14 (4)

堆
duī
heap,
pile
49;32　11 (2)

唯
wéi wěi
solely;
[yes-man]
58;30　11 (4)

难
難 nán nàn
difficult; nasty;
disaster; blame
35;172　10 (1)

雅
yǎ
proper; elegant;
your (polite)
99;172　12 (4)

推
tuī
push; grind; to clip; deduce;
shirk; postpone; elect; esteem
55;64　11 (1)

维
維 wéi
hold together;
maintain; &
77;120　11 (2)

摊
攤 tān
spread out;
booth, stall; &
55;64　13 (3)

雌
cí
female
-
208;172　14 (4)

滩
灘 tān
beach, sands;
shoals, rapids
40;85　13 (3)

雄
xióng
male; mighty,
grand; hero
208;172　12 (2)

雕
diāo
carve, engrave;
vulture, eagle
208;172　16 (3)

浦
pǔ
river bank,
river mouth
40;85　10 (-)

埔
pǔ
[Huangpu]
-
49;32　10 (4)

捕
bǔ
catch, seize,
arrest
55;64　10 (2)

辅
輔 fǔ
assist
-
100;159　11 (1)

铺
鋪 pū pù
spread; pave;
store, shop
147;167　12 (2)

1	41
2	42
3	43
4	44
5	45
6	46
7	47
8	48
9	49
10	50
11	51
12	52
13	53
14	54
15	**55**
16	56
17	57
18	58
19	59
20	60
21	61
22	62
23	63
24	64
25	65
26	66
27	67
28	68
29	69
30	70
31	71
32	72
33	73
34	74
35	75
36	76
37	77
38	78
39	79
40	80

占

沾 zhān
wet; moisten; stain; touch
40;85 8 (3)

站 zhàn
station; (bus) stop; to stand
126;117 10 (1)

粘 *黏 zhān nián
glue; sticky; paste up
159;119 11 (2)

贴 貼 tiē
paste; nestle; subsidize
106;154 9 (2)

帖 tiē tiě tiè
docile; fitting; note, card
57;50 8 (4)

钻 鑽 zuān zuàn
penetrate, bore, drill; diamond
147;167 10 (2)

各

洛 luò
(a river)
-
40;85 9 (-)

格 gé
grid; standard; subdivision
94;75 10 (2)

略 lüè
slightly; omit; plan; seize; &
142;102 11 (2)

胳 gē gé
[arm]
-
118;130 10 (2)

骆 駱 luò
[camel]
-
75;187 9 (3)

路 lù
road, route; way; region; &
196;157 13 (1)

赂 賂 lù
[bribe]
-
106;154 10 (4)

铭 銘 míng
inscription; engrave
147;167 11 (4)

㕣

沿 yán yàn
along; follow; border, edge
40;85 8 (2)

铅 鉛 qiān
lead (the metal)
147;167 10 (1)

船 chuán
boat, ship
182;137 11 (1)

召

昭 zhāo
clear, evident
103;72 9 (-)

绍 紹 shào
continue
-
77;120 8 (1)

招 zhāo
beckon; invite; recruit; incur; provoke; confess; a trick
55;64 8 (2)

台

冶 yě
smelt
-
8;15 7 (3)

治 zhì
control; peace; cure; study; &
40;85 8 (1)

怡 yí
happy (literary)
41;61 8 (-)

抬 tái
raise, lift
55;64 8 (1)

始 shǐ
beginning
-
73;38 8 (1)

胎 tāi
embryo; birth; a tire; padding
118;130 9 (-)

合

恰 qià
suitable; exactly
41;61 9 (3)

洽 qià
harmonious; discuss
40;85 9 (4)

哈 hā hǎ hà
exhale; Aha!; laugh
58;30 9 (1)

拾 shí
pick up, collect; ten
55;64 9 (1)

给 給 gěi jǐ
give; for (someone); allow; supply; ample
77;120 9 (1)

份	扮	纷	粉	吩	盼
fèn	bàn	紛 fēn	fěn	fēn	pàn
portion, share	disguise, dress up as	in profusion; confused	dust, powder; white; pink	[command, order]	hope for; look
21;9 6 (2)	55;64 7 (2)	77;120 7 (2)	159;119 10 (2)	58;30 7 (2)	141;109 9 (2)

怜	冷	伶	龄
憐 lián	lěng	líng	齡 líng
pity, sympathy; pamper	cold, frosty; rare; deserted	actor (archaic); [clever; bereft]	age, years, duration
41;61 8 (2)	8;15 7 (1)	21;9 7 (4)	206;211 13 (2)

玲	铃	岭	吟
líng	鈴 líng	嶺 lǐng	yín
[tinkling of jade]; exquisite, deft]	bell	mountain peak, ridge, range	chant, recite; (animal's) roar
88;96 9 (4)	147;167 10 (2)	60;46 8 (4)	58;30 7 (4)

沧	枪	舱	抢
滄 cāng	槍 qiāng	艙 cāng	搶 qiǎng qiāng
deep blue (sea)	gun; spear, lance	cabin, hold (on ship)	snatch; vie for; to rush; scrape
40;85 7 (-)	94;75 8 (2)	182;137 10 (3)	55;64 7 (2)

论	沦	抡	伦	轮
論 lùn lún	淪 lún	掄 lūn lún	倫 lún	輪 lún
discuss; theory; decide; &	sink; be reduced to	brandish; choose	series; peer; (feudal) ethics	wheel; take turns
10;149 6 (1)	40;85 7 (-)	55;64 7 (4)	21;9 6 (-)	100;159 8 (2)

陀	蛇	舵	驼
tuó	shé yí	duò	駝 tuó
[(spinning) top]	snake	rudder, helm	camel; hump-backed
33;170 7 (-)	174;142 11 (2)	182;137 11 (4)	75;187 8 (3)

1	41
2	42
3	43
4	44
5	45
6	46
7	47
8	48
9	49
10	50
11	51
12	52
13	53
14	54
15	55
16	**56**
17	57
18	58
19	59
20	60
21	61
22	62
23	63
24	64
25	65
26	66
27	67
28	68
29	69
30	70
31	71
32	72
33	73
34	74
35	75
36	76
37	77
38	78
39	79
40	80

出巾市

拙	础	帅	沛	肺
zhuō	礎 chǔ	帥 shuài	pèi	fèi
clumsy; my (humble)	plinth, base	commander; smart, graceful	copious -	lungs
55;64 8 (4)	136;112 10 (1)	57;50 5 (4)	40;85 7 (4)	118;130 8 (2)

赤東竞攵匕

赫	辣	兢	敲	能
hè	là	jīng	qiāo	néng
impressive -	spicy, acrid; vicious	[conscientious]	knock, strike, hit	able to; energy capability
190;155 14 (4)	186;160 14 (3)	12;10 14 (4)	218;66 14 (2)	37;130 10 (1)

亡兒关宛

忙	貌	联	豌	
máng	mào	聯 lián	wān	
busy; hurried, hasty	view; face, appearance	unite, join, link up	[pea] -	
41;61 6 (1)	198;153 14 (2)	163;128 12 (1)	191;151 15 (4)	

厶大夫

私	弘	驮	肤	扶
sī	hóng	馱 tuó duò	膚 fū	fú
private; selfish; secret, illicit	great, grand; enlarge	carry (on back, of animals)	skin; [superficial]	hold on to; help
149;115 7 (2)	71;57 5 (-)	75;187 6 (3)	118;130 8 (2)	55;64 7 (2)

史女乂

驶	妆	汝	赵	
駛 shǐ	妝 zhuāng	rǔ	趙 zhào	
(of a vehicle) to go; to speed	adorn; apply make-up	you (literary)	(surname)	
75;187 8 (3)	42;38 6 (4)	40;85 6 (-)	189;156 9 (3)	

井甘

讲	耕	甜	钳	
講 jiǎng	*畊 gēng	tián	鉗 拑 qián	
speak, discuss, tell, explain; &	plow -	sweet; (sleep) soundly	pincers, pliers; clamp; restrain	
10;149 6 (1)	176;127 10 (3)	177;99 11 (2)	147;167 10 (4)	

勿勾芻

吻	物	构	钩	鞠
wěn	wù	構 gòu	鉤 gōu	jū
lips; kiss; animal's mouth	thing; content, substance	construct, compose	hook -	to rear, bring up; nourish
58;30 7 (3)	110;93 8 (1)	94;75 8 (2)	147;167 9 (3)	212;177 17 (

夕多争

矽	夥	够	静	
xī	huǒ	*夠 gòu	靜 jìng	
silicon -	many (literary) (see Table 1)	enough; attain; rather, quite	still, calm, quiet	
136;112 8 (-)	142;36 15 (-)	64;36 11 (1)	202;174 14 (1)	

■

军

于开聿更

巴艮

亏元民

廴羊

风

手毛毛

乾 qián male (archaic) (see Table 1) 203;5 11 (-)	辉 輝 huī radiance; shine 172;159 12 (2)

汇 匯彙 huì gather, meet; remit (money) 40;22 5 (3)	吁 *籲 yù xū plead; groan; Oh! 58;30 6 (4)	研 yán grind; study, research 136;112 9 (1)	拜 bài pay a visit; bow to 111;64 9 (2)	鞭 biān whip - 212;177 18 (4)

犯 fàn offense; attack; criminal 69;94 5 (2)	肥 féi fat; baggy; fertile; fertilizer 118;130 8 (2)	把 bǎ bà to hold; control; a handle; & 55;64 7 (1)	服 fú clothes; serve; obey; & 118;74 8 (1)	报 報 bào report; reply; newspaper 55;32 7 (1)

仁 rén benevolence; kernel 21;9 4 (4)	污 *汙污 wū dirt, filth; smear; corrupt 40;85 6 (2)	玩 wán play; trifle with; enjoy; resort to 88;96 8 (1)	氓 méng máng the common people 43;83 8 (3)

弱 ruò weak; inferior; a bit less 71;57 10 (2)	疑 yí doubt - 39;103 14 (2)	解 jiě jiè xiè untie; explain; solve; dispel; & 201;148 13 (1)

钢 鋼 gāng gàng steel; sharpen 147;167 9 (1)	枫 楓 fēng maple - 94;75 8 (-)	飘 飄 piāo flutter; drift on the wind 121;182 15 (2)

稣 穌 sū revive - 210;115 13 (-)	掰 bāi break (with the fingers) 111;64 12 (4)	耗 hào use up; dawdle; bad news 176;127 10 (3)	托 *託 tuō entrust; pretext; support; & 55;64 6 (2)

豁 huō huò crack; forsake; open; exempt 199;150 17 (4)

、

、

'

之	广	户	良	义	以
zhī	廣 guǎng	hù	liáng	義 yì	yǐ
(particle, object pronoun)	wide, broad; spread; many	door; family; bank account	good; very	justice; meaning; &	using; so as to according to; &
1;4 3 (1)	44;53 3 (1)	86;63 4 (1)	184;138 7 (2)	25;123 3 (1)	23;9 4 (1)

主	永	心	必	书	启 → 3
zhǔ	yǒng	xīn	bì	書 shū	启 → 3
master, host, lord; manage; &	eternal, forever	heart; core; feelings	necessarily; certainly	write; letter, book, document	疠 → 3
88;3 5 (1)	1;85 5 (1)	81;61 4 (1)	1;61 5 (1)	3;73 4 (1)	问 → 3

斗	头	术	求	为	亩 → 6
*鬥 dòu dǒu	頭 tóu tou	*術 shù zhú	qiú	為 wéi wèi	亩 → 6
fight; dovetail; dipper; &	head; top; first; chief; end; &	art, technique, skill; method	beg, request; seek	do, act, act as; become; be equal to; for the sake of	
82;68 4 (2)	52;181 5 (1)	94;75 5 (1)	1;85 7 (1)	1;86 4 (1)	

尤	龙	发	戈	戊	我
yóu	龍 lóng	發 髮 fā fà	gē	wù	wǒ
especially; blame, fault	dragon; imperial	emit; become; develop; hair; &	lance, spear, (an old weapon)	5th; HS	I, me, my, we, our
53;43 4 (1)	137;212 5 (2)	35;105 5 (1)	101;62 4 (4)	138;62 5 (-)	101;62 7 (1)

白	自	血	身	向	囱
bái	zì	xuè xiě	shēn	*嚮 xiàng	cōng
white; blank, in vain; gratis; &	self; oneself; from; certainly	blood -	body, torso; life; oneself	facing; towards; direction; &	[chimney] -
150,106 5 (1)	180;132 6 (1)	181;143 6 (2)	200;158 7 (1)	4;30 6 (1)	4;31 7 (3)

乌	鸟	岛	舟	盘	兜
烏 wū	鳥 niǎo	島 dǎo	zhōu	盤 pán	dōu
crow; black, dark	bird -	island -	boat (literary)	dish, tray; coil; examine; build	pocket; bag; wrap; solicit; &
4;86 4 (4)	152;196 5 (2)	60;46 7 (2)	182;137 6 (4)	182;108 11 (2)	29;10 11 (4)

皂	泉	皇	息	臭	鼻
zào	quán	huáng	xī	chòu xiù	bí
soap; black	spring, fountain	emperor, sovereign	breath; cease; news; grow; &	stink; disgusting	nose -
150;106 7 (2)	150;85 9 (4)	150;106 9 (2)	180;61 10 (1)	180;132 10 (2)	226;209 14 (2

卑	鬼	粤	奥	长
bēi	guǐ	yuè	ào	長 cháng zhǎng
low, inferior, modest	ghost; stealthy; sinister; &	Guangdong -	profound; hard to understand	long; long-term; steadily; forte; grow; senior, chief; get, acquire
12;24 8 (4)	216;194 9 (2)	4;119 12 (4)	52;37 12 (3)	4;168 4 (1)

弟	兑	总	单	兽	曾
dì	duì	總 zǒng	單 dān	獸 shòu	céng zēng
younger brother	to exchange; to dilute	chief; anyway; always; sum up	single, alone; list; (bed) sheet	beast -	formerly; great (grandchild)
24;57 7 (1)	24;10 7 (3)	81;120 9 (1)	24;30 8 (1)	24;94 11 (3)	103;73 12 (2)

丫	米	半	炎	脊
yā	mǐ	bàn	yán	jǐ jí
fork (in tree), bifurcation	rice; meter (length)	half, semi-; partly	hot; blazing; inflammation	backbone, spine; ridge
24;2 3 (-)	159;119 6 (1)	3;24 5 (1)	83;86 8 (4)	118;130 10 (4)

兰	羊	并	关	养
蘭 lán	yáng	併並 bìng	關 guān	養 yǎng
orchid -	sheep; goat	actually; also; merge; equally	shut; switch off; involve; &	maintain; raise, nurture; &
24;140 5 (3)	157;123 6 (1)	24;9 6 (2)	24;169 6 (1)	24;184 9 (2)

益	首	兼	兹	慈
yì	shǒu	jiān	*兹 zī	cí
benefit; profit; increasingly	head; chief, first; indict	concurrent; both; double	this; now; year (literary)	kind, loving, merciful
146;108 10 (2)	24;185 9 (1)	24;12 10 (3)	24;140 9 (-)	81;61 13 (4)

前	煎	剪	普	奠	尊
qián	jiān	jiǎn	pǔ	diàn	zūn
front, in front of, forward; former	fry, boil, simmer	scissors; clip, trim; wipe out	universal -	settle (a place); funeral offerings	senior; esteem, respect
24;18 9 (1)	80;86 13 (3)	27;18 11 (2)	103;72 12 (2)	52;37 12 (3)	54;41 12 (2)

盖	姜	羡	羞	差
蓋 gài	薑 jiāng	xiàn	xiū	chà chā chāi cī
lid, cover; affix; surpass; build	ginger -	envy, admire	shy; ashamed	differ; err; wrong; difference; lacking; errand
157;140 11 (2)	157;140 9 (4)	157;123 12 (2)	157;123 10 (4)	157;48 9 (1)

养	美	善	着
養 yǎng	měi	shàn	zháo zhāo zhuó zhe
maintain; raise, nurture; &	beautiful; America	good; expert; apt to; friendly	touch; catch (cold); burn; to wear; use, apply; -ing; &
24;184 9 (2)	157;123 9 (2)	157;30 12 (2)	157;109 11 (1)

1	41
2	42
3	43
4	44
5	45
6	46
7	47
8	48
9	49
10	50
11	51
12	52
13	53
14	54
15	55
16	56
17	57
18	**58**
19	59
20	60
21	61
22	62
23	63
24	64
25	65
26	66
27	67
28	68
29	69
30	70
31	71
32	72
33	73
34	74
35	75
36	76
37	77
38	78
39	79
40	80

小

少 shǎo shào
few; lacking;
Stop!; young; &
79;42 4 (1)

尘 塵 chén
dust, dirt; this
(mortal) world
79;32 6 (3)

尖 jiān
tip, pinnacle;
sharp, pointed
79;42 6 (2)

劣 liè
inferior,
poor quality
79;19 6 (3)

雀 què qiǎo
sparrow
-
79;172 11 (4)

省 shěng xǐng
save; omit; province;
visit; aware; introspection
79;109 9 (1)

⺍

尚 shàng
esteem,
respect; yet
79;42 8 (3)

肖 xiào xiāo
resemble
-
79;130 7 (4)

当 當 噹 dāng dàng
act as; when, whilst; ought;
regard as; equal to; proper; &
79;102 6 (1)

类 類 lèi
kind, type;
similar to
159;181 9 (2)

粪 糞 fèn
dung,
excrement
159;119 12 (3)

米 mǐ
rice;
meter (length)
159;119 6 (1)

光 guāng
light; glory; scenery; bare;
smooth; depleted; alone
172;10 6 (2)

⺍

尝 嘗 cháng
to taste, test;
ever, already
139;30 9 (2)

学 學 xué
study, learn;
knowledge; &
74;39 8 (1)

觉 覺 jué jiào
feel; conscious;
realize; sleep
107;147 9 (1)

党 黨 dǎng
political party;
club, gang
139;203 10 (2)

堂 táng
hall, court;
cousin
139;32 11 (1)

掌 zhǎng
palm (of hand);
control
139;64 12 (1)

常 cháng
often; constant;
normal
139;50 11 (1)

裳 cháng shang
a skirt
(ancient)
139;145 14 (4)

赏 賞 shǎng
bestow; reward
appreciate
139;154 12 (3)

⺍

兴 興 xīng xìng
start; prosper;
excitement
24;134 6 (1)

誉 譽 yù
reputation;
praise
185;149 13 (4)

举 舉 jǔ
raise; praise; deed; cite;
entire; behavior; choose; start
227;134 9 (1)

学 學 xué
study, learn;
knowledge; &
74;39 8 (1)

觉 覺 jué jiào
feel; conscious;
realize; sleep
107;147 9 (1)

个	介	伞	企	众	仓
個 gè gě	jiè	傘 sǎn	qǐ	眾 衆 zhòng	倉 cāng
(measure word); item; individual	between; take seriously	umbrella -	expect, await; stand on tiptoe	numerous; a crowd	warehouse, granary
23;9 3 (1)	23;9 4 (1)	23;9 6 (2)	23;9 6 (2)	23;109 6 (2)	23;9 4 (3)

全	金	余	舍
quán	jīn	*餘 yú	捨 shě shè
completely; whole, all	gold; metal; money	remainder, surplus; after	abandon; house, shed; &
23;11 6 (1)	209;167 8 (2)	23;9 7 (2)	23;135 8 (1)

今	令	合	会
jīn	lìng lǐng	hé gě	會 huì kuài
now, present; today; modern	command; your (resp); &	join; add up to; shut; to suit; &	meet; meeting; union, society; going to; know how to; &
23;9 4 (1)	23;9 5 (2)	23;30 6 (1)	23;73 6 (1)

念	含	贪	俞	命
*唸 niàn	hán	貪 tān	yú	mìng
study; recite; think of, yearn	contain; hold in mouth	corrupt; greedy; covet	(surname) -	life; command; destiny; assign
81;61 8 (1)	58;30 7 (2)	106;154 8 (4)	23;9 9 (-)	23;30 8 (2)

食	盒	拿	愈	禽
shí sì	hé	ná	*瘉 癒 yù	qín
eat; food, meal; edible; eclipse	box, case, casket	grasp; using; treat as; &	get well; better; more and more	birds -
217;184 9 (1)	146;108 11 (2)	111;64 10 (1)	81;61 13 (3)	23;114 12 (4)

分	公
fēn fèn	gōng
small unit; part; divide; duty; &	public; official; general; impartial; metric units; male (animal)
24;18 4 (1)	24;12 4 (1)

岔	贫	盆	翁
chà	貧 pín	pén	wēng
branch off, turn off	poor, destitute; talkative	basin, pot, tub	old man, father, father in law
60;46 7 (4)	106;154 8 (3)	146;108 9 (2)	183;124 10 (3)

父	谷	斧	爷	爸	爹
fù	*穀 gǔ	fǔ	爺 yé	bà	diē
father -	valley; grain, cereal	axe -	father; uncle, grandpa (polite)	father -	father, dad (colloq)
108;88 4 (1)	199;150 7 (3)	108;69 8 (4)	108;88 6 (2)	108;88 8 (1)	108;88 10 (3)

1	41
2	42
3	43
4	44
5	45
6	46
7	47
8	48
9	49
10	50
11	51
12	52
13	53
14	54
15	55
16	56
17	57
18	58
19	**59**
20	60
21	61
22	62
23	63
24	64
25	65
26	66
27	67
28	68
29	69
30	70
31	71
32	72
33	73
34	74
35	75
36	76
37	77
38	78
39	79
40	80

一 一

二 èr	**三** sān	**云** *雲 yún	**元** yuán	**示** shì	**亏** 虧 kuī
two	three	cloud	first; chief; unit; yuan	show; notify	deficit; unfair; thanks to; &
-	-	-			
11;7 2 (1)	2;1 3 (1)	11;7 4 (1)	11;10 4 (1)	132;113 5 (1)	11;141 3 (3)
灭 滅 miè	**丽** 麗 lì	**画** 畫 huà	**豆** dòu	**买** 買 mǎi	
snuff out; wipe out; drown	beautiful	picture; (of Ch char) stroke	beans, pulses	buy	
83;85 5 (2)	2;198 7 (2)	38;102 8 (1)	191;151 7 (2)	5;154 6 (1)	
丁 dīng zhēng	**不** bù bú	**平** píng	**下** xià xia		
4th; HS; man, population	no, not, un-; can't	flat, even, level; calm; average	below, down; descend; unload; next; inferior; send; decide; &		
2;1 2 (3)	95;1 4 (1)	2;51 5 (1)	16;1 3 (1)		
开 開 kāi kai	**牙** yá	**无** 無 wú	**于** *於 yú	**干** *乾 幹 gān gàn	
open; start; operate; &	tooth; ivory	without; not; nothing; &	in, at, to, from, than	dry; futile; adopt (child); main part, trunk; do, work; fight	
51;169 4 (1)	99;92 4 (2)	53;86 4 (2)	11;7 3 (2)	11;51 3 (1)	
万 *萬 wàn mò	**歹** dǎi	**瓦** wǎ wà	**丐** gài	**天** tiān	
ten thousand; many; utterly	bad, evil	(roof) tile; earthenware	beg; beggar (literary)	sky, Heaven; God; day; season; weather; nature, natural	
2;1 3 (1)	97;78 4 (4)	98;98 4 (3)	2;1 4 (-)	90;37 4 (1)	
石 shí dàn	**百** bǎi	**死** sǐ	**至** zhì	**严** 嚴 yán	
stone, rock; inscription	a hundred; numerous	die; death; rigid	until, up to; arrive at	tight; strict, severe	
136;112 5 (2)	150;106 6 (1)	97;78 6 (1)	171;133 6 (2)	168;30 7 (2)	
丙 bǐng	**页** 頁 yè	**面** *麵 麪 miàn	**耍** shuǎ	**夏** xià	
3rd; HS	page	face; surface; extent; flour; &	to play	summer	
2;1 5 (3)	170;181 6 (1)	2;176 9 (1)	169;126 9 (3)	65;35 10 (1)	
两 兩 liǎng	**而** ér	**雨** yǔ	**再** zài	**更** gèng gēng	
two, a couple; both; a few; &	and; due to; but; (from …) to	rain	again; further; more; before; &	even more; to change	
2;11 7 (1)	169;126 6 (1)	204;173 8 (1)	2;13 6 (1)	2;73 7 (1)	

千 qiān
thousand; numerous
12;24 3 (1)

升 *昇 shēng
rise, raise; promote; liter
4;24 4 (2)

禾 hé
grain, cereal; rice
149;115 5 (4)

币 幣 bì
money -
57;50 4 (2)

乏 fá
deficiency; exhausted
4;4 4 (2)

壬 rén
9th; HS
49;33 4 (-)

系 *係 繫 xì
fasten; system; department; &
77;120 7 (1)

乎 hū
(suffix particle)
2;4 5 (2)

手 shǒu
hand; by hand; hold; person
111;64 4 (1)

毛 máo
fur, hair, wool; scared; rough; gross (profit); 1/10 yuan; &
112;82 4 (1)

乖 guāi
obedient; quick-witted
4;4 8 (3)

乘 chéng shèng
ride; multiply; make use of
149;4 10 (2)

秉 bǐng
grasp; control (literary)
149;115 8 (4)

垂 chuí
droop; hang down
4;32 8 (3)

重 chóng zhòng
repeat; heavy; to stress; &
4;166 9 (1)

熏 xūn xùn
smoke -
80;86 14 (4)

乔 喬 qiáo
tall; disguise
90;30 6 (4)

丢 diū
lose; throw away
133;1 6 (1)

悉 xī
know; all, entire
197;61 11 (2)

番 fān
a time, a turn
197;102 12 (3)

舌 → 61

乐 樂 yuè lè
music; enjoy; happy
4;75 5 (1)

氏 shì
family name; surname; née
122;83 4 (3)

丘 qiū
mound, grave
4;1 5 (3)

我 wǒ
I, me, my, we, our
101;62 7 (1)

么 麼 me
[what; such as] (suffix)
4;200 3 (1)

妥 tuǒ
arranged; appropriate
116;38 7 (3)

采 *採 cǎi cài
pick, pluck, select; &
197;165 8 (2)

受 shòu
receive, accept; endure
116;29 8 (2)

爱 愛 ài
love; be fond of; cherish; apt to
116;61 10 (1)

爵 jué
nobility; wine cup
116;87 17 (-)

秃 tū
bald; blunt; unsatisfactory
149;115 7 (4)

季 jì
season, quarterly
149;39 8 (2)

秀 xiù
beautiful; excellent
149;115 7 (2)

委 wěi wēi
appoint; indirect; &
149;38 8 (2)

香 xiāng
fragrant; appetizing; heartily; perfume, incense; popular
215;186 9 (1)

否 fǒu pǐ
deny; not; evil; censure
95;30 7 (2)

歪 wāi
crooked, askew; devious
95;77 9 (2)

甭 béng
don't; needn't -
95;101 9 (3)

厂 厂 ㇒

乞	每	舞	复
qǐ	měi	wǔ	*復複覆 fù
beg	each, every;	dance	duplicate, repeat; complex;
-	habitually	-	resume; reply; revenge
20;5 3 (4)	20;80 7 (1)	20;136 14 (1)	20;60 9 (1)

气	氛	氧	氮	氢	与
氣 qì	fēn	yǎng	dàn	氫 qīng	與 yǔ yù yú
air, gas, breath;	atmosphere,	oxygen	nitrogen	hydrogen	and; with; to;
odor; enrage; &	vapor	-	-	-	help; give; &
109;84 4 (1)	109;84 8 (3)	109;84 10 (3)	109;84 12 (4)	109;84 9 (4)	2;134 3 (2)

午	矢	年	乍	行
wǔ	shǐ	nián	zhà	xíng háng
noon;	arrow;	year; annual;	suddenly;	go; do, perform; capable; OK;
EB	vow	age; New Year	at first; extend	for now; line; (business) firm
20;24 4 (1)	148;111 5 (-)	20;51 6 (1)	20;4 5 (-)	62;144 6 (1)

冤	罕	写	买
yuān	hän	寫 xiě xiè	買 mǎi
injustice; bad	rare	write;	buy
luck; hatred	-	draw; depict	
18;14 10 (3)	18;122 7 (4)	18;40 5 (1)	5;154 6 (1)

军	冥	冠	尔
軍 jūn	míng	guàn guān	爾 ěr
army,	dark; deep;	precede; crown,	you; like that,
troops	stupid; Hades	hat; champion	that (literary)
18;159 6 (2)	18;14 10 (-)	18;14 9 (2)	79;89 5 (3)

色	免	兔	危	负
sè shǎi	miǎn	tù	wēi	負 fù
color; scene;	avoid; exempt;	rabbit,	danger;	to shoulder; suffer; rely on
looks; lust; &	dismiss	hare	near death	minus; owe; fail; be defeated
27;139 6 (1)	27;10 7 (2)	27;10 8 (2)	27;26 6 (1)	27;154 6 (1)

争	急	龟	鱼	角
爭 zhēng	jí	龜 guī jūn	魚 yú	jiǎo jué
compete (for),	quick; urgent;	tortoise,	fish	angle, corner; 1/10 yuan; horn;
argue (about)	hurry; annoyed	turtle	-	role; actor; contend
27;87 6 (2)	81;61 9 (1)	27;213 7 (4)	210;195 8 (1)	201;148 7 (1)

象	鲁
*像 xiàng	魯 lǔ
elephant;	stupid;
be like; shape	rude
27;152 11 (2)	210;195 12 (4)

多
duō
many;
more; over-; &
64;36 6 (1)

名
míng
name;
renown; famous
64;30 6 (1)

冬
dōng
winter;
drum sound
65;15 5 (1)

条 條 tiáo
twig; clause;
slip of paper
65;75 7 (1)

备 備 bèi
prepare, equip;
fully
65;9 8 (1)

务 務 wù
affair, business;
work at
65;19 5 (1)

各
gè
each,
every
65;30 6 (1)

灸
jiū
moxibustion
(Ch. medicine)
83;86 7 (3)

圣 聖 shèng
sacred; sage;
Majesty
35;128 5 (3)

桑
sāng
mulberry
tree
94;75 10 (4)

叠 *疊 疉 dié
pile up;
repeat
35;29 13 (2)

予
yǔ yú
grant,
bestow
31;6 4 (3)

矛
máo
spear,
lance
155;110 5 (2)

柔
róu
soft, pliable;
gentle
155;75 9 (3)

勇
yǒng
brave
-
31;19 9 (2)

承
chéng
undertake;
indebted; &
5;64 8 (2)

子
zǐ zi
child; son; egg, seed;
person; thing; EB
74;39 3 (1)

矣
yǐ
(particle,
archaic)
37;111 7 (-)

允
yǔn
allow;
equitable
37;10 4 (2)

台 *臺 檯 颱 tái
platform, stage; support;
desk; (TV) station; Taiwan
37;30 5 (2)

怠
dài
idle,
lazy
81;61 9 (4)

垒 壘 lěi
rampart, fort;
build
49;32 9 (4)

叁
sān
three
-
37;28 8 (4)

参 參 cān cēn shēn
join in; consult,
refer; ginseng
37;28 8 (1)

乒
pīng
gunshot sound;
[ping-pong]
4;4 6 (2)

乓
pāng
banging sound;
[ping-pong]
4;3 6 (2)

兵
bīng
soldier; army;
military; arms
24;12 7 (2)

岳
yuè
high mountain;
wife's parents
60;46 8 (4)

1	41
2	42
3	43
4	44
5	45
6	46
7	47
8	48
9	49
10	50
11	51
12	52
13	53
14	54
15	55
16	56
17	57
18	58
19	59
20	60
21	**61**
22	62
23	63
24	64
25	65
26	66
27	67
28	68
29	69
30	70
31	71
32	72
33	73
34	74
35	75
36	76
37	77
38	78
39	79
40	80

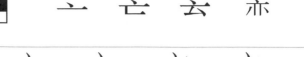
六	亡	之	方	立	亢
liù	wáng	zhī	fāng	lì	kàng
six	die; lose; flee; subjugate	(particle, object pronoun)	direction; place; square; &	to stand; to set up; at once; &	proud, haughty excessively
-	43;8 3 (3)	1;4 3 (1)	85;70 4 (1)	126;117 5 (1)	9;8 4 (4)
9;12 4 (1)					

文	交
wén	jiāo
writing; culture; rite; civilian; &	exchange; meet; join; befriend; to hand over; mutual; &
84;67 4 (1)	9;8 6 (1)

衣	玄	亥	市	亦	夜
yī	xuán	hài	shì	yì	yè
garment, clothes, cover	black, dark; profound	EB	market; city	also, too (literary)	night
161;145 6 (1)	9;95 5 (-)	9;8 6 (-)	9;50 5 (1)	162;8 6 (4)	9;36 8 (1)

亩	言	卒	率	裔
mǔ	yán	zú	shuài lǜ	yì
mu (unit of land area, 1/6 acre)	word; speech; say, talk	soldier; servant; finish; die	to lead; frank; rate, ratio; &	posterity; far-off land (literary)
9;102 7 (2)	185;149 7 (1)	9;24 8 (-)	9;95 11 (2)	161;145 13 (-)

离	衷	衰	裹	襄	片
lí	zhōng	shuāi	guǒ	xiāng	piàn piān
depart; apart; distant from	sincere; heartfelt	grow weak, decline	wrap; bind up	assist (literary)	sheet, slice; fragment; film
9;172 10 (1)	9;145 10 (3)	9;145 10 (3)	9;145 14 (3)	9;145 17 (-)	114;91 4 (1)

忘	妄	盲	赢
wàng wáng	wàng	máng	yíng
forget	absurd; presumptuous	blind, blindly	win (game); profit
-	43;38 6 (4)	43;109 8 (3)	43;154 17 (1)
43;61 7 (1)			

充	弃	畜	育
chōng	*棄 qì	xù chù	yù yō
full, ample; act as	discard, abandon	raise (animals); livestock	give birth to; raise, rear
9;10 6 (2)	9;55 7 (2)	142;102 10 (4)	118;130 8 (1)

恋	弯	变	蛮
戀 liàn	彎 wān	變 biàn	蠻 mán
love, romance	bend, curve; curved	change, transform	fierce; rugged
162;61 10 (2)	162;57 9 (2)	162;149 8 (1)	162;142 12 (4)

■

齐
齊 qí
alike; together;
neat; ready; &
160;210 6 (1)

斋
齋 zhāi
to fast, abstain;
a room; &
84;210 10 (-)

产
産 chǎn
give birth to;
produce
126;100 6 (1)

辛
xīn
hardship; bitter,
acrid; 8th; HS
186;160 7 (1)

亲
親 qīn qìng
parent, relative;
dear to; kiss; &
126;147 9 (1)

帝
dì
God;
emperor
9;50 9 (2)

旁
páng
side;
besides, other
85;70 10 (1)

商
shāng
merchant;
trade; discuss
9;30 11 (1)

竞
競 jìng
compete
-
126;117 10 (2)

音
yīn
sound, tone;
news
211;180 9 (1)

章
zhāng
chapter; rules;
badge, seal
211;117 11 (1)

竟
jìng
finish; finally;
surprisingly; &
211;117 11 (2)

意
yì
idea; a desire;
opinion; expect
211;61 13 (1)

童
tóng
child; virgin;
bare (hills)
126;117 12 (2)

彦
彥 yàn
a good man
(literary)
63;59 9 (-)

亨
hēng
successful,
go smoothly
9;8 7 (-)

享
xiǎng
enjoy
-
9;8 8 (2)

烹
pēng
boil, cook,
quick-fry
80;86 11 (4)

京
jīng
capital (city);
Beijing
9;8 8 (2)

哀
āi
grief, sorrow;
to pity
9;30 9 (3)

高
gāo
tall, high; loud;
expensive
218;189 10 (1)

亭
tíng
pavilion,
kiosk, stall
9;8 9 (3)

亮
liàng
bright; shine;
enlighten; &
9;8 9 (1)

毫
háo
hair; milli-;
(not) at all; &
112;82 11 (2)

豪
háo
hero; bold,
wilful; despot
9;152 14 (3)

膏
gāo gào
fat, grease, oil;
lubricate; &
218;130 14 (3)

宀 宁宀宄宄宄

宀

宁 寧 níng nìng
tranquil;
Nanjing; prefer
45;40 5 (3)

宇 yǔ
house; eaves;
(outer) space
45;40 6 (3)

字 zì
word, (written)
character; &
45;39 6 (1)

它 *牠 tā
it
-
45;40 5 (1)

宅 zhái
residence
-
45;40 6 (3)

农 農 nóng
agriculture;
peasant
18;161 6 (1)

宋 sòng
Song
(dynasty)
45;40 7 (3)

牢 láo
prison; secure,
durable
45;93 7 (3)

安 ān
peace; calm,
safe; install; &
45;40 6 (1)

定 dìng
decide; calm;
book (seats); &
45;40 8 (1)

宝 寶 bǎo
precious;
your (polite)
45;40 8 (2)

家 *傢 jiā
household;
specialist; &
45;40 10 (1)

宜 yí
appropriate;
should
45;40 8 (1)

官 guān
an official;
organ (of body)
45;40 8 (2)

宙 zhòu
(universal) time;
cosmos
45;40 8 (3)

审 審 shěn
examine, try
(case); careful
45;40 8 (3)

宀

穴 xué
hole; cave;
lair; grave
128;116 5 (4)

灾 災 zāi
disaster
-
45;86 7 (2)

实 實 shí
solid, real;
seed, fruit
45;40 8 (1)

宛 wǎn
winding,
tortuous
45;40 8 (-)

宿 sù xiǔ xiù
stay
overnight
45;40 11 (1)

寂 jì
still, quiet;
lonely
45;40 11 (3)

寝 寢 qǐn
sleep; bedroom;
mausoleum
45;40 13 (-)

宀宀宄

守 shǒu
keep watch,
guard; nearby
45;40 6 (2)

宏 hóng
great, vast,
grand
45;40 7 (3)

宠 寵 chǒng
dote on,
pamper
45;40 8 (-)

寇 kòu
bandit;
invader
45;40 11 (4)

宰	宪	案	害	寄	宵
zǎi	憲 xiàn	àn	hài	jì	xiāo
to rule, govern; to butcher	law, statute; constitution	table; proposal; (legal) case; &	harm; murder; get (illness) &	send, mail; entrust; rely on	night -
45;40 10 (4)	45;61 9 (3)	45;75 10 (2)	45;40 10 (2)	45;40 11 (1)	45;40 10 (3)

宽	寞	寒	塞	寨	赛
寬 kuān	mò	hán	sāi sài sè	zhài	賽 sài
broad; lenient; relaxed; well off	lonely; deserted	cold; shiver; poor, needy	stopper; jam in; strategic place	stockade, camp	contest, game; to rival, surpass
45;40 10 (2)	45;40 13 (3)	45;40 12 (1)	45;32 13 (3)	45;40 14 (4)	45;154 14 (1)

完	宗	宣	富	寅	寡
wán	zōng	xuān	fù	yín	guǎ
whole, intact; finish; use up	ancestor; clan; purpose; model	proclaim; drain off	rich, wealthy	EB -	few; rare; insipid; widow
45;40 7 (1)	45;40 8 (3)	45;40 9 (2)	45;40 12 (1)	45;40 11 (-)	45;40 14 (3)

室	宫	宴	寓	宾	
shì	宮 gōng	yàn	yù	賓 bīn	
a room -	palace, temple; womb	banquet; at ease; entertain	reside, abode; moral (of story)	guest -	
45;40 9 (1)	45;40 9 (3)	45;40 10 (1)	45;40 12 (3)	45;154 10 (2)	

客	密	蜜	察		
kè	mì	mì	chá		
guest, visitor, customer; &	closely; dense; precise; secret	honey; sweet, candied	examine, inspect		
45;40 9 (1)	45;40 11 (2)	45;142 14 (2)	45;40 14 (2)		

空	究	突	帘	穷	窄
kōng kòng	jiū	tū	*簾 lián	窮 qióng	zhǎi
sky, air; in vain; empty, vacant	investigate; after all	abrupt; rush at; protruding	screen, curtain	poor; limit; extremely	narrow; petty; hard up
128;116 8 (1)	128;116 7 (1)	128;116 9 (1)	128;50 8 (3)	128;116 7 (2)	128;116 10 (2)

穿	容	窜	窃	窑	
chuān	róng	竄 cuàn	竊 qiè	窯 yáo	
penetrate; wear, put on	contain; permit, tolerate; looks	flee; amend	steal; furtive, secretly	kiln; cave; pit	
128;116 9 (1)	45;40 10 (1)	128;116 12 (3)	128;116 9 (4)	128;116 11 (3)	

窝	窗	窿	窟	交	
窩 wō	chuāng	lóng	kū	jiāo	
nest, lair, pit; to bend; &	window -	[hole; deficit]	hole, cave; den	exchange; meet; join; befriend; to hand over; &	
128;116 12 (4)	128;116 12 (1)	128;116 16 (3)	128;116 13 (3)	9;8 6 (1)	

艹

芯 xìn xīn core; pith 50;140 7 (-)	芦 lú lǚ reed - 50;140 7 (4)	芳 fāng fragrant; good name 50;140 7 (4)	芒 máng wáng awn (beard of barley) 50;140 6 (4)	芝 zhī [sesame; iris] 50;140 6 (4)	茂 mào luxuriant; splendid 50;140 8 (4)
菩 pú [Bodhi tree, Buddha] 50;140 11 (-)	蒂 dì base (of a fruit) 50;140 12 (4)	荒 huāng neglect; famine; desolate; & 50;140 9 (3)	蓄 xù store up; grow (beard) 50;140 13 (4)	蓉 róng [hibiscus] Chengdu 50;140 13 (-)	萱 xuān [tawny daylily] 50;140 12 (-)
苦 kǔ bitter; pain, suffering 50;140 8 (1)	著 zhù outstanding; book; write 50;140 11 (2)	萧 xiāo desolate - 50;140 11 (-)	菁 jīng lush; essence 50;140 11 (-)	荔 lì [lychee] - 50;140 9 (4)	
茅 máo cogon grass - 50;140 8 (3)	茎 jīng stem, stalk (of plant) 50;140 8 (4)	苹 píng [apple] - 50;140 8 (1)	葬 zàng bury - 50;140 12 (4)	蕾 lěi bud - 50;140 16 (4)	
萬 wàn ten thousand - 50;140 12 (-)	萝 luó vine, ivy; [radish] 50;140 11 (2)	薯 shǔ cassava, yam, potato 50;140 16 (4)	蔑 *miè nothing; disdain (literary) 50;140 14 (3)		
菜 cài vegetable; food; (meal) course 50;140 11 (1)	萎 wěi wěi decline, wane, wither 50;140 11 (-)	蕃 fán fān luxuriant; foreigner; & 50;140 15 (-)	薰 xūn fragrance (literary) 50;140 17 (-)	董 dǒng director, trustee 50;140 12 (4)	
芬 fēn fragrant - 50;140 7 (4)	茶 chá tea - 50;140 9 (1)	苍 cāng green; blue; gray, ashen 50;140 7 (3)	惹 rě provoke, incite, stir up 81;61 12 (2)	葱 cōng onion; green 50;140 12 (4)	
蓝 lán la blue, indigo 50;140 13 (1)	蕉 jiāo broad-leaf plant; [banana] 50;140 15 (1)	蒸 zhēng evaporate; to steam (food) 50;140 13 (3)	葵 kuí sunflower; mallow 50;140 12 (4)	蔡 cài (surname) - 50;140 14 (-)	

劳	荣	营	萤	莺
勞 láo	榮 róng	營 yíng	螢 yíng	鶯 yīng
toil; fatigue; good deed; &	thrive; honor	operate; seek; barracks; &	firefly -	oriole, warbler
134;19 7 (1)	134;75 9 (2)	134;86 11 (2)	134;142 11 (-)	134;196 10 (-)

 蒙

*濛矇 mēng méng měng
cheat; guess; unconscious;
cover; ignorant; misty; Mongolia
134;140 13 (3)

草	莫	葛
cǎo	mò	gé gě
grass, straw; rough, careless	no, not; Don't!	kudzu vine, creeping plant
50;140 9 (1)	50;140 10 (4)	50;140 12 (3)

墓	幕	募	慕	暮
mù	mù	mù	mù	mù
tomb, grave	screen, curtain; act (of play)	solicit, enlist; raise (funds)	admire; yearn for	dusk, evening; late on
50;32 13 (3)	50;50 13 (3)	50;19 12 (-)	50;61 14 (2)	50;72 14 (4)

共	昔	恭	巷	黄
gòng	xī	gōng	xiàng hàng	黃 huáng
collectively, together; share	the past, former	respectful, reverent	lane, alley	yellow -
93;12 6 (1)	93;72 8 (-)	93;61 10 (4)	93;49 9 (3)	93;201 11 (1)

带	革	某	燕	曹
帶 dài	gé	mǒu	yàn yān	cáo
belt, zone; to lead; carry; &	leather, hide; to change; expel	a certain (thing, person)	swallow (bird)	people (of some kind) (literary)
57;50 9 (1)	212;177 9 (2)	135;75 9 (2)	93;86 16 (3)	103;73 11 (4)

艹

芯 xìn xīn core; pith 50;140 7 (-)	苏 sū revive; ('su' sound) 50;140 7 (4)	花 huā flower; flowery; expend; & 50;140 7 (1)	荷 hé hè lotus; burden; to shoulder 50;140 10 (4)	蔼 ǎi friendly - 50;140 14 (4)	蒋 jiǎng (surname) 50;140 12 (4)
茫 máng vast, vague; perplexed 50;140 9 (4)	范 *範 fàn example, model; scope 50;118 8 (2)	荡 dàng flush away; a pool; swing; & 50;140 9 (4)	莎 suō [nutgrass] 50;140 10 (-)	萍 píng duckweed - 50;140 11 (4)	
菠 bō [spinach; pineapple] 50;140 11 (3)	落 luò là lào fall; drop; omit; lag behind; & 50;140 12 (2)	薄 báo bó bò flimsy; meager; unkind; & 50;140 16 (2)			
获 huò get, obtain; reap; capture 50;94 10 (2)	茄 qié jiā eggplant, aubergine 50;140 8 (4)	菇 gū mushroom - 50;140 11 (4)	菲 fēi fěi luxuriant, rich; unworthy, poor 50;140 11 (-)	莉 lì [jasmine] - 50;140 10 (-)	藉 jí [cluttered] (see Table 1) 50;140 17 (-)
萨 sà ('sa' sound); (surname) 50;140 11 (4)	荫 yìn yīn shaded; chilly 50;140 9 (-)	蕴 yùn contain; stored up (literary) 50;140 15 (4)	药 yào medicine; chemicals 50;140 9 (1)	苑 yuàn garden; cultural center (literary) 50;140 8 (-)	
萌 méng sprout, bud, germinate 50;140 11 (4)	薛 xuē (surname) - 50;140 16 (-)	藤 téng rattan cane; vine, creeper 50;140 18 (4)			
葫 hú [gourd] - 50;140 12 (4)	蒜 suàn garlic - 50;140 13 (4)	蔬 shū vegetables - 50;140 15 (2)	薪 xīn salary; firewood 50;140 16 (4)	蔽 bì shelter, conceal 50;140 14 (4)	

艾	芙	英	芽	节
ài yì	fú	yīng	yá	節 jié jiē
artemisia plant	[lotus, hibiscus]	hero; English	bud, shoot, sprout	segment; node, joint; festival; agenda; economize; &
50;140 5 (4)	50;140 7 (-)	50;140 8 (1)	50;140 7 (3)	50;118 5 (1)

艺	茂	莱
藝 yì	mào	萊 lái
skill; art	luxuriant; splendid	('le' sound); [radish]
50;140 4 (1)	50;140 8 (4)	50;140 10 (-)

茧	芭	苗	萬
繭 jiǎn	bā	miáo	wàn
cocoon; callus	('ba' sound); (a herb)	seedling; small fry; vaccine	ten thousand (see Table 1)
50;120 9 (4)	50;140 7 (4)	50;140 8 (3)	50;140 12 (-)

若	荐	芹	蔗	蘑	藏
ruò	薦 jiàn	qín	zhè	mó	cáng zàng
as if; like; seem	recommend -	[celery] -	sugar cane -	mushroom -	conceal; store; scriptures
50;140 8 (3)	50;140 9 (3)	50;140 7 (4)	50;140 14 (4)	50;140 19 (4)	50;140 17 (2)

菊	萄	葡
jú	táo	pú
chrysanthemum -	grape -	[grape] -
50;140 11 (4)	50;140 11 (3)	50;140 12 (3)

莲	蓬
蓮 lián	péng
lotus -	disheveled; fluffy
50;140 10 (4)	50;140 13 (3)

菌
jùn jūn
mushroom; fungus; bacteria
50;140 11 (2)

1	41
2	42
3	43
4	44
5	45
6	46
7	47
8	48
9	49
10	50
11	51
12	52
13	53
14	54
15	55
16	56
17	57
18	58
19	59
20	60
21	61
22	62
23	63
24	64
25	**65**
26	66
27	67
28	68
29	69
30	70
31	71
32	72
33	73
34	74
35	75
36	76
37	77
38	78
39	79
40	80

竹

ⅡⅡ

竿 gān
rod, pole, cane
178;118 9 (4)

笑 xiào
laugh, smile; ridicule
178;118 10 (1)

笔 筆 bǐ
write; pen; (of Ch char) stroke
178;118 10 (1)

笨 bèn
stupid, dull; clumsy
178;118 11 (2)

策 cè
plan, scheme; urge, spur on
178;118 12 (2)

第 dì
number (as in 'No. 3')
178;118 11 (

笋 筍 sǔn
bamboo shoot
178;118 10 (4)

笃 篤 dǔ
sincere; serious (illness)
178;118 9 (-)

笆 bā
basket; bamboo fence
178;118 10 (4)

笛 dí
flute, whistle
178;118 11 (4)

符 fú
accord with; symbol
178;118 11 (2)

筷 kuài
chopsticks
-
178;118 13 (2)

筑 *築 zhù zhú
build; Guiyang
178;118 12 (2)

筛 篩 shāi
sift, sieve
178;118 12 (4)

筋 jīn
muscle, tendon
178;118 12 (3)

箱 xiāng
box, case, trunk
178;118 15 (

簸 bǒ bò
winnow; winnowing fan
178;118 19 (4)

籍 jí
register, record; domicile
178;118 20 (3)

簿 bù
book, register
178;118 19 (-)

等 děng
etc.; grade; await; equal
178;118 12 (1)

管 guǎn
tube, pipe, flute; attend to; &
178;118 14 (2)

答 dá dā
respond, answer
178;118 12 (1)

签 簽 籤 qiān
sign, autograph; label, sticker
178;118 13 (2)

箭 jiàn
arrow
-
178;118 15 (2)

篱 籬 lí
hedge, fence
178;118 16 (

筝 箏 zhēng
zheng (zither); [kite]
178;118 12 (4)

算 suàn
count, reckon; count as; &
178;118 14 (1)

箩 籮 luó
bamboo basket
178;118 14 (4)

篮 籃 lán
basket
-
178;118 16 (1)

筹 籌 chóu
plan, prepare; counter, token
178;118 13 (4)

笼 籠 lóng lǒng
cage, basket; envelope; trunk
178;118 11 (3)

篇 piān
piece of paper; (written) article
178;118 15 (1)

筒 tǒng
cylinder, tube
178;118 12 (3)

简 簡 jiǎn
abbreviated; simple; letter
178;118 13 (1)

筐 kuāng
basket
-
178;118 12 (

ⅡⅡ

览 覽 lǎn
see, to view; read
107;147 9 (1)

监 監 jiān jiàn
supervise; prison
146;108 10 (3)

鉴 鑒 鑑 jiàn
mirror, reflect; inspect; warn
209;167 13 (3)

贤 賢 xián able and virtuous 106;154 8 (4)	肾 腎 shèn kidney - 118;130 8 (4)	紧 緊 jǐn tight; taut; strict; urgent 77;120 10 (1)

癸 guǐ HS 10th; 154;105 9 (-)	凳 dèng bench, stool 154;16 14 (3)	登 dēng register; publish; ascend; step on; get on or off (vehicle); & 154;105 12 (2)

占 *佔 zhàn zhān seize, occupy; comprise; & 16;25 5 (1)	贞 貞 zhēn pure; loyal; chaste 16;154 6 (4)	点 點 diǎn a little; o'clock; dot, point; & 80;203 9 (1)	卢 盧 lú (surname) - 16;108 5 (4)	卡 kǎ qiǎ get stuck; checkpoint 16;25 5 (1)

卓 zhuō tall, erect; eminent 16;24 8 (4)	桌 zhuō table - 94;75 10 (1)	与 與 yǔ yù yú and; with; to; help; give; & 2;134 3 (2)	上 shàng shang shǎng above, on, up; ascend; go to; previous; first; put in position; & 16;1 3 (1)	虍 → 33

步 bù step, pace; walk; situation 102;77 7 (1)	齿 齒 chǐ tooth - 206;211 8 (3)	肯 kěn willing; consent 102;130 8 (2)

岂 豈 qǐ (particle, literary) 60;151 6 (4)	岁 歲 suì year, years old 60;77 6 (1)	崇 chóng lofty, dignified; esteem 60;46 11 (2)	嵩 sōng high, lofty (mountain) 60;46 13 (-)	出 chū exit; go out; to issue, produce, vent; exceed; occur; expenditure 61;17 5 (1)

岩 *巖 yán rock; cliff 60;46 8 (3)	炭 tàn charcoal - 60;86 9 (4)	岸 àn shore, coast; river bank 60;46 8 (2)	崖 yá cliff, precipice 60;46 11 (3)	岗 崗 gǎng mound; sentry 60;46 7 (3)

崔 cuī (surname) - 60;46 11 (4)	崭 嶄 zhǎn high; [brand new] 60;46 11 (3)	嵌 qiàn inlay, embed 60;46 12 (4)	崩 bēng collapse, burst 60;46 11 (4)	巍 wēi lofty, towering (mountain) 60;46 20 (-)

1	41
2	42
3	43
4	44
5	45
6	46
7	47
8	48
9	49
10	50
11	51
12	52
13	53
14	54
15	55
16	56
17	57
18	58
19	59
20	60
21	61
22	62
23	63
24	64
25	65
26	**66**
27	67
28	68
29	69
30	70
31	71
32	72
33	73
34	74
35	75
36	76
37	77
38	78
39	79
40	80

十 土 士 生

十

古	支	克	丧	南	市
gǔ	zhī	kè	喪 sāng sàng	nán	shì
ancient; old fashioned	branch; erect, prop up; pay; &	able to; subdue; gram; digest; &	mourning; lose	south -	market; city
12;30 5 (2)	12;65 4 (1)	12;10 7 (1)	12;30 8 (3)	12;24 9 (1)	9;50 5 (1)

直	真	衷	辜	卖	索
*直 zhí	*眞 zhēn	zhōng	gū	賣 mài	suǒ
straight; direct; frank; upright; &	true, genuine; really; clearly	sincere, heartfelt	guilt; crime	sell; betray; show off; strive	rope, cable; search; ask for
12;24 8 (1)	12;12 10 (1)	9;145 10 (3)	186;160 12 (3)	12;154 8 (1)	77;120 10 (3)

妻	惠	囊
qī	huì	náng
wife -	favor, kindness	bag, pocket
73;38 8 (2)	81;61 12 (4)	12;30 22 (4)

土

赤	寺	去
chì	sì	qù qu
red; bare; loyal	temple -	go, depart; away; discard; last (year)
190;155 7 (3)	49;41 6 (4)	133;28 5 (1)

击	走	幸	袁	卖	者 → 3
擊 jí	zǒu	*倖 xìng	yuán	賣 mài	
strike, hit, attack	walk, go; depart; leak out	good fortune; luckily; rejoice	(surname) -	sell; betray; show off; strive	
38;64 5 (2)	189;156 7 (1)	49;51 8 (1)	49;145 10 (4)	12;154 8 (1)	

士

吉	志	声	壳	壶
jí	*誌 zhì	聲 shēng	殼 ké qiào	壺 hú
lucky, auspicious	intention; recall; annals; sign	sound, voice, tone; fame	shell, husk, crust, casing	pot, kettle, flask
49;30 6 (4)	49;61 7 (1)	49;128 7 (1)	49;79 7 (3)	49;33 10 (2)

壹	喜	嘉
yī	xǐ	jiā
one -	happy event; happy; liking for	good, fine; praise
49;33 12 (4)	49;30 12 (1)	49;30 14 (4)

生

告	先	靠
gào	xiān	kào
notify; accuse; request	first; ahead; early; deceased	lean on; rely on; keep to; near
58;30 7 (1)	29;10 6 (1)	205;175 15 (2)

麦 麥 mài wheat; cereals 188;199 7 (2)	**素** sù basic; habitual; vegetable; & 89;120 10 (2)	**表** *錶 biǎo list, form, chart; to show; gauge; (wrist) watch; surface; cousin; & 89;145 8 (1)		
责 責 zé duty; require; reprove; punish 89;154 8 (1)	**青** qīng green; blue 202;174 8 (1)	**毒** dú poison, drugs; malicious 89;80 9 (3)		

共 gòng collectively, together; share 93;12 6 (1)	**恭** gōng respectful, reverent 93;61 10 (4)	**巷** xiàng hàng lane, alley 93;49 9 (3)	**昔** xī the past, former 93;72 8 (-)	**黄** 黃 huáng yellow - 93;201 11 (1)

杰 *傑 jié hero; outstanding 94;75 8 (4)	**李** lǐ plum - 94;75 7 (2)	**杏** xìng apricot - 94;75 7 (4)	**查** chá zhā investigate, check, look up 94;75 9 (1)	**森** sēn forested; dark, gloomy 94;75 12 (2)

奋 奮 fèn raise; rouse; zealous 52;37 8 (2)	**夺** 奪 duó by force; seize; strive 52;37 6 (2)	**奇** qí jī weird; surprise; odd (number) 52;37 8 (2)	**夸** *誇 kuā praise; brag; exaggerate 52;37 6 (3)	**奈** nài [in vain; do (to someone)] 52;37 8 (3)

太 tài excessive, too, over-; utmost 52;37 4 (1)	**态** 態 tài form; attitude; condition, state 81;61 8 (1)	**牵** 牽 qiān lead (by the hand); involve 52;93 9 (2)	**奔** bēn bèn rush, run, flee; head for 52;37 8 (3)	**套** tào cover, sheath; knot; coax; & 52;37 10 (2)	**奢** shē extravagant, excessive 52;37 11 (4)

奉 fèng serve; proffer; obey; revere; & 130;37 8 (4)	**泰** tài peaceful, calm; extreme, -most 130;85 10 (4)	**秦** qín Qin (dynasty); Shaanxi 130;115 10 (4)	**奏** zòu play music; achieve; & 130;37 9 (4)	**春** chūn springtime; vitality 130;72 9 (1)	**蠢** chūn stupid; wriggle 130;142 21 (3)

拳 quán fist; boxing 158;64 10 (3)	**眷** juàn family, dependant 158;109 11 (-)	**卷** *捲 juǎn juàn roll up; roll (of); book, dossier 158;26 8 (2)	**券** quàn xuàn ticket, certificate; arch 158;18 8 (4)	**养** 養 yǎng maintain; raise; nurture; & 24;184 9 (2)

1	41		
2	42		
3	43		
4	44		
5	45		
6	46		
7	47		
8	48		
9	49		
10	50		
11	51		
12	52		
13	53		
14	54		
15	55		
16	56		
17	57		
18	58		
19	59		
20	60		
21	61		
22	62		
23	63		
24	64		
25	65		
26	66		
27	**67**		
28	68		
29	69		
30	70		
31	71		
32	72		
33	73		
34	74		
35	75		
36	76		
37	77		
38	78		
39	79		
40	80		

口 品 四 田

口

足 zú
foot; leg; ample
196;157 7 (1)

另 lìng
separate, other
58;30 5 (2)

兄 xiōng
elder brother
58;10 5 (2)

只 *隻 祇 zhǐ zhī
only, merely; one (of a pair)
58;30 5 (1)

吊 *弔 diào
suspend, hoist; condole; revoke
58;30 6 (2)

号 號 hào háo
number; date; sign; horn; &
58;141 5 (1)

吴 *吳 wú
(old kingdom); (surname)
58;30 7 (3)

呆 dāi ái
dull, stupid; stay
58;30 7 (2)

呈 chéng
to present, show, offer
58;30 7 (4)

吕 呂 lǚ
(surname) -
58;30 6 (4)

员 員 yuán
person, -er; member
58;30 7 (1)

虽 雖 suī
although; even if
58;172 9 (1)

品 pǐn
grade, quality; goods; to savor
58;30 9 (2)

品

咒 zhòu
a charm, spell, curse
30;30 8 (-)

哭 kū
cry, weep
96;30 10 (1)

骂 罵 mà
curse, rebuke
75;122 9 (2)

器 qì
utensil; talent; organ (of body)
58;30 16 (1)

嚣 囂 xiāo
clamor -
58;30 18 (-)

四

罚 罰 fá
punish -
145;122 9 (3)

罪 zuì
crime; guilt, blame; suffering
145;122 13 (3)

罗 *羅 囉 luó luō
net; sift; collect; display; &
145;122 8 (4)

罢 罷 bà
stop; dismiss
145;122 10 (3)

署 shǔ
office; arrange; to sign; proxy
145;122 13 (3)

罩 zhào
cover, (lamp) shade
145;122 13 (3)

置 *寘 zhì
put, place, install; buy
145;122 13 (2)

蜀 shǔ
Sichuan -
145;142 13 (-)

田

果 guǒ
fruit; result; sure enough; &
94;75 8 (1)

男 nán
man, male; son
142;102 7 (1)

界 jiè
boundary; scope; world
142;102 9 (1)

畏 wèi
fear; respect
142;102 9 (4)

思 sī
think, thought
142;61 9 (1)

里 *裏 裡 lǐ lǐ
in, inside; mile, 1/2 km; &
195;166 7 (1)

胃 wèi
stomach -
142;130 9 (2)

累 lèi lěi léi
toil; tired; pile up; implicate; &
142;120 11 (1)

愚 yú
foolish, stupid; to dupe
81;61 13 (3)

贯 貫 guàn
pierce; link up; birthplace
106;154 8 (2)

黑 hēi
black; dark; shady, sinister
223;203 12 (1)

墨 mò
black; ink; writing; learning
223;32 15 (2)

旦
dàn
day;
dawn
103;72 5 (3)

早
zăo
early; morning;
before; long ago
103;72 6 (1)

旱
hàn
drought;
(dry) land
103;72 7 (3)

是
shì
is, are; indeed;
yes, correct
213;72 9 (1)

易
yì
easy; amiable;
exchange
103;72 8 (1)

星
xīng
star, planet;
particle
103;72 9 (1)

显
顯 xiăn
obvious;
to display; &
103;181 9 (2)

晃
huàng huăng
sway; dazzle;
(pass) in a flash
103;72 10 (3)

昌
chāng
prosperous,
thriving
103;72 8 (4)

晕
暈 yūn yùn
dizzy;
to faint
103;72 10 (3)

晨
chén
morning
-
103;72 11 (1)

冒
mào
emit; take risk;
bold; fraud
104;13 9 (1)

景
jĭng
scenery;
revere; situation
103;72 12 (2)

暴
bào
violent; cruel;
stand out
103;72 15 (3)

暑
shŭ
hot
weather
103;72 12 (2)

量
liáng liàng
measure;
capacity
103;166 12 (2)

曼
màn
prolonged;
graceful
103;73 11 (-)

昆
kūn
elder
brother
103;72 8 (3)

昂
áng
high, soaring;
hold (head) high
103;72 8 (4)

晶
jīng
brilliant;
crystal
103;72 12 (4)

最
zuì
most,
utmost
103;73 12 (1)

要
yào yāo
want, ask for; if;
need, must; &
166;146 9 (1)

栗
lì
chestnut;
tremble
166;75 10 (4)

票
piào
ticket, note, bill;
ballot; hostage
166;113 11 (1)

贾
賈 gŭ
merchant;
to do business
166;154 10 (-)

覆
fù
cover; capsize
(see Table 1)
166;146 18 (4)

雪
xuě
snow; avenge,
set right
204;173 11 (1)

雷
léi
thunder
-
204;173 13 (2)

需
xū
need, require;
requirement
204;173 14 (1)

雨
yŭ
rain
-
204;173 8 (1)

零
líng
zero; tiny bit;
fall (leaves)
204;173 13 (1)

雾
霧 wù
fog,
mist
204;173 13 (2)

霉
méi
mold,
mildew
204;173 15 (3)

震
zhèn
shake, quake;
shocked
204;173 15 (3)

雹
báo
hail,
hailstone
204;173 13 (4)

霍
huò
quickly,
suddenly
204;173 16 (4)

霖
lín
downpour,
heavy rain
204;173 16 (-)

霜
shuāng
frost
-
204;173 17 (3)

露
lù lòu
reveal;
dew; syrup
204;173 21 (2)

霸
bà
tyrant, overload;
dominate
204;173 21 (4)

霞
xiá
rosy clouds, at
dawn or sunset
204;173 17 (4)

1 41
2 42
3 43
4 44
5 45
6 46
7 47
8 48
9 49
10 50
11 51
12 52
13 53
14 54
15 55
16 56
17 57
18 58
19 59
20 60
21 61
22 62
23 63
24 64
25 65
26 66
27 67
28 **68**
29 69
30 70
31 71
32 72
33 73
34 74
35 75
36 76
37 77
38 78
39 79
40 80

中 虫	忠 zhōng loyal, devoted 105;61 8 (3)	贵 貴 guì expensive, precious 105;154 9 (1)	患 huàn afflicted; hardship; worry 81;61 11 (3)	
米 火 炎 匕	粪 糞 fèn dung, excrement 159;119 12 (3)	类 類 lèi kind, type; similar to 159;181 9 (2)	炎 yán hot; blazing; inflammation 83;86 8 (4)	脊 jǐ jí backbone, spine; ridge 118;130 10 (4)	旨 zhǐ aim, intention; decree 39;72 6 (4)
九 车 龙 戈	杂 雜 zá miscellaneous; to mix, blend 94;172 6 (1)	轰 轟 hōng bang, boom; bombard 100;159 8 (4)	聋 聾 lóng deaf - 137;128 11 (4)	袭 襲 xí raid; follow suit 137;145 11 (3)	尧 堯 yáo (a legendary chieftain) 29;32 6 (-)
艹 业 卅	革 gé leather, hide; to change; expel 212;177 9 (2)	燕 yàn yān swallow (bird) 93;86 16 (3)	凿 鑿 záo zuò chisel; mortise; make a hole 140;167 12 (3)	带 帶 dài belt, zone; to lead; carry; & 57;50 9 (1)	
甚 甘 弗	其 qí he, she, it; that; his, her, its; & 24;12 8 (1)	甚 shèn shén very; more; [what?] 2;99 9 (3)	基 jī foundation, base, basis 49;32 11 (1)	某 mǒu a certain (thing, person) 135;75 9 (2)	费 費 fèi fees; consume, use up; waste 106;154 9 (2)
久 勿 乍	灸 jiǔ moxibustion (Ch. medicine) 83;86 7 (3)	忽 hū neglect, ignore; suddenly 81;61 8 (1)	怎 zěn How?, Why? - 81;61 9 (1)		
乂 臼	杀 殺 shā kill; fight; reduce; very 25;79 6 (2)	希 xī hope; rare 25;50 7 (1)	鼠 shǔ rat, mouse 225;208 13 (4)	舅 jiù uncle; brother in law 179;134 13 (3)	
巛 珏 羽 非	巢 cháo nest - 78;47 11 (-)	瑟 sè se (Chinese zither) 88;96 13 (-)	翠 cuì green; jade; kingfisher 183;124 14 (4)	翼 yì wing - 183;124 17 (4)	斐 fěi [striking]; ('fi' sound) 205;67 12 (2)

肀 尹				
灵	寻	肃	隶	君
靈 líng	尋 xún xín	蕭 sù	隸 lì	jūn
clever; effective; spirit; fairy, elf	seek -	solemn; respectful	subordinate, servant, slave	monarch; gentleman; Mr.
70;173 7 (2)	70;41 6 (2)	124;129 8 (2)	124;171 8 (3)	58;30 7 (4)

疋 彐 可 子				
买	蛋	录	哥	孟
買 mǎi	dàn	錄 lù	gē	mèng
buy	egg; oval	record; employ	older brother	first -
5;154 6 (1)	156;142 11 (1)	70;167 8 (1)	58;30 10 (1)	74;39 8 (3)

刀 刃 乃 及 已				
召	忍	孕	盈	忌
zhào	rěn	yùn	yíng	jì
call, summon	endure; hardheartedly	pregnant	full of; surplus	jealousy; fear; abstain from
27;30 5 (2)	81;61 7 (2)	74;39 5 (4)	146;108 9 (4)	72;61 7 (4)

王 工				
吾	弄	汞	贡	无
wú	nòng lòng	gǒng	貢 gòng	無 wú
I, we, my, our (literary)	handle; get; do; play with; alley	mercury -	contribute; pay tribute	without; not; nothing; &
58;30 7 (-)	88;55 7 (2)	48;85 7 (4)	48;154 7 (2)	53;86 4 (2)

亚				
吞	蚕	晋	恶	严
tūn	蠶 cán	晉 jìn	惡 噁 è ě wù	嚴 yán
swallow, gulp; to annex	silkworm -	promote; advance; enter	evil; fierce; nauseous; hate	tight; strict, severe
90;30 7 (3)	90;142 10 (3)	168;72 10 (4)	168;61 10 (3)	168;30 7 (2)

几 云 而				
贝	见	朵	至	耍
貝 bèi	見 jiàn	duǒ	zhì	shuǎ
sea shell -	see; meet, visit; evident; opinion	(measure word) -	until, up to; arrive at	to play -
106;154 4 (4)	107;147 4 (1)	30;75 6 (2)	171;133 6 (2)	169;126 9 (3)

目 壬 氏				
导	异	鼎	丢	昏
導 dǎo	*異 yì	dǐng	diū	hūn
direct, guide; transmit	different; strange	cauldron; tripod, tripartite	lose; throw away	dusk; confused; dim; to faint
72;41 6 (1)	72;55 6 (2)	141;206 12 (-)	133;1 6 (1)	122;72 8 (2)

冋 冊 里				
聂	骨	贯	黑	墨
聶 niè	骨 gǔ gú gū	貫 guàn	hēi	mò
(surname) -	bone; skeleton, framework	pierce; link up; birthplace	black; dark; shady, sinister	black; ink; writing; learning
163;128 10 (4)	214;188 9 (2)	106;154 8 (2)	223;203 12 (1)	223;32 15 (2)

1	41
2	42
3	43
4	44
5	45
6	46
7	47
8	48
9	49
10	50
11	51
12	52
13	53
14	54
15	55
16	56
17	57
18	58
19	59
20	60
21	61
22	62
23	63
24	64
25	65
26	66
27	67
28	68
29	**69**
30	70
31	71
32	72
33	73
34	74
35	75
36	76
37	77
38	78
39	79
40	80

丶

乓
pīng
gunshot sound;
[ping-pong]
4;4　6 (2)

丶

乒
pāng
banging sound;
[ping-pong]
4;3　6 (2)

头　頭 tóu tou
head; top; first,
chief; end; &
52;181　5 (1)

买　買 mǎi
buy

5;154　6 (1)

实　實 shí
solid, real;
seed, fruit
45;40　8 (1)

卖　賣 mài
sell; betray;
show off; strive
12;154　8 (1)

太
tài
excessive, too,
over-; utmost
52;37　4 (1)

底
dǐ
bottom, base;
end; rough copy
44;53　8 (2)

凡
fán
common,
ordinary; every
30;16　3 (2)

舟
zhōu
boat
(literary)
182;137　6 (4)

为　為 wéi wèi
do, act, act as; become;
be equal to; for the sake of
1;86　4 (1)

丿

少
shǎo shào
few; lacking;
Stop!; young; &
79;42　4 (1)

步
bù
step, pace;
walk; situation
102;77　7 (1)

参　參 cān cēn shēn
join in; consult,
refer; ginseng
37;28　8 (1)

⬚少 → 44

丨

个　個 gè gě
(measure word);
item; individual
23;9　3 (1)

爪
zhǎo zhuǎ
claw,
talon
116;87　4 (4)

丫
yā
fork (in tree),
bifurcation
24;2　3 (-)

乙

乞
qǐ
beg
-
20;5　3 (4)

艺　藝 yì
skill;
art
50;140　4 (1)

无　無 wú
without; not;
nothing; &
53;86　4 (2)

匕

它
*牠 tā
it
-
45;40　5 (1)

尼
ní
Buddhist nun;
('ni' sound)
67;44　5 (4)

死
sǐ
die; death;
rigid
97;78　6 (1)

毙　斃 bì
die;
kill
123;66　10 (4)

七

皂
zào
soap;
black
150;106　7 (2)

龙　龍 lóng
dragon;
imperial
137;212　5 (2)

宠　寵 chǒng
dote on,
pamper
45;40　8 (-)

笼　籠 lóng lǒng
cage, basket;
envelope; trunk
178;118　11 (3)

冬	寒	枣	尽		
dōng	hán	棗 zǎo	盡 儘 jìn jǐn		
winter; drum sound	cold; shiver; poor, needy	date (palm); jujube	used up; entire; utmost; &		
65;15 5 (1)	45;40 12 (1)	167;75 8 (4)	117;108 6 (2)		

辛	卒	宰	幸	毕	华
xīn	zú	zǎi	*倖 xìng	畢 bì	華 huá huà
hardship; bitter, acrid; 8th; HS	soldier; servant; finish; die	to rule, govern; to butcher	good fortune; luckily; rejoice	finish, complete	splendid; China; your (polite); &
186;160 7 (1)	9;24 8 (-)	45;40 10 (4)	49;51 8 (1)	123;102 6 (2)	12;140 6 (3)

率	辜	翠	哗		
shuài lǜ	gū	cuì	嘩 譁 huā huá		
to lead; frank; rate, ratio; &	guilt; crime	green; jade; kingfisher	clamor, noise		
9;95 11 (2)	186;160 12 (3)	183;124 14 (4)	58;30 9 (3)		

早	旱	罩	单	卑	呈 → 74
zǎo	hàn	zhào	單 dān	bēi	
early; morning; before; long ago	drought; (dry) land	cover, (lamp) shade	single, alone; list; (bed) sheet	low, inferior, modest	
103;72 6 (1)	103;72 7 (3)	145;122 13 (3)	24;30 8 (1)	12;24 8 (4)	

卓	草	章	干		
zhuō	cǎo	zhāng	*乾 幹 gān gàn		
tall, erect; eminent	grass, straw; rough, careless	chapter; rules; badge, seal	dry; futile; adopt (child); main part, trunk; do, work; fight		
16;24 8 (4)	50;140 9 (1)	211;117 11 (1)	11;51 3 (1)		

辱	寻	尊	夺	导	
rǔ	尋 xún xín	zūn	奪 duó	導 dǎo	
disgrace; to insult	seek -	senior; esteem, respect	by force; seize; strive	direct, guide; transmit	
187;161 10 (3)	70;41 6 (2)	54;41 12 (2)	52;37 6 (2)	72;41 6 (1)	

守	等	筹	寺	寿	
shǒu	děng	籌 chóu	sì	壽 shòu	
keep watch, guard; nearby	etc.; grade; await; equal	plan, prepare; counter, token	temple -	longevity; age; birthday; funeral	
45;40 6 (2)	178;118 12 (1)	178;118 13 (4)	49;41 6 (4)	54;33 7 (3)	

八 乂 人

八

六	穴	兴	共	只
liù	xué	興 xīng xìng	gòng	*隻 祇 zhǐ zhī
six	hole; cave; lair; grave	start; prosper; excitement	collectively, together; share	only, merely; one (of a pair)
-	128;116 5 (4)	24;134 6 (1)	93;12 6 (1)	58;30 5 (1)
9;12 4 (1)				

兵	宾	冥	其	
bīng	賓 bīn	míng	qí	
soldier; army; military; arms	guest	dark; deep; stupid; Hades	he, she, it; that; his, her, its; &	
24;12 7 (2)	45;154 10 (2)	18;14 10 (-)	24;12 8 (1)	

典	具	真	寅	黄
diǎn	jù	*眞 zhēn	yín	黃 huáng
reference book; ceremony; &	tool, utensil; possess	true, genuine; really; clearly	EB	yellow
24;12 8 (1)	24;12 8 (2)	12;12 10 (1)	45;40 11 (-)	93;201 11 (1)

粪	冀	翼	舆	贝 → 7
糞 fèn	jì	yì	輿 yú	
dung, excrement	look forward to (literary)	wing	public; territory	
159;119 12 (3)	24;12 16 (4)	183;124 17 (4)	24;159 14 (4)	

乂

父	义	文	艾	交
fù	義 yì	wén	ài yì	jiāo
father	justice; meaning; &	writing; culture; rite; civilian; &	artemisia plant	exchange; meet; join; befriend; to hand over; mutual; &
-	25;123 3 (1)	84;67 4 (1)	50;140 5 (4)	9;8 6 (1)
108;88 4 (1)				

斐	岗	风	冈
fěi	崗 gǎng	風 fēng	岡 gǎng
[striking]; ('fi' sound)	mound; sentry	wind; scenery; habits; news	ridge (of hill)
205;67 12 (-)	60;46 7 (3)	121;182 4 (1)	19;46 4 (4)

人

贝	闪	肉	质	内	呆 → 7
貝 bèi	閃 shǎn	ròu	質 zhì	nèi	天 → 7
sea shell	flash; lightning; dodge; sprain	meat, flesh; pulp	quality, nature; simple; query	inside, inner; one's wife	灾 → 7
-	46;169 5 (2)	19;130 6 (1)	22;154 8 (2)	19;11 4 (1)	贝 → 7
106;154 4 (4)					

亥	窝
hài	窩 wō
EB	nest, lair, pit; to bend; &
-	128;116 12 (4)
9;8 6 (-)	

介 jiè
between;
take seriously
23;9 4 (1)

乔 喬 qiáo
tall;
disguise
90;30 6 (4)

齐 齊 qí
alike; together;
neat; ready; &
160;210 6 (1)

界 jiè
boundary;
scope; world
142;102 9 (1)

养 養 yǎng
maintain; raise,
nurture; &
24;184 9 (2)

鼻 bí
nose
-
226;209 14 (2)

肃 肅 sù
solemn;
respectful
124;129 8 (2)

萧 蕭 xiāo
desolate
-
50;140 11 (-)

异 → 77

允 yǔn
allow;
equitable
37;10 4 (2)

先 xiān
first; ahead;
early; deceased
29;10 6 (1)

充 chōng
full, ample;
act as
9;10 6 (2)

元 yuán
first; chief;
unit; yuan
11;10 4 (1)

光 guāng
light; glory; scenery; bare;
smooth; depleted; alone
172;10 6 (2)

兄 xiōng
elder
brother
58;10 5 (2)

见 見 jiàn
see; meet, visit;
evident; opinion
107;147 4 (1)

尧 堯 yáo
(a legendary
chieftain)
29;32 6 (-)

完 wán
whole, intact;
finish; use up
45;40 7 (1)

宪 憲 xiàn
law, statute;
constitution
45;61 9 (3)

无 無 wú
without; not;
nothing; &
53;86 4 (2)

兑 duì
to exchange;
to dilute
24;10 7 (3)

克 kè
able to; subdue;
gram; digest; &
12;10 7 (1)

党 黨 dǎng
political party;
club, gang
139;203 10 (2)

竞 競 jìng
compete
-
126;117 10 (2)

竟 jìng
finish; finally;
surprisingly; &
211;117 11 (2)

览 → 77

晃 huàng huǎng
sway; dazzle;
(pass) in a flash
103;72 10 (3)

兜 dōu
pocket; bag;
wrap; solicit; &
29;10 11 (4)

免 miǎn
avoid; exempt;
dismiss
27;10 7 (2)

兔 tù
rabbit,
hare
27;10 8 (2)

冤 yuān
injustice; bad
luck; hatred
18;14 10 (3)

荒 huāng
neglect; famine;
desolate; &
50;140 9 (3)

鬼 guǐ
ghost; stealthy;
sinister; &
216;194 9 (2)

冠 guàn guān
precede; crown;
hat; champion
18;14 9 (2)

寇 kòu
bandit,
invader
45;40 11 (4)

秃 tū
bald; blunt;
unsatisfactory
149;115 7 (4)

壳 殼 ké qiào
shell, husk,
crust, casing
49;79 7 (3)

凭 憑 píng
lean on, rely on;
evidence; &
30;61 8 (3)

咒 zhòu
a charm, spell,
curse
30;30 8 (-)

凳 dèng
bench,
stool
154;16 14 (3)

亮 liàng
bright; shine;
enlighten; &
9;8 9 (1)

小

尔 爾 ěr
you; like that, that (literary)
79;89 5 (3)

示 shì
show; notify
132;113 5 (1)

京 jīng
capital (city); Beijing
9;8 8 (2)

景 jīng
scenery; revere; situation
103;72 12 (2)

乐 樂 yuè lè
music; enjoy; happy
4;75 5 (1)

荒 huāng
neglect; famine; desolate; &
50;140 9 (3)

示

奈 nài
[in vain; do (to someone)]
52;37 8 (3)

崇 chóng
lofty, dignified; esteem
60;46 11 (2)

票 piào
ticket, note, bill; ballot; hostage
166;113 11 (1)

禁 jìn jīn
prohibit; endure, bear
132;113 13 (2)

祭 jì
mourn; worship; sacrifice
132;113 11 (-)

察 chá
examine, inspect
45;40 14 (2)

蔡 cài
(surname)
-
50;140 14 (-)

小

恭 gōng
respectful, reverent
93;61 10 (4)

慕 mù
admire; yearn for
50;61 14 (2)

灬

杰 *傑 jié
hero; outstanding
94;75 8 (4)

点 點 diǎn
a little; o'clock; dot, point; &
80;203 9 (1)

烹 pēng
boil, cook; quick-fry
80;86 11 (4)

煮 zhǔ
to cook, boil
80;86 12 (2)

黑 hēi
black; dark; shady, sinister
223;203 12 (1)

熏 xūn xùn
smoke
-
80;86 14 (4)

煎 jiān
fry, boil, simmer
80;86 13 (3)

燕 yàn yān
swallow (bird)
93;86 16 (3)

蒸 zhēng
evaporate; to steam (food)
50;140 13 (3)

蕉 jiāo
broad-leaf plant; [banana]
50;140 15 (1)

薰 xūn
fragrance (literary)
50;140 17 (-)

蔗 zhè
sugar cane
-
50;140 14 (4)

焦 jiāo
burnt, scorched; anxious
208;86 12 (3)

烈 liè
intense, fiery; self-sacrificing
80;86 10 (2)

然 rán
correct; but; so; this; -ly
80;86 12 (1)

热 熱 rè
heat, thermo-; fever; craze
80;86 10 (1)

熟 shú shóu
ripe; cooked, processed; familiar; skilled; deeply
80;86 15 (1)

熬 āo áo
endure; to boil, stew
80;86 14 (3)

煞 shà shā
demon; very; stop; reduce
80;86 13 (-)

熊 xióng
a bear
-
80;86 14 (2)

熙 xī
bright; happy; thriving
80;86 14 (-)

照 zhào
shine; reflect; photo; license; according to; towards; &
80;86 13 (1)

心

志	忠	忌	忍	忽	怎
*誌 zhì	zhōng	jì	rěn	hū	zěn
intention; recall; annals; sign	loyal, devoted	jealousy; fear; abstain from	endure; hardheartedly	neglect, ignore; suddenly	How?, Why? -
49;61 7 (1)	105;61 8 (3)	72;61 7 (4)	81;61 7 (1)	81;61 8 (1)	81;61 9 (1)

思	恳	患	惠	恶	
sī	懇 kěn	huàn	huì	惡 噁 è ě wù	
think, thought	sincerely; beseech	afflicted; hardship; worry	favor, kindness	evil; fierce; nauseous; hate	
142;61 9 (1)	184;61 10 (2)	81;61 11 (3)	81;61 12 (4)	168;61 10 (3)	

忘	恋	总	息	意	慈
wàng wáng	戀 liàn	總 zǒng	xī	yì	cí
forget -	love, romance	chief; anyway; always; sum up	breath; cease; news; grow; &	idea; a desire; opinion; expect	kind, loving, merciful
43;61 7 (1)	162;61 10 (2)	81;120 9 (1)	180;61 10 (1)	211;61 13 (1)	81;61 13 (4)

态	急	惫	惹	葱	慧
態 tài	jí	憊 bèi	rě	蒽 cōng	huì
form; attitude; condition, state	quick, urgent; hurry; annoyed	exhausted, tired out	provoke, incite; stir up	onion; green	intelligent, wise
81;61 8 (1)	81;61 9 (1)	81;61 12 (4)	81;61 12 (2)	50;140 12 (4)	81;61 15 (3)

念	愈	怠	悉	愚	悬
*唸 niàn	*瘉癒 yù	dài	xī	yú	懸 xuán
study; recite; think of, yearn	get well; better; more and more	idle, lazy	know; all, entire	foolish, stupid; to dupe	hang; pending; far apart; &
81;61 8 (1)	81;61 13 (3)	81;61 9 (4)	197;61 11 (4)	81;61 13 (4)	81;61 11 (3)

您	悠	惩	悲	恐	怨
nín	yōu	懲 chéng	bēi	kǒng	yuàn
you (polite)	leisurely; long lasting; distant	punish -	sad, sorrow, compassion	fear; terrify	resent; blame; complain
81;61 11 (1)	81;61 11 (2)	81;61 12 (4)	205;61 12 (2)	81;61 10 (2)	81;61 9 (3)

怒	恕	想	愁	慰	憋
nù	shù	xiǎng	chóu	wèi	biē
anger, fury; raging	forgive, excuse	think; want to; miss, long for	worry -	to console; be relieved	stifle, hold back
81;61 9 (2)	81;61 10 (-)	81;61 13 (1)	81;61 13 (1)	81;61 15 (2)	81;61 15 (4)

感	惑	思	恩	瑟	
gǎn	huò	sī	ēn	sè	
feel, touch; be moved, grateful	mislead; be puzzled	think, thought	favor, kindness	se (Chinese zither)	
81;61 13 (1)	81;61 12 (4)	142;61 9 (1)	81;61 10 (4)	88;96 13 (-)	

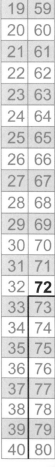

1	41
2	42
3	43
4	44
5	45
6	46
7	47
8	48
9	49
10	50
11	51
12	52
13	53
14	54
15	55
16	56
17	57
18	58
19	59
20	60
21	61
22	62
23	63
24	64
25	65
26	66
27	67
28	68
29	69
30	70
31	71
32	**72**
33	73
34	74
35	75
36	76
37	77
38	78
39	79
40	80

一

二
èr
two
-
11;7 2 (1)

三
sān
three
-
2;1 3 (1)

兰 蘭 lán
orchid
24;140 5 (3)

从
叢 cóng
crowd, group,
clump; thicket
2;29 5 (3)

丝
絲 sī
silk; thread;
tiny amount
2;120 5 (2)

旦
dàn
day;
dawn
103;72 5 (3)

鱼
魚 yú
fish
-
210;195 8 (1)

叁
sān
three
-
37;28 8 (4)

些
xiē
few; some;
a bit
11;7 8 (1)

查
chá zhā
investigate,
check, look up
94;75 9 (1)

宣
xuān
proclaim;
drain off
45;40 9 (2)

昼 晝 zhòu
daytime
-
117;72 9 (4)

萱
xuān
[tawny
daylily]
50;140 12 (-)

立
lì
to stand; to set
up; at once; &
126;117 5 (1)

豆
dòu
beans,
pulses
191;151 7 (2)

竖 豎 shù
vertical,
upright
126;151 9 (4)

壹
yī
one
-
49;33 12 (4)

登
dēng
register; publish; ascend;
step on; get on or off (vehicle); &
154;105 12 (2)

签 簽 籤 qiān
sign, autograph;
label, sticker
178;118 13 (2)

鉴 鑒 鑑 jiàn
mirror, reflect;
inspect; warn
209;167 13 (3)

应 應 yīng yìng
should; agree;
respond; cope
44;61 7 (1)

坯
pī
semi-finished
product
49;32 8 (4)

坦
tǎn
level, smooth;
calm; candid
49;32 8 (3)

担 擔 dān dàn
undertake;
burden
55;64 8 (2)

渣
zhā
shards; dregs,
sediment
40;85 12 (3)

与
與 yǔ yù yú
and; with; to;
help; give; &
2;134 3 (2)

写
寫 xiě xiè
write;
draw; depict
18;40 5 (1)

乌 烏 wū
crow;
black, dark
4;86 4 (4)

鸟
鳥 niǎo
bird
-
152;196 5 (2)

莺 鶯 yīng
oriole,
warbler
134;196 10 (-)

鹰
鷹 yīng
eagle,
hawk
152;196 18 (

马
馬 mǎ
horse
-
75;187 3 (1)

笃
篤 dǔ
sincere;
serious (illness)
178;118 9 (-)

骂
罵 mà
curse,
rebuke
40;122 9 (2)

驾 駕 jià
to harness;
drive (vehicle)
75;187 8 (1)

或
huò
or; either;
perhaps
101;62 8 (1)

吗 → 49
鸣 → 54

止
zhǐ
stop, halt;
until; limited to
102;77 4 (2)

上
shàng shang shǎng
above, on, up; ascend; go to;
previous; first; put in position; &
16;1 3 (1)

土
tǔ
soil, ground;
local, native; &
49;32 3 (2)

士
shì
person; knight;
scholar; &
49;33 3 (2)

生
shēng
give birth; grow; life; livelihood;
raw, unripe, un-; student; &
4;100 5 (1)

工
gōng
to work, worker;
industry; skill
48;48 3 (1)

巫
wū
witch,
wizard
48,48 7 (4)

王
wáng
king
-
88;96 4 (2)

玉
yù
jade;
your (polite)
131;96 5 (2)

正
zhèng zhēng
correct, straight, upright, proper;
exactly; main, chief; January; &
102;77 5 (1)

五
wǔ
five
-
2;7 4 (1)

互
hù
mutual
-
2;7 4 (1)

且
qiě
as well as;
for a while
2;1 5 (1)

丑
*醜 chǒu
ugly;
disgraceful; EB
2;1 4 (3)

卫
衛 wèi
protect,
defend, guard
32;144 3 (2)

丘
qiū
mound,
grave
4;1 5 (3)

壬
rén
9th;
HS
49;33 4 (-)

垂
chuí
droop;
hang down
4;32 8 (3)

重
chóng zhòng
repeat; heavy;
to stress; &
4;166 9 (1)

业
業 yè
business;
already
140;75 5 (1)

亚
亞 yà
inferior;
Asia
168;7 6 (3)

壶
壺 hú
pot, kettle,
flask
49;33 10 (2)

显
顯 xiǎn
obvious;
to display; &
103;181 9 (2)

鉴
鑒 鑑 jiàn
mirror, reflect;
inspect; warn
209;167 13 (3)

宜
yí
appropriate;
should
45;40 8 (1)

直
*直 zhí
straight; direct;
frank; upright; &
12;24 8 (1)

置
*置 zhì
put, place,
install; buy
145;122 13 (2)

叠
*疊 疉 dié
pile up;
repeat
35;29 13 (2)

𡉀 ⟶ 75
𡌅 ⟶ 75
𡈼 ⟶ 75
疋 ⟶ 75
皿 ⟶ 80

丁

宁	亭	予
寧 níng nìng	tíng	yǔ yú
tranquil;	pavilion,	grant,
Nanjing; prefer	kiosk, stall	bestow
45;40 5 (3)	9;8 9 (3)	31;6 4 (3)

干

竿	旱	宇	岸	南
gān	hàn	yǔ	àn	nán
rod, pole,	drought;	house; eaves;	shore, coast,	south
cane	(dry) land	(outer) space	river bank	-
178;118 9 (4)	103;72 7 (3)	45;40 6 (3)	60;46 8 (2)	12;24 9 (1)

火

灸	灵	焚	烫	炎
jiǔ	靈 líng	fén	燙 tàng	yán
moxibustion	clever; effective;	burn	scald, burn;	hot; blazing;
(Ch. medicine)	spirit; fairy, elf	-	to iron, perm	inflammation
83;86 7 (3)	70;173 7 (2)	83;86 12 (-)	83;86 10 (2)	83;86 8 (4)

灭	炭	氮	灾	灰
滅 miè	tàn	dàn	災 zāi	huī
snuff out;	charcoal	nitrogen	disaster	ash, dust; gray;
wipe out; drown	-	-	-	disheartened
83;85 5 (2)	60;86 9 (4)	109;84 12 (4)	45;86 7 (2)	14;86 6 (2)

大

尖	类	契	奖	奥	奠
jiān	類 lèi	qì	獎 獎 jiǎng	ào	diàn
tip, pinnacle;	kind, type;	contract; agree;	praise, reward,	profound; hard	settle (a place
sharp, pointed	similar to	carve (literary)	encourage	to understand	funeral offerin
79;42 6 (2)	159;181 9 (2)	52;37 9 (-)	52;37 9 (2)	52;37 12 (3)	52;37 12 (3)

头	买	实	卖	矣
頭 tóu tou	買 mǎi	實 shí	賣 mài	yǐ
head; top; first,	buy	solid, real;	sell; betray;	(particle,
chief; end; &	-	seed, fruit	show off; strive	archaic)
52;181 5 (1)	5;154 6 (1)	45;40 8 (1)	12;154 8 (1)	37;111 7 (-)

天

吴	笑	癸	奏	葵
*吳 wú	xiào	guǐ	zòu	kuí
(old kingdom);	laugh, smile;	HS	play music;	sunflower;
(surname)	ridicule	10th;	achieve; &	mallow
58;30 7 (3)	178;118 10 (1)	154;105 9 (-)	130;37 9 (4)	50;140 12 (4)

丰

奉	举
fèng	舉 jǔ
serve; proffer;	raise; praise; deed; cite;
obey; revere; &	entire; behavior; choose; start
130;37 8 (4)	227;134 9 (1)

十

弄
nòng lòng
handle; get; do;
play with; alley
88;55 7 (2)

弊
bì
malpractice;
disadvantage
51;55 14 (4)

异
*異 yì
different;
strange
72;55 6 (2)

算
suàn
count, reckon;
count as; &
178;118 14 (1)

奔
bēn bèn
rush, run, flee;
head for
52;37 8 (3)

葬
zàng
bury
-
50;140 12 (4)

并
併並 bìng
actually; also;
merge; equally
24;9 6 (2)

弃
*棄 qì
discard,
abandon
9;55 7 (2)

鼻
bí
nose
-
226;209 14 (2)

木

宋
sòng
Song
(dynasty)
45;40 7 (3)

杀
殺 shā
kill; fight;
reduce; very
25;79 6 (2)

条
條 tiáo
twig; clause;
slip of paper
65;75 7 (1)

杂
雜 zá
miscellaneous;
to mix, blend
94;172 6 (1)

朵
duǒ
(measure word)
-
30;75 6 (2)

某
mǒu
a certain
(thing, person)
135;75 9 (2)

呆
dāi ái
dull, stupid;
stay
58;30 7 (2)

果
guǒ
fruit; result;
sure enough; &
94;75 8 (1)

栗
lì
chestnut;
tremble
166;75 10 (4)

桌
zhuō
table
-
94;75 10 (1)

巢
cháo
nest
-
78;47 11 (-)

亲
親 qīn qìng
parent, relative;
dear to; kiss; &
126;147 9 (1)

案
àn
table; proposal;
(legal) case; &
45;75 10 (2)

寨
zhài
stockade,
camp
45;40 14 (4)

茶
chá
tea
-
50;140 9 (1)

荣
榮 róng
thrive;
honor
134;75 9 (2)

菜
cài
vegetable; food;
(meal) course
50;140 11 (1)

采
*採 cǎi cài
pick, pluck,
select; &
197;165 8 (2)

柔
róu
soft, pliable;
gentle
155;75 9 (3)

桑
sāng
mulberry
tree
94;75 10 (4)

秦
qín
Qin (dynasty);
Shaanxi
130;115 10 (4)

笨
bèn
stupid, dull;
clumsy
178;118 11 (2)

染
rǎn
dye; pollute;
catch (disease)
94;75 9 (2)

柒
qī
seven
-
94;75 9 (4)

渠
qú
ditch,
channel
94;85 10 (2)

梁
*樑 liáng
bridge; ridge;
roof beam
94;75 11 (2)

粱
liáng
millet
(literary)
159;119 13 (3)

集
jí
gather, collect;
market
208;172 12 (1)

桨
槳 jiǎng
oar,
paddle
94;75 10 (4)

柴
chái
firewood
-
94;75 10 (2)

梨
lí
pear
-
94;75 11 (2)

架
jià
erect; prop up;
shelf, rack; &
94;75 9 (2)

土

圣
聖 shèng
sacred; sage;
Majesty
35;128 5 (3)

至
zhì
until, up to;
arrive at
171;133 6 (2)

垄
壟 lǒng
ridge
(in paddy field)
137;32 8 (3)

基
jī
foundation,
base, basis
49;32 11 (1)

垦
墾 kěn
cultivate;
reclaim (land)
184;32 9 (4)

里
*裏裡 li lǐ
in, inside;
mile, 1/2 km; &
195;166 7 (1)

在
zài
exist; be -ing;
at; depends; &
14;32 6 (1)

堂
táng
hall, court;
cousin
139;32 11 (1)

童
tóng
child; virgin;
bare (hills)
126;117 12 (2)

室
shì
a room
-
45;40 9 (1)

塞
sāi sài sè
stopper; jam in;
strategic place
45;32 13 (3)

墓
mù
tomb,
grave
50;32 13 (3)

垒
壘 lěi
rampart, fort;
build
49;32 9 (4)

至
zhì
until, up to;
arrive at
171;133 6 (2)

量
liáng liàng
measure;
capacity
103;166 12 (2)

墨
mò
black; ink;
writing; learning
223;32 15 (2)

崖
yá
cliff,
precipice
60;46 11 (3)

尘
塵 chén
dust, dirt; this
(mortal) world
79;32 6 (3)

坐
zuò
sit; ride on;
recoil; &
49;32 7 (1)

坚
堅 jiān
strong; resolute;
stronghold
49;32 7 (1)

堡
bǎo
fortress
-
49;32 12 (4)

垫
墊 diàn
cushion; to pay
(for now); &
49;32 9 (3)

型
xíng
mold, model,
type, template
49;32 9 (2)

坠
墜 zhuì
fall; sag,
weighed down
49;32 7 (-)

堕
墮 duò
sink,
fall
49;32 11 (4)

壁
bì
wall
-
49;32 16 (2)

塑
sù
model,
mold
49;32 13 (2)

牛

牢
láo
prison; secure;
durable
45;93 7 (3)

牵
牽 qiān
lead (by the
hand); involve
52;93 9 (2)

犁
*犂 lí
plow
-
110;93 11 (4)

车

军
軍 jūn
army,
troops
18;159 6 (2)

晕
暈 yūn yùn
dizzy;
to faint
103;72 10 (3)

辈
輩 bèi
people; lifetime,
generation
205;159 12 (3)

空 kōng kòng
sky, air; in vain; empty, vacant
128;116 8 (1)

茎 (莖) jīng
stem, stalk (of plant)
50;140 8 (4)

氢 (氫) qīng
hydrogen
-
109;84 9 (4)

左 zuǒ
left (hand); different; wrong
14;48 5 (1)

差 chà chā chāi cī
differ; err; wrong; difference; lacking; errand
157;48 9 (1)

主 zhǔ
master, host, lord; manage; &
88;3 5 (1)

全 quán
completely; whole, all
23;11 6 (1)

呈 chéng
to present, show, offer
58;30 7 (4)

皇 huáng
emperor, sovereign
150;106 9 (2)

望 wàng
hope; gaze; visit; repute; &
88;74 11 (1)

宝 (寶) bǎo
precious; your (polite)
45;40 8 (2)

歪 wāi
crooked, askew; devious
95;77 9 (2)

整 zhěng
entire; orderly; repair; punish
192;66 16 (1)

定 dìng
decide; calm; book (seats); &
45;40 8 (1)

是 shì
is, are; indeed; yes, correct
213;72 9 (1)

走 zǒu
walk, go; depart; leak out
189;156 7 (1)

楚 chǔ
clear, distinct; pain
156;75 13 (1)

足 zú
foot; leg; ample
196;157 7 (1)

币 (幣) bì
money
-
57;50 4 (2)

市 shì
market; city
9;50 5 (1)

吊 *弔 diào
suspend, hoist; condole; revoke
58;30 6 (2)

帝 dì
God; emperor
9;50 9 (2)

帘 *簾 lián
screen, curtain
128;50 8 (3)

布 *佈 bù
cloth; spread; deploy; declare
14;50 5 (1)

带 (帶) dài
belt, zone; to lead; carry; &
57;50 9 (1)

常 cháng
often; constant; normal
139;50 11 (1)

蒂 dì
base (of a fruit)
50;140 12 (4)

幕 mù
screen, curtain; act (of play)
50;50 13 (3)

帮 (幫) bāng
help, assist; gang; &
57;50 9 (1)

希 xī
hope; rare
25;50 7 (1)

击 (擊) jí
strike, hit, attack
38;64 5 (2)

出 chū
exit; go out; to issue, produce, vent; exceed; occur; expenditure
61;17 5 (1)

岔 chà
branch off, turn off
60;46 7 (4)

岳 yuè
high mountain; wife's parents
60;46 8 (4)

密 mì
closely; dense; precise; secret
45;40 11 (2)

岛 (島) dǎo
island
-
60;46 7 (2)

窟 kū
hole, cave; den
128;116 13 (3)

1	41
2	42
3	43
4	44
5	45
6	46
7	47
8	48
9	49
10	50
11	51
12	52
13	53
14	54
15	55
16	56
17	57
18	58
19	59
20	60
21	61
22	62
23	63
24	64
25	65
26	66
27	67
28	68
29	69
30	70
31	71
32	72
33	73
34	74
35	**75**
36	76
37	77
38	78
39	79
40	80

又 夂 女 夕

又

支 zhī
branch; erect,
prop up; pay; &
12;65 4 (1)

変 變 biàn
change,
transform
162;149 8 (1)

受 shòu
receive, accept;
endure
116;29 8 (2)

曼 màn
prolonged;
graceful
103;73 11 (-)

凤 鳳 fèng
phoenix
-
30;196 4 (4)

皮 pí
skin, leather;
outer layer; &
153;107 5 (2)

友 yǒu
friend
-
14;29 4 (1)

发 發 髪 fā fà
emit; become;
develop; hair; &
35;105 5 (1)

爱 愛 ài
love; be fond of;
cherish; apt to
116;61 10 (1)

夂

麦 麥 mài
wheat;
cereals
188;199 7 (2)

夏 xià
summer
-
65;35 10 (1)

复 *復褐覆 fù
duplicate, repeat; complex;
resume; reply; revenge
20;60 9 (1)

女

安 ān
peace; calm;
safe; install; &
45;40 6 (1)

妥 tuǒ
arranged;
appropriate
116;38 7 (3)

委 wěi wēi
appoint;
indirect; &
149;38 8 (2)

耍 shuǎ
to play
-
169;126 9 (3)

要 yào yāo
want, ask for; if;
need, must; &
166;146 9 (1)

妄 wàng
absurd;
presumptuous
43;38 6 (4)

宴 yàn
banquet; at
ease; entertain
45;40 10 (1)

妻 qī
wife
-
73;38 8 (2)

姜 薑 jiāng
ginger
-
157;140 9 (4)

萎 wēi wěi
decline, wane,
wither
50;140 11 (-)

姿 zī
looks; posture;
gesture
73;38 9 (3)

婆 pó
old woman;
mother in law
73;38 11 (3)

娶 qǔ
marry
(a woman)
73;38 11 (3)

婴 嬰 yīng
baby,
infant
73;38 11 (3)

夕

岁 歲 suì
year,
years old
60;77 6 (1)

多 duō
many;
more; over-; &
64;36 6 (1)

梦 夢 mèng
dream
-
64;36 11 (2)

爹 diē
father, dad
(colloq)
108;88 10 (3)

萝 蘿 luó
vine, ivy;
[radish]
50;140 11 (2)

箩 籮 luó
bamboo
basket
178;118 14 (4)

罗 *羅 囉 luó luō
net; sift; collect;
display; &
145;122 8 (4)

另	男	务 (務)	劣	穷 (窮)	劳 (勞)
lìng	nán	wù	liè	qióng	láo
separate, other	man, male; son	affair, business; work at	inferior, poor quality	poor; limit; extremely	toil; fatigue; good deed; &
58;30 5 (2)	142;102 7 (1)	65;19 5 (1)	79;19 6 (3)	128;116 7 (2)	134;19 7 (1)
努	势 (勢)	舅	勇	雾 (霧)	募
nǔ	shì	jiù	yǒng	wù	mù
exert oneself; bulge	power; gesture; appearance; &	uncle; brother in law	brave –	fog, mist	solicit, enlist, raise (funds)
28;19 7 (1)	28;19 8 (2)	179;134 13 (3)	31;19 9 (2)	204;173 13 (2)	50;19 12 (-)

分	芬	券	氛
fēn fèn	fēn	quàn xuàn	fēn
small unit; part; divide; duty; &	fragrant –	ticket, certificate; arch	atmosphere, vapor
24;18 4 (1)	50;140 7 (4)	158;18 8 (4)	109;84 8 (3)
劈	剪	寡	
pī pǐ	jiǎn	guǎ	
split; strike; right up against	scissors; clip; trim; wipe out	few; rare; insipid; widow	
27;18 15 (4)	27;18 11 (2)	45;40 14 (3)	

令	零	琴
lìng lǐng	líng	qín
command; your (resp); &	zero; tiny bit; fall (leaves)	zither; stringed instrument
23;9 5 (2)	204;173 13 (1)	88;96 12 (3)

学 (學)	李	季	孕
xué	lǐ	jì	yùn
study, learn; knowledge; &	plum –	season, quarterly	pregnant –
74;39 8 (1)	94;75 7 (2)	149;39 8 (2)	74;39 5 (4)

拿	掌	拳	挚 (摯)	攀	擎
ná	zhǎng	quán	zhì	pān	qíng
grasp; using; treat as; &	palm (of hand); control	fist; boxing	sincere (literary)	climb; implicate	lift up, hold up, raise
111;64 10 (1)	139;64 12 (1)	158;64 10 (3)	111;64 10 (4)	111;64 19 (3)	111;64 16 (-)

笔 (筆)	毫	髦	尾
bǐ	háo	máo	wěi
write; pen; (of Ch char) stroke	hair; milli-; (not) at all; &	[fashionable] –	tail, end
178;118 10 (1)	112;82 11 (2)	220;190 14 (4)	67;44 7 (2)

水　水　糸　氏　伐　衣

水

泉
quán
spring, fountain
150;85 9 (4)

汞
gǒng
mercury
-
48;85 7 (4)

浆 漿 jiāng jiàng
thick liquid, syrup; starch
125;85 10 (3)

尿
niào suī
urine; urinate
67;44 7 (4)

聚
jù
assemble, get together
163;128 14 (3)

水

求
qiú
beg, request; seek
1;85 7 (1)

录 錄 lù
record; employ
70;167 8 (1)

隶 隸 lì
subordinate, servant, slave
124;171 8 (3)

泰
tài
peaceful, calm; extreme, -most
130;85 10 (4)

暴
bào
violent; cruel; stand out
103;72 15 (3)

黎
lí
multitude (literary)
149;202 15 (3

糸

紫
zǐ
purple
-
77;120 12 (2)

繁
fán
numerous; propagate
77;120 17 (2)

紧 緊 jǐn
tight; taut; strict; urgent
77;120 10 (1)

絮
xù
cotton wadding; garrulous
77;120 12 (4)

系 *係 繫 xì
fasten; system; department; &
77;120 7 (1)

累
lèi lěi léi
toil; tired; pile up; implicate; &
142;120 11 (1)

索
suǒ
rope, cable; search; ask for
77;120 10 (3)

素
sù
basic; habitual; vegetable; &
89;120 10 (2)

氏

畏
wèi
fear; respect
142;102 9 (4)

丧 喪 sāng sàng
mourning; lose
12;30 8 (3)

长 長 cháng zhǎng
long; long-term; steadily; forte; grow; senior, chief; get, acquire
4;168 4 (1)

伐

衣
yī
garment, clothes, cover
161;145 6 (1)

农 農 nóng
agriculture; peasant
18;161 6 (1)

哀
āi
grief, sorrow; to pity
9;30 9 (3)

袁
yuán
(surname)
-
49;145 10 (4)

衰
shuāi
grow weak, decline
9;145 10 (3)

衷
zhōng
sincere, heartfelt
9;145 10 (3)

裹
guǒ
wrap; bind up
9;145 14 (3)

囊
náng
bag, pocket
12;30 22 (4)

襄
xiāng
assist (literary)
9;145 17 (-)

表 *錶 biǎo
list, form, chart; to show; gauge; (wrist) watch; surface; cousin; &
89;145 8 (1)

衣

裳
cháng shang
a skirt (ancient)
139;145 14 (4)

袭 襲 xí
raid; follow suit
137;145 11 (3)

袋
dài
bag, sack, pocket
161;145 11 (2)

裂
liè
crack, split, rip
161;145 12 (3)

装 裝 zhuāng
pretend; act out; dress up; outfit; to pack, load; install
161;145 12 (1)

幺	玄	么	公
yāo	xuán	麼 me	gōng
one (on dice; when speaking)	black, dark; profound	[what; such as] (suffix)	public; official; general; impartial; metric units; male (animal)
76;52 3 (-)	9;95 5 (-)	4;200 3 (1)	24;12 4 (1)

罢	套	县	丢	去
罷 bà	tào	縣 縣 xiàn	diū	qù qu
stop; dismiss	cover, sheath; knot; coax; &	county, district	lose; throw away	go, depart; away; discard; last (year)
145;122 10 (3)	52;37 10 (2)	37;120 7 (2)	133;1 6 (2)	133;28 5 (1)

宏	瓜	云	尝	会
hóng	gua	*雲 yún	嘗 cháng	會 huì kuài
great, vast, grand	melon, gourd	cloud -	to taste, test; ever, already	meet; meeting; union, society; going to; know how to; &
45;40 7 (3)	151;97 5 (2)	11;7 4 (1)	139;30 9 (2)	23;73 6 (1)

览	宽	觅	觉
覽 lǎn	寬 kuān	覓 mì	覺 jué jiào
see, to view; read	broad; lenient; relaxed; well off	seek -	feel; conscious; realize; sleep
107;147 9 (1)	45;40 10 (2)	116;147 8 (-)	107;147 9 (1)

贞	页	贡	责	负
貞 zhēn	頁 yè	貢 gòng	責 zé	負 fù
pure; loyal; chaste	page -	contribute; pay tribute	duty; require; reprove; punish	to shoulder; suffer; rely on minus; owe; fail; be defeated
16;154 6 (4)	170;181 6 (1)	48;154 7 (2)	89;154 8 (1)	27;154 6 (1)

员	贵	贯	贾	费	贤
員 yuán	貴 guì	貫 guàn	賈 gǔ	費 fèi	賢 xián
person, -er; member	expensive, precious	pierce; link up; birthplace	merchant; to do business	fees; consume, use up; waste	able and virtuous
58;30 7 (1)	105;154 9 (1)	106;154 8 (2)	166;154 10 (-)	106;154 9 (2)	106;154 8 (4)

货	贷	贸	贺	资
貨 huò	貸 dài	貿 mào	賀 hè	資 zī
commodity, goods; money	lend; borrow; evasive; forgive	trade, commerce	congratulate; greetings	money; provide; subsidize; aptitude; qualifications
106;154 8 (2)	106;154 9 (4)	106;154 9 (2)	106;154 9 (2)	106;154 10 (2)

贪	贫	赏	赛	赞	质
貪 tān	貧 pín	賞 shǎng	賽 sài	贊 讚 zàn	質 zhì
corrupt; greedy; covet	poor, destitute; talkative	bestow; reward; appreciate	contest; game; to rival, surpass	to praise, favor, support	quality, nature; simple; query
106;154 8 (4)	106;154 8 (3)	139;154 12 (3)	45;154 14 (1)	106;154 16 (2)	22;154 8 (2)

1 41 / 2 42 / 3 43 / 4 44 / 5 45 / 6 46 / 7 47 / 8 48 / 9 49 / 10 50 / 11 51 / 12 52 / 13 53 / 14 54 / 15 55 / 16 56 / 17 57 / 18 58 / 19 59 / 20 60 / 21 61 / 22 62 / 23 63 / 24 64 / 25 65 / 26 66 / 27 67 / 28 68 / 29 69 / 30 70 / 31 71 / 32 72 / 33 73 / 34 74 / 35 75 / 36 76 / 37 **77** / 38 78 / 39 79 / 40 80

口 口

占	古	杏	吉	告
*佔 zhàn zhān	gǔ	xìng	jí	gào
seize, occupy; comprise; &	ancient; old fashioned	apricot -	lucky, auspicious	notify; accuse; request
16;25 5 (1)	12;30 5 (2)	94;75 7 (4)	49;30 6 (4)	58;30 7 (1)

呂	吾	吞	否	召	舌
呂 lǚ	wú	tūn	fǒu pǐ	zhào	shé
(surname) -	I, we, my, our (literary)	swallow, gulp; to annex	deny; not; evil; censure	call, summon	tongue -
58;30 6 (4)	58;30 7 (-)	90;30 7 (3)	95;30 7 (2)	27;30 5 (2)	177;135 6 (2)

各	台
gè	*臺檯颱 tái
each, every	platform, stage; support; desk; (TV) station; Taiwan
65;30 6 (1)	37;30 5 (2)

售	咨	哲	唇
shòu	諮 zī	zhé	*脣 chún
sell -	consult	wise; philosopher	lips -
208;30 11 (3)	58;149 9 (4)	58;30 10 (2)	187;30 10 (3)

言	害	容	宮	客	喜
yán	hài	róng	宮 gōng	kè	xǐ
word; speech; say, talk	harm; murder; get (illness); &	contain; permit, tolerate; looks	palace, temple; womb	guest, visitor, customer; &	happy event; happy; liking for
185;149 7 (1)	45;40 10 (2)	45;40 10 (1)	45;40 9 (3)	45;40 9 (1)	49;30 12 (1)

苦	菩	蓉	營	答
kǔ	pú	róng	營 yíng	dá dā
bitter; pain, suffering	[Bodhi tree, Buddha]	[hibiscus]; Chengdu	operate; seek; barracks; &	respond, answer
50;140 8 (1)	50;140 11 (-)	50;140 13 (-)	134;86 11 (2)	178;118 12 (1)

合	含	舍	谷	兽	善
hé gě	hán	捨 shě shè	*穀 gǔ	獸 shòu	shàn
join; add up to; shut; to suit; &	contain; hold in mouth	abandon; house, shed; &	valley; grain, cereal	beast -	good; expert; apt to; friendly
23;30 6 (1)	58;30 7 (2)	23;135 8 (1)	199;150 7 (3)	24;94 11 (3)	157;30 12 (2)

誉	誓	譬	警
譽 yù	shì	pì	jǐng
reputation; praise	oath, vow	example, analogy	warn; vigilant; police
185;149 13 (4)	185;149 14 (4)	185;149 20 (3)	185;149 19 (2)

石
shí dàn
stone, rock;
inscription
136;112 5 (2)

右
yòu
right (hand)
-
14;30 5 (1)

名
míng
name;
renown; famous
64;30 6 (1)

君
jūn
monarch;
gentleman; Mr.
58;30 7 (4)

后
*後 **hòu**
back, behind,
after; empress
22;30 6 (1)

启
啓 **qǐ**
open, begin;
enlighten
86;30 7 (2)

岩
*巖 **yán**
rock;
cliff
60;46 8 (3)

碧
bì
green; blue
(literary)
136;112 14 (4)

奇
qí jī
weird; surprise;
odd (number)
52;37 8 (2)

寄
jì
send, mail;
entrust; rely on
45;40 11 (1)

哥
gē
older
brother
58;30 10 (1)

向
*嚮 **xiàng**
facing; towards;
direction; &
4;30 6 (1)

同
tóng tòng
same, equal;
together, with
19;30 6 (1)

周
*週 **zhōu**
circuit; week;
thoughtful; &
19;30 8 (1)

问
問 **wèn**
ask; ask after;
interrogate
46;30 6 (1)

尚
shàng
esteem,
respect; yet
79;42 8 (3)

商
shāng
merchant;
trade; discuss
9;30 11 (1)

高
gāo
tall, high; loud;
expensive
218;189 10 (1)

嵩
sōng
high, lofty
(mountain)
60;46 13 (-)

筒
tǒng
cylinder,
tube
178;118 12 (3)

阁
閣 **gé**
pavilion;
Excellency; &
46;169 9 (4)

官
guān
an official;
organ (of body)
45;40 8 (2)

管
guǎn
tube, pipe, flute;
attend to; &
178;118 14 (2)

1	41
2	42
3	43
4	44
5	45
6	46
7	47
8	48
9	49
10	50
11	51
12	52
13	53
14	54
15	55
16	56
17	57
18	58
19	59
20	60
21	61
22	62
23	63
24	64
25	65
26	66
27	67
28	68
29	69
30	70
31	71
32	72
33	73
34	74
35	75
36	76
37	77
38	**78**
39	79
40	80

曰

白 bái
white; blank, in vain; gratis; &
150;106 5 (1)

旨 zhǐ
aim, intention; decree
39;72 6 (4)

昔 xī
the past, former
93;72 8 (-)

昏 hūn
dusk; confused; dim; to faint
122;72 8 (2)

香 xiāng
fragrant; appetizing; heartily; perfume, incense; popular
215;186 9 (1)

音 yīn
sound, tone; news
211;180 9 (1)

者 zhě
person, -er, -ist; this
92;125 8 (1)

春 chūn
springtime; vitality
130;72 9 (1)

奢 shē
extravagant, excessive
52;37 11 (4)

普 pǔ
universal
-
103;72 12 (2)

曾 céng zēng
formerly; great (grandchild)
103;73 12 (2)

著 zhù
outstanding; book; write
50;140 11 (2)

薯 shǔ
cassava, yam, potato
50;140 16 (4)

暮 mù
dusk, evening; late on
50;72 14 (4)

曹 cáo
people (of some kind) (literary)
103;73 11 (4)

晋 jin
promote; advance; enter
168;72 10 (4)

昌 chāng
prosperous, thriving
103;72 8 (4)

暑 shǔ
hot weather
103;72 12 (2)

署 shǔ
office; arrange; to sign; proxy
145;122 13 (3)

鲁 lǔ
stupid; rude
210;195 12 (4)

馨 xīn
fragrance (literary)
215;186 20 (-)

皆 jiē
all, every (literary)
123;106 9 (4)

暂 zàn
temporary; brief
103;72 12 (2)

替 tì
substitute; on behalf of
103;73 12 (2)

智 zhì
wisdom, wit
103;72 12 (3)

间 jiān jiàn
between; room; to separate; &
46;169 7 (1)

简 jiǎn
abbreviated; simple; letter
178;118 13 (-)

目

首 shǒu
head; chief, first; indict
24;185 9 (1)

眷 juàn
family, dependant
158;109 11 (-)

盲 máng
blind, blindly
43;109 8 (3)

冒 mào
emit; take risk; bold; fraud
104;13 9 (1)

省 shěng xǐng
save; omit; province; visit; aware; introspection
79;109 9 (1)

督 dū
supervise
-
141;109 13 (3)

瞥 piē
glimpse; dart a look at
141;109 16 (4)

看 kàn kān
watch; look at; look after; &
141;109 9 (1)

眉 méi
eyebrow
-
141;109 9 (3)

着 zháo zhāo zhuó zhe
touch; catch (cold); burn; to wear; use, apply; -ing; &
157;109 11 (1)

且

宜 yí
appropriate; should
45;40 8 (1)

叠 曡 疊 dié
pile up; repeat
35;29 13 (2)

查 chá zhā
investigate, check, look up
94;75 9 (1)

直 zhí
straight; direct; frank; upright; &
12;24 8 (1)

置 zhì
put, place, install; buy
145;122 13 (2)

虫 group

茧 繭 jiǎn
cocoon; callus
50;140 9 (4)

蚕 蠶 cán
silkworm
-
90;142 10 (3)

蛮 蠻 mán
fierce; rugged
162;142 12 (4)

蛋 dàn
egg; oval
156;142 11 (1)

萤 螢 yíng
firefly
-
134;120 11 (-)

虽 雖 suī
although; even if
58;172 9 (1)

蜜 mì
honey; sweet, candied
45;142 14 (2)

蟹 xiè
crab
-
174;142 19 (-)

月 group

肯 kěn
willing; consent
102;130 8 (2)

育 yù yō
give birth to; raise, rear
118;130 8 (1)

青 qīng
green; blue
202;174 8 (1)

骨 骨 gǔ gú gū
bone; skeleton, framework
214;188 9 (2)

胃 wèi
stomach
-
142;130 9 (2)

有 yǒu yòu
have, possess; there is / are; &
14;74 6 (1)

肖 xiào xiāo
resemble
-
79;130 7 (4)

脊 jǐ jí
backbone, spine; ridge
118;130 10 (4)

宵 xiāo
night
-
45;40 10 (3)

膏 gāo gào
fat, grease, oil; lubricate; &
218;130 14 (3)

菁 jīng
lush; essence
50;140 11 (-)

肩 jiān
shoulder
-
86;130 8 (2)

肾 腎 shèn
kidney
-
118;130 8 (4)

臂 bì bei
arm
(of the body)
118;130 17 (4)

背 bèi bēi
the back; turn one's back on; by rote; to shoulder; &
118;130 9 (2)

巴 group

仓 倉 cāng
warehouse, granary
23;9 4 (3)

苍 蒼 cāng
green; blue; gray, ashen
50;140 7 (3)

卷 *捲 juǎn juàn
roll up; roll (of); book, dossier
158;26 8 (2)

危 wēi
danger; near death
27;26 6 (1)

巷 xiàng hàng
lane, alley
93;49 9 (3)

雹 báo
hail, hailstone
204;173 13 (4)

色 sè shǎi
color; scene; looks; lust; &
27;139 6 (1)

芭 bā
('ba' sound); (a herb)
50;140 7 (4)

笆 bā
basket; bamboo fence
178;118 10 (4)

爸 bà
father
-
108;88 8 (1)

1 41
2 42
3 43
4 44
5 45
6 46
7 47
8 48
9 49
10 50
11 51
12 52
13 53
14 54
15 55
16 56
17 57
18 58
19 59
20 60
21 61
22 62
23 63
24 64
25 65
26 66
27 67
28 68
29 69
30 70
31 71
32 72
33 73
34 74
35 75
36 76
37 77
38 78
39 79
40 80

■ 耳 母 田 皿

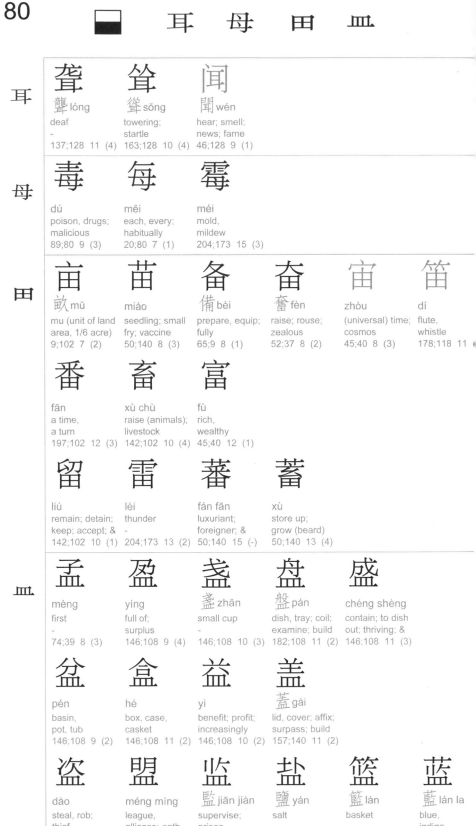

耳

聋 聾 lóng
deaf
-
137;128 11 (4)

耸 聳 sǒng
towering;
startle
163;128 10 (4)

闻 聞 wén
hear; smell;
news; fame
46;128 9 (1)

母

毒 dú
poison, drugs;
malicious
89;80 9 (3)

每 měi
each, every;
habitually
20;80 7 (1)

霉 méi
mold,
mildew
204;173 15 (3)

田

亩 畝 mǔ
mu (unit of land
area, 1/6 acre)
9;102 7 (2)

苗 miáo
seedling; small
fry; vaccine
50;140 8 (3)

备 備 bèi
prepare, equip;
fully
65;9 8 (1)

奋 奮 fèn
raise; rouse;
zealous
52;37 8 (2)

宙 zhòu
(universal) time;
cosmos
45;40 8 (3)

笛 dí
flute,
whistle
178;118 11

番 fān
a time,
a turn
197;102 12 (3)

畜 xù chù
raise (animals);
livestock
142;102 10 (4)

富 fù
rich,
wealthy
45;40 12 (1)

留 liú
remain; detain;
keep; accept; &
142;102 10 (1)

雷 léi
thunder
-
204;173 13 (2)

蕃 fán fān
luxuriant;
foreigner; &
50;140 15 (-)

蓄 xù
store up;
grow (beard)
50;140 13 (4)

皿

孟 mèng
first
-
74;39 8 (3)

盈 yíng
full of;
surplus
146;108 9 (4)

盏 盞 zhǎn
small cup
-
146;108 10 (3)

盘 盤 pán
dish, tray; coil;
examine; build
182;108 11 (2)

盛 chéng shèng
contain; to dish
out; thriving; &
146;108 11 (3)

盆 pén
basin,
pot, tub
146;108 9 (2)

盒 hé
box, case,
casket
146;108 11 (2)

益 yì
benefit; profit;
increasingly
146;108 10 (2)

盖 蓋 gài
lid, cover; affix;
surpass; build
157;140 11 (2)

盗 dào
steal, rob;
thief
146;108 11 (2)

盟 méng míng
league,
alliance; oath
146;108 13 (3)

监 監 jiān jiàn
supervise;
prison
146;108 10 (3)

盐 鹽 yán
salt
-
146;108 10 (2)

篮 籃 lán
basket
-
178;118 16 (1)

蓝 藍 lán la
blue,
indigo
50;140 13 (

丶方夕

究	芳	旁	参
jiū	fāng	páng	参 cān cēn shēn
investigate; after all	fragrant; good name	side; besides, other	join in; consult, refer; ginseng
128;116 7 (1)	50;140 7 (4)	85;70 10 (1)	37;28 8 (1)

毛禾乑必

窄	宅	秦	聚	瑟
zhǎi	zhái	qín	jù	sè
narrow; petty; hard up	residence	Qin (dynasty); Shaanxi	assemble, get together	se (Chinese zither)
128;116 10 (2)	45;40 6 (3)	130;115 10 (4)	163;128 14 (3)	88;96 13 (-)

而瓦死

鼻	斋	需	瓷	毙
bí	齋 zhāi	xū	cí	斃 bì
nose	to fast, abstain; a room; &	need, require; requirement	porcelain	die; kill
226;209 14 (2)	84;210 10 (-)	204;173 14 (1)	98;98 10 (3)	123;66 10 (4)

酉叩

穿	酱	器	嚣	豁
chuān	醬 jiàng	qì	囂 xiāo	huō huò
penetrate; wear, put on	sauce, paste; soy sauce	utensil; talent; organ (of body)	clamor	crack; forsake; open; exempt
128;116 9 (1)	193;164 13 (2)	58;30 16 (1)	58;30 18 (-)	199;150 17 (4)

才己弓

亨	矛	茅	岂	弯
hēng	máo	máo	豈 qǐ	彎 wān
successful, go smoothly	spear, lance	cogon grass	(particle, literary)	bend, curve; curved
9;8 7 (-)	155;110 5 (2)	50;140 8 (3)	60;151 6 (4)	162;57 9 (2)

乃卫

气	秀	爷	节
氣 qì	xiù	爺 yé	節 jié jiē
air, gas, breath; odor; enrage; &	beautiful; excellent	father; uncle, grandpa (polite)	segment; node; joint; festival; agenda; economize; &
109;84 4 (1)	149;115 7 (2)	108;88 6 (2)	50;118 5 (1)

土彐

笋	雪	当
筍 sǔn	xuě	當 噹 dāng dàng
bamboo shoot	snow; avenge, set right	act as; when, whilst; ought; regard as; equal to; proper; &
178;118 10 (4)	204;173 11 (1)	79;102 6 (1)

㐄金食

琴	黎	鉴	餐
qín	lí	鑒 鑑 jiàn	cān
zither; stringed instrument	multitude (literary)	mirror, reflect; inspect; warn	eat; food; meal
88;96 12 (3)	149;202 15 (3)	209;167 13 (3)	217;184 16 (2)

1	41
2	42
3	43
4	44
5	45
6	46
7	47
8	48
9	49
10	50
11	51
12	52
13	53
14	54
15	55
16	56
17	57
18	58
19	59
20	60
21	61
22	62
23	63
24	64
25	65
26	66
27	67
28	68
29	69
30	70
31	71
32	72
33	73
34	74
35	75
36	76
37	77
38	78
39	79
40	80

APPENDIX: Traditional Characters

This appendix contains all the traditional character equivalents of the characters in the main pages 1–80 (but not repeating those which are unchanged on simplification). The appendix uses the same method as the main book (except there is no thumbnail index) and has its own finder chart, opposite.

If a particular traditional character you are looking for is not in the appendix, this means that it is identical to the simplified character. Thus it is to be found on the main pages. Indeed, in the case of some traditional characters, you might prefer to try looking in the main pages 1–80 first: either for simple characters (which are often unchanged) or where you can try guessing what the simplified character will be like. (For example, any character with the traditional radical 訁 on the left hand side is likely to simplify to something with the modern radical 讠.)

For each traditional character the information given is in the following sequence: the simplified form(s); pronunciation(s); traditional radical (the numbers referring to Table 4 at the back of the book); stroke-count; and the page number where the simplified character appears (so you can look it up in the main part of the book).

If two traditional characters simplify to the same simplified character, then as a rule the simplified character will inherit both meanings and both pronunciations. (Typically the pronunciations will be the same anyway, or will differ only in tone.)

Variants and older versions of some characters are still around, and some are given in the appendix. There are also variants of character components such as: 昷 (昷), 令 (令), and 尋 (尋).

You will also sometimes see older forms of some of the traditional radicals. For example: 忄 (忄), 艹 (艹) and 辶 (辶).

For the appendix, I have applied the historical conventions for stroke-count often used by dictionaries for traditional characters: these sometimes differ from the actual number of strokes used to write the characters. Note the stroke-counts for the following components:

Radical:	阝	艹	辶	廴
Stroke-count for simplified characters:	2	3	2	2
Stroke-count for traditional characters:	3	4	3	3

Watch out also for: 乏 巨 垂 瓦 及 鬼

Even for simplified characters, stroke-counts can be tricky: be careful with characters containing the following components, for example: 世 甘 冊 釆.

A1	彡 夕 丨 刂 忄 火	
A2	氵	
A3	亻 彳 扌 上 土 人	
A4	扌	
A5	犭 孑 弓 巾 山 女 阝	
A6	木 禾 釆 米 爿 牛 夫	
A7	丁 工 王 矢 岳 方 礻 衤	
A8	糸	
A9	金	
A10	口 日 目 貝 田	
A11	耳 歹 石 足 酉 車 卓 幸 虫	
A12	月 舟 身 自 血 臣 臣 區 食	
A13	言	
A14	馬 魚 莫 骨 豐	
A15	other ◧	

A16	◳	
A17	◰ ◱	
A18	■ ◧ ◨ ◨ ◪ ◫ ⊞ ■	

◫ (black left)
A19	丶 丿 丨 卜 ⺄ 刂 乚 七 屯 也	
A20	十 寸 少 弋 戈 主 交 方 亥 京	
A21	羊 并 人 夾 犬 力 丸 夬	
A22	丁 干 几 長 王 氏 刀 己 司 勺 包 句	
A23	欠 攵 反 斤 殳 辛 馬 鳥 隹	
A24	占 由 甫 見 且 丑 弓 頁	
A25	卩 阝 艮 鬼 風 冊 區 各 令	
A26	other ◧	

■ (black top)
A27	八 丷 八 半 人 亠 西 人 卩 亇	
A28	亠 宀 穴 十 士 大 止 山	
A29	卄 竹 羽 炏	
A30	口 吅 四 目 目 田 西 雨 聿 髟	
A31	other ◘	

□ (black bottom)
A32	八 儿 彡 一 灬 心	
A33	火 大 木 巿 山 十 寸 キ 牛 土	
A34	糸 水 氏 衣 又 夂 女 力 手	
A35	口 曰 田 月 皿 虫 車 貝 見	
A36	other ◻	

■ 冫 彡 丿 丨

冫

凍 馮 氷
冻 dòng　冯 féng　冰 bīng
15　10　[45]　187　12　[3]　85　5　[3]

彡

須
须 xū
181　12　[1]

丿

順
顺 shùn
181　12　[48]

丨

鬥
斗 dòu
191　10　[1]

恆
恒 héng
61 9 [2]

慚
慚 cán
61 14 [2]

懶
懶 lǎn
61 19 [2]

悽
凄 qī
61 11 [3]

憤
愤 fèn
61 16 [2]

憐
怜 lián
61 15 [2]

憶
忆 yì
61 16 [2]

懷
怀 huái
61 19 [2]

惱
恼 nǎo
61 12 [2]

慘
惨 cǎn
61 14 [2]

懼
惧 jù
61 21 [2]

慣
惯 guàn
61 14 [2]

憫
悯 mǐn
61 15 [49]

煉
炼 liàn
86 13 [3]

燒
烧 shāo
86 16 [3]

煩
烦 fán
86 13 [3]

煙
烟 yān
86 13 [3]

燭
烛 zhú
86 17 [3]

煥
焕 huàn
86 13 [3]

燦
灿 càn
86 17 [3]

爍
烁 shuò
86 19 [3]

燈
灯 dēng
86 16 [3]

爛
烂 làn

爐
炉 lú

氵 氿 沇 沇 沇 沇

氵

氾 泛 fàn
85 5 [48]

決 决 jué
15 7 [46]

汙 污 wū
85 6 [7]

污 污 wū
85 6 [7]

冲 冲 chōng
15 7 [52]

洩 泄 xiè
85 9 [7]

淵 渊 yuān
85 12 [7]

沇

鴻 鸿 hóng
196 17 [54]

測 测 cè
85 12 [42]

漸 渐 jiàn jiān
85 14 [51]

瀰 弥 mí
85 20 [14]

漲 涨 zhǎng zhàng
85 14 [7]

滌 涤 dí
85 14 [6]

濺 溅 jiàn
85 18 [43]

澱 淀 diàn
85 16 [5]

灘 滩 tān
85 22 [7]

澀 涩 sè
85 17 [6]

沇

淚 泪 lèi
85 11 [7]

滬 沪 hù
85 14 [5]

瀝 沥 lì
85 19 [7]

濾 滤 lù
85 18 [7]

沇

洶 汹 xiōng
85 9 [52]

沇

汎 泛 fàn
85 6 [48]

潤 润 rùn
85 15 [7]

減 减 jiǎn
0 12 [43]

滅 灭 miè
85 13 [60]

日

涼 凉 liáng liàng 15 11 [54]	滾 滚 gǔn 85 14 [5]	濟 济 jǐ jì 85 17 [5]	濱 滨 bīn 85 17 [5]	瀉 泻 xiè 85 18 [6]
滬 沪 hù 85 14 [5]	淚 泪 lèi 85 11 [7]	澳 澳 ào 85 16 [5]		
淒 凄 qī 15 11 [3]	澆 浇 jiāo 85 15 [5]	濤 涛 tāo 85 17 [7]	潰 溃 kuì 85 15 [5]	湊 凑 còu 15 12 [3]	淺 浅 qiǎn 85 11 [5]
滿 满 mǎn 85 14 [5]	漢 汉 hàn 85 14 [7]	溝 沟 gōu 85 13 [7]	濃 浓 nóng 85 16 [5]	
濛 蒙 méng 85 17 [64]	瀟 潇 xiāo 85 20 [5]	滯 滞 zhì 85 14 [6]		
況 况 kuàng 15 8 [3]	渦 涡 wō 85 12 [6]	湯 汤 tāng 85 12 [49]	濕 湿 shī 85 17 [6]	澤 泽 zé 85 16 [55]	濁 浊 zhuó 85 16 [7]
溼 湿 shī 85 13 [6]	湧 涌 yǒng 85 12 [6]	淨 净 jìng 15 11 [6]		
渾 浑 hún 85 12 [6]	沒 没 méi mò 85 7 [6]	漁 渔 yú 85 14 [6]	滲 渗 shèn 85 14 [5]	淪 沦 lún 85 11 [56]	滄 沧 cāng 85 13 [56]
澇 涝 lào 85 15 [5]	澀 涩 sè 85 17 [6]	潔 洁 jié 85 15 [5]	潛 潜 qián 85 15 [5]	濫 滥 làn 85 17 [6]
潑 泼 pō 85 15 [41]	灑 洒 sǎ 85 22 [7]	灣 湾 wān 85 25 [5]		

■▮ 亻

俠 侠 xiá 9 9 [9]	倆 俩 liǎ liǎng 9 10 [9]	僞 伪 wěi 9 11 [9]			
傾 倾 qīng 9 13 [48]	們 们 men 9 10 [9]	條 条 tiáo 75 11 [61]	倣 仿 fǎng 9 10 [8]	側 侧 cè 9 11 [9]	儲 储 chǔ 9 17 [9]
佔 占 zhàn zhān 9 7 [66]	偵 侦 zhēn 9 11 [8]	傢 家 jiā 9 12 [63]	億 亿 yì 9 15 [42]	偽 伪 wěi 9 11 [9]	
倖 幸 xing 9 10 [67]	債 债 zhài 9 13 [8]	儘 尽 jǐn 9 16 [36]	偉 伟 wěi 9 11 [45]	傳 传 chuán zhuàn 9 13 [46]	
併 并 bìng 9 8 [74]	儀 仪 yí 9 15 [8]	償 偿 cháng 9 17 [8]	僕 仆 pú 9 14 [9]	僅 仅 jǐn 9 13 [51]	備 备 bèi 9 12 [61]
侶 侣 lǚ 9 9 [8]	優 优 yōu 9 17 [45]	價 价 jià jie 9 15 [8]	僑 侨 qiáo 9 15 [8]	係 系 xì 9 9 [60]	僞 伪 wěi 9 14 [9]
傷 伤 shāng 9 13 [8]	倫 伦 lún 9 10 [8]	儉 俭 jiǎn 9 15 [8]	傑 杰 jié 9 12 [67]		
佈 布 bù 9 7 [32]	備 备 bèi 9 12 [61]	傭 佣 yòng yōng 9 13 [9]			
個 个 gè gě 9 10 [59]					

佛 佛 fú 　 60 8 [9]

復 复 fù 　 60 12 [76]

後 后 hòu 　 60 9 [78]

從 从 cóng cōng 　 60 11 [30]

徑 径 jìng 　 60 10 [10]

術 术 shù zhú 　 144 11 [41]

衒 衒 xián 　 167 14 [10]

衝 冲 chòng 　 144 15 [52]

衛 卫 wèi 　 144 15 [39]

徵 征 zhēng 　 60 15 [10]

徹 彻 chè 　 60 14 [10]

協 协 xié 　 24 8 [10]

頃 顷 qǐng 　 181 11 [48]

塊 块 kuài 　 32 13 [10]

壞 坏 huài 　 32 19 [47]

壇 坛 tán 　 32 16 [10]

墳 坟 fén 　 32 15 [44]

壜 坛 tán 　 32 19 [10]

壜 坛 tán 　 32 9 [10]

壩 坝 bà 　 32 24 [48]

場 场 chǎng cháng 　 32 12 [49]

夾 夹 jiā jiá gā 　 37 7 [38]

來 来 lái lai 　 9 8 [38]

扣 扣 扣 扣 扣

扣

拑	挾	揀
钳 qián	挟 xié	拣 jiǎn
64 8 [21]	64 10 [13]	64 12 [13]

扣

掛	攤	擲	擬	攏
挂 guà	摊 tān	掷 zhì zhī	拟 nǐ	拢 lǒng
64 11 [55]	64 22 [55]	64 18 [54]	64 17 [13]	64 19 [45]

扣

據	擴
据 jù jū	扩 kuò
64 16 [13]	64 18 [13]

扣

擱	攔
搁 gē gé	拦 lán
64 17 [49]	64 20 [11]

扣

摳
抠 kōu
64 14 [13]

搗
搗 dǎo
64 13 [11]

擁
拥 yōng
64 16 [13]

擠
挤 jǐ
64 17 [11]

擰
拧 níng nǐng nìng
64 17 [11]

撓
挠 náo
64 15 [11]

摟
搂 lōu lǒu
64 14 [11]

攜
携 xié
64 21 [12]

撲
扑 pū
64 15 [13]

捲
卷 juǎn
64 11 [67]

擋
挡 dǎng dàng
64 16 [11]

拐
拐 guǎi
64 8 [12]

損
损 sǔn
64 13 [12]

揚
扬 yáng
64 12 [49]

擾
扰 rǎo
64 18 [45]

擇
择 zé zhái
64 16 [12]

擺
摆 bǎi
64 18 [12]

攝
摄 shè
64 21 [12]

掃
扫 sǎo sào
64 11 [52]

採
采 cǎi
64 11 [74]

掙
挣 zhèng zhēng
64 11 [12]

撫
抚 fǔ
64 15 [13]

揮
挥 huī
64 12 [12]

搖
摇 yáo
64 13 [12]

換
换 huàn
64 12 [12]

擔
担 dān dàn
64 16 [12]

攙
搀 chān
64 20 [12]

捨
舍 shě shè
64 11 [78]

掄
抡 lūn lún
64 11 [12]

撿
捡 jiǎn
64 16 [12]

搶
抢 qiǎng qiāng
64 13 [56]

拚
拼 pīn
64 8 [11]

摻
掺 chān
64 14 [12]

撚
捻 niǎn
64 15 [12]

攆
撵 niǎn
64 18 [12]

撈
捞 lāo
64 15 [11]

撥
拨 bō
64 15 [41]

攢
攒 zǎn cuán
64 22 [12]

攪
搅 jiǎo
64 23 [11]

攬
揽 lǎn
64 24 [12]

■ 犭 孑 弓 巾 山

犭

狹	狽	猶	獲	獨	獵
狭 xiá	狈 bèi	犹 yóu	获 huò	独 dú	猎 liè
94 10 [46]	94 10 [14]	94 12 [14]	94 17 [65]	94 16 [14]	94 18 [14]

獅	獄	豬	貓
狮 shī	狱 yù	猪 zhū	猫 māo máo
94 13 [14]	94 14 [46]	152 15 [14]	153 16 [14]

孑

孫	預
孙 sūn	预 yù
39 10 [41]	181 13 [48]

弓

張	彈	強
张 zhāng	弹 tán dàn	强 qiáng qiǎng jiàng
57 11 [43]	57 15 [14]	57 11 [14]

彌	疆
弥 mí	强 qiáng qiǎng jiàng
57 17 [50]	57 16 [14]

巾

帳	幟
帐 zhàng	帜 zhì
50 11 [14]	50 15 [55]

山

峽	嶼
峡 xiá	屿 yǔ
46 10 [14]	46 17 [14]

女

阝

妳 你奶 nǐ nǎi 38 8 [9]

媽 妈 mā 38 13 [22]

嫻 娴 xián 38 15 [22]

嫺 娴 xián 38 15 [22]

姙 妊 rèn 38 9 [22]

嬸 婶 shěn 38 18 [22]

孃 娘 niáng 38 20 [22]

娛 娱 yú 38 10 [22]

婦 妇 fù 38 11 [22]

嬭 奶 nǎi 38 17 [22]

嬌 娇 jiāo 38 15 [22]

陣 阵 zhèn 170 10 [22]

陳 陈 chén 170 11 [22]

陝 陕 shǎn 170 10 [46]

隙 隙 xì 170 11 [22]

陸 陆 liù lù 170 11 [22]

隊 队 duì 170 12 [22]

陽 阳 yáng 170 12 [22]

階 阶 jiē 170 12 [22]

際 际 jì 170 14 [22]

隱 隐 yǐn 170 17 [22]

險 险 xiǎn 170 16 [22]

陰 阴 yīn 170 11 [22]

陰 阴 yīn 170 12 [22]

隨 随 suí 170 16 [22]

木

棟 栋 dòng 75 12 [45]
柵 栅 zhà shān 75 9 [17]

樹 树 shù 75 16 [17]
橢 椭 tuǒ 75 16 [17]

樓 楼 lóu 75 15 [16]
棲 栖 qī 75 12 [17]
檯 台 tái 75 18 [78]
檸 柠 níng 75 18 [16]
樁 桩 zhuāng 75 15 [17]
棧 栈 zhàn 75 12 [43]

樣 样 yàng 75 15 [16]
檔 档 dàng 75 17 [16]
樸 朴 pǔ 75 16 [17]
權 权 quán 75 22 [17]
橫 横 héng hèng 75 16 [16]
構 构 gòu 75 14 [17]

桿 杆 gān gǎn 75 11 [47]
楊 杨 yáng 75 13 [17]
楞 棱 léng 75 13 [16]
標 标 biāo 75 15 [16]
極 极 jí 75 13 [17]
橘 桔 jú 75 16 [16]

橋 桥 qiáo 75 16 [16]
檢 检 jiǎn 75 17 [16]
槍 枪 qiāng 75 14 [16]

樑 梁 liáng 75 15 [74]
櫻 樱 yīng 75 21 [16]

櫥 橱 chú 75 19 [17]
機 机 jī 75 16 [17]

樞 枢 shū 75 15 [17]
櫃 柜 guì 75 18 [17]

楓 枫 fēng 75 13 [17]
欄 栏 lán 75 21 [16]

稜	積	稈	種
棱 léng	积 jī	秆 gǎn	种 zhǒng zhòng
115 13 [16]	115 16 [18]	115 12 [18]	115 14 [52]
穢	穫	穩	稱
秽 huì	获 huò	稳 wěn	称 chēng chèn
115 18 [18]	115 19 [65]	115 19 [18]	115 14 [50]

釋
释 shì
·165 20 [18]

糧	糰
粮 liáng	团 tuán
119 18 [53]	119 20 [37]

牠	犧
它 tā	牺 xī
93 7 [70]	93 21 [52]

壯	妝	狀	將	牆
壮 zhuàng	妆 zhuāng	状 zhuàng	将 jiāng jiàng	墙 qiáng
33 7 [3]	38 7 [3]	94 8 [3]	41 11 [3]	90 17 [10]

規
规 guī
147 11 [48]

丁	頂 頂 dǐng 181 11 [19]					
工	項 项 xiàng 181 12 [48]					
王	珊 珊 shān 96 9 [19]	現 现 xiàn 96 11 [48]	瑪 玛 mǎ 96 14 [49]	瓏 珑 lóng 96 20 [19]	環 环 huán 96 17 [47]	瓊 琼 qióng 96 18 [19]
矢	矯 矫 jiǎo jiáo 111 17 [20]					
缶	罎 坛 tán 121 22 [10]	罈 坛 tán 121 18 [10]				

於
于 yú
70 8 [39]

視
視 shì
147 11 [20]

祇
只 zhǐ
112 8 [68]

祕
秘 mì
113 10 [18]

祐
佑 yòu
113 10 [9]

禍
祸 huò
113 14 [20]

禪
禅 chán shàn
113 17 [20]

禮
礼 lǐ
113 18 [20]

禱
祷 dǎo
113 18 [20]

補
补 bǔ
145 12 [20]

裡
里 li lǐ
145 12 [75]

褲
裤 kù
145 15 [20]

襯
衬 chèn
145 21 [43]

複
复 fù
145 14 [76]

襖
袄 ǎo
145 18 [20]

襪
袜 wà
145 20 [45]

襬
摆 bǎi
145 20 [12]

糸□

糾	紀	紅	級	納	純
纠 jiū	纪 jì	红 hóng gōng	级 jí	纳 nà	纯 chún
120 8 [15]	120 9 [15]	120 9 [15]	120 10 [49]	120 10 [15]	120 10 [42]

紙	紐	組	細	紳	緬
纸 zhǐ	纽 niǔ	组 zǔ	细 xì	绅 shēn	缅 miǎn
120 10 [15]	120 10 [53]	120 11 [15]	120 11 [15]	120 11 [52]	120 15 [15]

練	絲	繩	繡
练 liàn	丝 sī	绳 shéng	绣 xiù
120 15 [15]	120 12 [73]	120 19 [15]	120 19 [15]

糸□

維	縱	綁	鄉
维 wéi	纵 zòng	绑 bǎng	乡 xiāng
120 14 [15]	120 17 [15]	120 13 [54]	163 12 [38]

繳	緻	緞	綴
缴 jiǎo	致 zhì	缎 duàn	缀 zhuì
120 19 [51]	133 15 [51]	120 15 [55]	120 14 [15]

糸□

纏
缠 chán
120 21 [15]

糸□

約	絨	織	纖
约 yuē yāo	绒 róng	织 zhī	纤 xiān
120 9 [50]	120 12 [15]	120 18 [15]	120 23 [15]

糸□

繼	縫
继 jì	缝 féng fèng
120 20 [15]	120 17 [15]

糸□

綢	綱	網	納
绸 chóu	纲 gāng	网 wǎng	纳 nà
120 14 [15]	120 14 [15]	120 14 [36]	120 10 [15]

紋	絞	紡	統	締	縴
纹 wén	绞 jiǎo	纺 fǎng	统 tǒng	缔 dì	纤 qiàn
120 10 [15]	120 12 [15]	120 10 [44]	120 11 [15]	120 15 [15]	120 17 [15]
綜	縮	編	綿	線	總
综 zōng zèng	缩 suō	编 biān	绵 mián	线 xiàn	总 zǒng
120 14 [15]	120 17 [15]	120 15 [15]	120 14 [15]	120 15 [15]	120 17 [58]
紗	結	緒	繞	績	續
纱 shā	结 jié jiē	绪 xù	绕 rào rǎo	绩 jī	续 xù
120 10 [44]	120 12 [15]	120 14 [15]	120 18 [15]	120 17 [15]	120 21 [15]
縛	縷	緯	繡	繃	
缚 fù	缕 lǚ	纬 wěi	绣 xiù	绷 bēng bèng běng	
120 16 [15]	120 17 [15]	120 15 [15]	120 19 [15]	120 17 [15]	
緣	綠	絲	綫		
缘 yuán	绿 lǜ lù	丝 sī	线 xiàn		
120 15 [15]	120 14 [15]	120 12 [73]	120 14 [15]		
絹	緝	紹	經	緬	
绢 juàn	缉 jī qī	绍 shào	经 jīng jìng	缅 miǎn	
120 13 [15]	120 15 [15]	120 11 [56]	120 13 [15]	120 15 [15]	
緩	綉				
缓 huǎn	锈 xiù				
120 15 [15]	120 13 [15]				
終	絡	絶	纔		
终 zhōng	络 luò	绝 jué	才 cái		
120 11 [15]	120 12 [15]	120 12 [15]	120 23 [38]		
紛	給	繪			
纷 fēn	给 gěi jǐ	绘 huì			
120 10 [15]	120 12 [15]	120 19 [15]			
綴					
缀 zhuì					
120 14 [15]					

針
针zhēn
167 10 [21]

釘
钉dīng dìng
167 10 [21]

鈍
钝dùn
167 12 [21]

鈣
钙gài
167 12 [21]

欽
钦qīn
76 12 [50]

鈾
铀yóu
167 13 [21]

鉗
钳qián
167 13 [21]

鈕
钮niǔ
167 12 [21]

銀
银yín
167 14 [53]

敘
叙xù
66 11 [31]

敍
叙xù
66 11 [31]

鍊
链liàn
167 17 [21]

鋪
铺pū pù
167 15 [21]

錘
锤chuí
167 17 [21]

鍾
钟zhōng
167 17 [21]

鏽
锈xiù
167 21 [21]

鍬
锹qiāo
167 17 [21]

鋤
锄chú
167 15 [21]

鍛
锻duàn
167 17 [21]

鋸
锯jù
167 16 [21]

鐮
镰lián
167 21 [21]

鍍
镀dù
167 17 [21]

鏟
铲chǎn
167 19 [21]

釣
钓diào
167 11 [21]

鉤
钩gōu
167 13 [21]

鉋
刨bào
167 13 [42]

鐵
铁tiě
167 21 [46]

鍵
键jiàn
167 17 [21]

鏈
链liàn
167 19 [21]

銅
铜tóng
167 14 [21]

鋼
钢gāng gàng
167 16 [21]

鍋
锅guō
167 17 [21]

日

鋅	鎊	鏡	鐘	鑲	錦
锌 xīn	镑 bàng	镜 jìng	钟 zhōng	镶 xiāng	锦 jǐn
167 15 [21]	167 18 [21]	167 19 [21]	167 20 [21]	167 25 [21]	167 16 [21]

鈔	鎮	錶	鑄	鏽	
钞 chāo	镇 zhèn	表 biǎo	铸 zhù	锈 xiù	
167 12 [21]	167 18 [21]	167 16 [67]	167 22 [21]	167 21 [21]	

錄	錢				
录 lù	钱 qián				
167 16 [77]	167 16 [21]				

銳	鎂	銷	鎖	錯	
锐 ruì	镁 měi	销 xiāo	锁 suǒ	错 cuò	
167 15 [21]	167 17 [21]	167 15 [21]	167 18 [21]	167 16 [21]	

鉛	鋁	鍋	錫	鑼	鏢
铅 qiān	铝 lǚ	锅 guō	锡 xī	锣 luó	镖 biāo
167 13 [21]	167 15 [21]	167 17 [21]	167 16 [21]	167 27 [21]	167 19 [21]

銘	鋒	銹			
铭 míng	锋 fēng	锈 xiù			
167 14 [21]	167 15 [21]	167 15 [21]			

鈴	鑰				
铃 líng	钥 yuè yào				
167 13 [21]	167 25 [21]				

鑑	鑽				
鉴 jiàn	钻 zuān zuàn				
167 22 [66]	167 27 [56]				

口

哑 哑 yǎ yā
30 11 [24]

嗎 吗 ma má mǎ
30 13 [24]

嘯 啸 xiào
30 16 [24]

喲 哟 yo yō
30 12 [24]

噸 吨 dūn
30 16 [42]

嚨 咙 lóng
30 19 [24]

嚇 吓 hè xià
30 17 [47]

嗚 呜 wū
30 13 [24]

鳴 鸣 míng
196 14 [54]

噢 噢 ō
30 16 [23]

噴 喷 pēn pèn
30 15 [23]

嘍 喽 lóu lou
30 14 [23]

嘯 啸 xiào
30 16 [24]

噹 当 dāng
30 16 [59]

嘩 哗 huá huā
30 15 [23]

嘆 叹 tàn
30 14 [24]

嘛 苏 sū
30 23 [65]

嚥 咽 yàn yān yè
30 19 [24]

噁 恶 ě wù
30 15 [72]

唸 念 niàn
30 11 [59]

喚 唤 huàn
30 12 [23]

囉 罗 luō
30 22 [68]

嘮 唠 láo
30 15 [23]

囑 嘱 zhǔ
30 24 [24]

嘰 叽 jī
30 15 [24]

嗎 吗 ma má mǎ
30 13 [24]

嗚 呜 wū
30 13 [24]

鳴 鸣 míng
196 14 [54]

吥 叫 jiào
30 7 [24]

嘔 呕 ǒu
30 14 [52]

日 目 貝 田

時 时 shí 72 10 [43]	曉 晓 xiǎo 72 16 [25]	暉 晖 huī 72 13 [25]	曠 旷 kuàng 72 19 [25]	曬 晒 shài 72 23 [25]

睜 睁 zhēng 109 13 [25]	瞭 了 liǎo liào 109 17 [39]	瞞 瞒 mán 109 16 [25]	矇 蒙 méng 109 19 [64]	眯 眯 mī mī 109 15 [25]	矚 瞩 zhǔ 109 25 [25]

財 财 cái 154 10 [28]	敗 败 bài 66 11 [28]	則 则 zé 18 9 [42]

貼 贴 tiē 154 12 [28]	賠 赔 péi 154 15 [28]	賭 赌 dǔ 154 15 [28]	賤 贱 jiàn 154 15 [43]	贖 赎 shú 154 22 [28]

贈 赠 zèng 154 19 [28]	購 购 gòu 154 17 [28]	賺 赚 zhuàn zuàn 154 17 [28]

賜 赐 cì 154 15 [28]	賬 账 帐 zhàng 154 15 [14]	貶 贬 biǎn 154 12 [28]	賂 赂 lù 154 13 [28]

販 贩 fàn 154 11 [28]	賄 贿 huì 154 13 [28]	賦 赋 fù 154 15 [43]	賊 贼 zéi 154 13 [43]

畊 耕 gēng 102 9 [18]	疇 畴 chóu 102 19 [25]	暢 畅 chàng 72 14 [49]

耳 歹 石 足 酉

耳

恥	聰	聽	職	聯
耻 chǐ	聪 cōng	听 tīng	职 zhí	联 lián
61 10 [25]	128 17 [25]	128 22 [51]	128 18 [25]	128 17 [25]

歹

殘	殲
残 cán	歼 jiān
78 12 [26]	78 21 [26]

石

碩	碼	確	碌
硕 shuò	码 mǎ	确 què	碌 lù liù
112 14 [48]	112 15 [26]	112 15 [26]	112 13 [26]

磚	礎	礦	礙
砖 zhuān	础 chǔ	矿 kuàng	碍 ài
112 16 [46]	112 18 [57]	112 20 [26]	112 19 [26]

足

跡	蹤	踐
迹 jī	踪 zōng	践 jiàn
157 13 [34]	157 18 [26]	157 15 [43]

躊	蹟	踴	躍
踌 chóu	迹 jī	踊 yǒng	跃 yuè
157 21 [26]	157 18 [34]	157 16 [26]	157 21 [26]

酉

醜	醞	釀
丑 chǒu	酝 yùn	酿 niàng niáng
164 17 [39]	164 17 [25]	164 24 [25]

車

軋	軒	軌	軟	斬
轧 yà zhá gá	轩 xuān	轨 guǐ	软 ruǎn	斩 zhǎn
159 8 [19]	159 10 [19]	159 9 [19]	159 11 [50]	69 11 [51]

軸	輔	輛	轍
轴 zhóu	辅 fǔ	辆 liàng	辙 zhé
159 12 [19]	159 14 [19]	159 15 [19]	159 18 [51]

較	轄	轉
较 jiào	辖 xiá	转 zhuǎn zhuàn
159 13 [19]	159 17 [19]	159 18 [46]

輯	輻	輕	轎	輪	輸
辑 jí	辐 fú	轻 qīng	轿 jiào	轮 lún	输 shū
159 16 [19]	159 16 [19]	159 14 [19]	159 19 [19]	159 15 [19]	159 16 [19]

卓

幹	韓
干 gàn	韩 hán
51 13 [39]	178 17 [29]

幸

執	報	親
执 zhí	报 bào	亲 qīn qìng
32 11 [13]	32 12 [13]	147 16 [74]

幸

辦	辮	辯
办 bàn	辫 biàn	辩 biàn
160 16 [1]	120 20 [54]	160 21 [37]

虫

螞	蝦	蟻	蠅	蟬	蠟
蚂 mǎ mà	虾 xiā	蚁 yǐ	蝇 yíng	蝉 chán	蜡 là
142 16 [29]	142 15 [29]	142 19 [29]	142 19 [29]	142 18 [29]	142 21 [29]

月

腫
肿 zhǒng
130 13 [52]

腳
脚 jiǎo
130 13 [54]

鵬
鹏 péng
196 19 [54]

勝
胜 shèng
19 12 [27]

騰
腾 téng tēng
187 20 [27]

臟
脏 zàng
130 22 [27]

膽
胆 dǎn
130 17 [27]

脹
胀 zhàng
130 12 [43]

腸
肠 cháng
130 13 [49]

臉
脸 liǎn
130 17 [27]

膠
胶 jiāo
130 15 [27]

腦
脑 nǎo
130 13 [27]

臘
腊 là xī
130 19 [27]

脈
脉 mài mò
130 10 [27]

膩
腻 nì
130 16 [27]

舟

艙
舱 cāng
137 16 [56]

艦
舰 jiàn
137 20 [28]

身

軀
躯 qū
158 18 [28]

自

帥
帅 shuài
50 9 [1]

師
师 shī
50 10 [1]

血

蠛
蔑 miè
143 21 [64]

頤 頤 yí 181 16 [48]				
臥 卧 wò 131 8 [41]	臨 临 lín 131 17 [1]			
歐 欧 ōu 76 15 [28]	毆 殴 ōu 79 15 [28]	鷗 鸥 ōu 196 22 [28]		
飪 饪 rèn 184 12 [20]	飲 饮 yǐn yìn 184 12 [20]	蝕 蚀 shí 142 14 [52]	餓 饿 è 184 15 [43]	
餃 饺 jiǎo 184 14 [20]	館 馆 guǎn 184 16 [20]	餅 饼 bǐng 184 14 [20]	饒 饶 ráo 184 20 [20]	饋 馈 kuì 184 20 [20]
餵 喂 wèi 184 17 [23]	饅 馒 mán 184 19 [20]			
餘 馀余 yú 184 15 [59]	餡 馅 xiàn 184 16 [20]	飾 饰 shì 184 13 [20]	饞 馋 chán 184 25 [20]	
飯 饭 fàn 184 12 [20]	飼 饲 sì 184 13 [20]	飽 饱 bǎo 184 13 [20]	饑 饥 jī 184 20 [20]	

訂 訂 訂 訂 訂 訂

計 计 jì 149 9 [4]	訂 订 dìng 149 9 [4]	記 记 jì 149 10 [49]	訣 诀 jué 149 11 [46]	訝 讶 yà 149 11 [4]	詛 诅 zǔ 149 12 [53]
許 许 xǔ 149 11 [4]	詐 诈 zhà 149 12 [50]	託 托 tuō 149 10 [13]	証 证 zhèng 149 12 [4]	評 评 píng 149 12 [47]	誣 诬 wū 149 14 [4]

訓 训 xùn 149 10 [4]	訛 讹 é 149 11 [42]	誰 谁 shuí shéi 149 15 [55]	誹 诽 fěi 149 15 [4]	謝 谢 xiè 149 17 [4]

訴 诉 sù 149 12 [4]	詭 诡 guǐ 149 13 [4]

討 讨 tǎo 149 10 [4]	訊 讯 xùn 149 10 [4]	詞 词 cí 149 12 [49]	詢 询 xún 149 13 [4]

試 试 shì 149 13 [4]	誡 诫 jiè 149 14 [43]	誠 诚 chéng 149 13 [4]	識 识 shí zhì 149 19 [4]	譏 讥 jī 149 19 [48]

謎 谜 mí mèi 149 17 [4]	誕 诞 dàn 149 15 [4]	譴 谴 qiǎn 149 21 [4]

調 调 tiáo diào 149 15 [4]	諷 讽 fěng 149 16 [4]

註 注 zhù 149 12 [44]	訪 访 fǎng 149 11 [44]	該 该 gāi 149 13 [4]	諒 谅 liàng 149 15 [54]	謗 谤 bàng 149 17 [4]	讓 让 ràng 149 24 [4]
詠 咏 yǒng 149 12 [23]	詫 诧 chà 149 13 [4]	誼 谊 yì 149 15 [4]	談 谈 tán 149 15 [4]	誇 夸 kuā 149 13 [67]	
詩 诗 shī 149 13 [4]	諸 诸 zhū 149 15 [4]	誌 志 zhì 149 14 [72]	請 请 qǐng 149 15 [4]	讀 读 dú dòu 149 22 [4]	
説 说 shuō shuì 149 14 [4]	詳 详 xiáng 149 13 [4]	譜 谱 pǔ 149 19 [4]	謙 谦 qiān 149 17 [4]	議 议 yì 149 20 [4]	護 护 hù 149 21 [11]
謀 谋 móu 149 16 [4]	諾 诺 nuò 149 16 [4]	謊 谎 huǎng 149 17 [4]	譁 哗 huá 149 19 [23]	謹 谨 jǐn 149 18 [4]	講 讲 jiǎng 149 17 [57]
誤 误 wù 149 14 [4]	課 课 kè 149 15 [4]	謂 谓 wèi 149 16 [4]	譯 译 yì 149 20 [4]	譚 谭 tán 149 19 [4]	
設 设 shè 149 11 [55]	認 认 rèn 149 14 [46]	語 语 yǔ 149 14 [4]	誦 诵 sòng 149 14 [4]	話 话 huà 149 13 [4]	誘 诱 yòu 149 14 [4]
詭 诡 guǐ 149 13 [4]	謠 谣 yáo 149 17 [4]	讒 谗 chán 149 24 [4]			
詮 诠 quán 149 13 [4]	診 诊 zhěn 149 13 [4]	論 论 lùn lún 149 15 [4]	訟 讼 sòng 149 11 [4]	誒 欸 ēi éi ěi èi ǎ 149 14 [50]	
諮 咨 zī 149 16 [78]	證 证 zhèng 149 19 [4]	諧 谐 xié 149 16 [4]	謬 谬 miù 149 18 [4]	讚 赞 zàn 154 26 [77]	

馬　魚

馬

駄	馳	駛
驮 tuó duò	驰 chí	驶 shǐ
187 13 [28]	187 13 [28]	187 15 [57]

駐	駭	駝	騎	騙	駿
驻 zhù	骇 hài	驼 tuó	骑 qí	骗 piàn	骏 jùn
187 15 [28]	187 16 [28]	187 15 [28]	187 18 [28]	187 19 [28]	187 17 [28]

駱	驕	騾	騷
骆 luò	骄 jiāo	骡 luó	骚 sāo
187 16 [56]	187 22 [28]	187 21 [28]	187 20 [28]

駁	驗	驟
驳 bó	验 yàn	骤 zhòu
187 14 [28]	187 23 [28]	187 24 [28]

驢	驅
驴 lǘ	驱 qū
187 25 [44]	187 21 [52]

魚

鮮	穌	鯨	鮑	觸
鲜 xiān xiǎn	稣 sū	鲸 jīng	鲍 bào	触 chù
195 17 [29]	115 16 [29]	195 19 [29]	195 16 [50]	148 20 [29]

莫

骨

豐

艱 艰 jiān 138 17 [53]	**歎** 叹 tàn 76 15 [24]	**難** 难 nán nàn 172 19 [55]
體 体 tǐ tī 188 23 [9]	**髒** 脏 zāng 188 23 [27]	**髓** 髓 suǐ 188 23 [31]
艶 艳 yàn 139 24 [30]	**豔** 艳 yàn 151 28 [30]	**豔** 艳 yàn 151 27 [30]

申 虫 亩	暢 畅 chàng 72 14 [49]	蝦 虾 xiā 142 15 [29]	畞 亩 mǔ 102 10 [62]		
光 皐 雇	輝 辉 huī 159 15 [18]	歸 归 guī 77 18 [1]	顧 顾 gù 181 21 [48]		
音 竞 音 亲 彦	韻 韵 yùn 180 19 [30]	競 竞 jìng 117 20 [62]	龍 龙 lóng 212 16 [33]	親 亲 qīn qìng 147 16 [74]	顔 颜 yán 181 18 [48]
屯 柬 皮	頓 顿 dùn 181 13 [48]	賴 赖 lài 154 16 [30]	頗 颇 pō 181 14 [48]		
真 夾 麥	顛 颠 diān 181 19 [48]	頰 颊 jiá 181 16 [48]	麵 面 miàn 199 20 [39]	麪 面 miàn 199 15 [39]	
売 棠 青 隶	殼 壳 ké qiào 79 12 [71]	穀 谷 gǔ 150 14 [59]	靜 静 jìng 174 16 [37]	隸 隶 lì 171 17 [77]	
雀 乡	鶴 鹤 hè 196 21 [30]	鄉 乡 xiāng 163 12 [38]			
步 虧 鹵 齒	頻 频 pín 181 16 [48]	虧 亏 kuī 141 17 [60]	鹹 咸 xián 197 20 [36]	齡 龄 líng 211 20 [30]	
昔 革	鵲 鹊 què 196 19 [54]	靭 韧 rèn 177 12 [49]			

頑 顽 wán 181 13 [48]	頭 头 tóu tou 181 16 [74]	門 门 mén 169 8 [1]	鬥 斗 dòu 191 10 [1]
預 预 yù 181 13 [48]	務 务 wù 19 11 [76]	鴉 鸦 yā 196 15 [19]	豬 猪 zhū 152 15 [14]
號 号 hào háo 141 13 [68]	鴨 鸭 yā 196 16 [54]	顆 颗 kē 181 17 [48]	飄 飘 piāo 182 20 [57]
縣 县 xiàn 120 16 [77]	縣 县 xiàn 120 16 [77]	願 愿 yuàn 181 19 [32]	
貓 猫 māo máo 153 16 [14]	鵝 鹅 é 196 18 [31]	鷄 鸡 jī 196 21 [54]	
夠 够 gòu 36 11 [57]	觸 触 chù 148 20 [29]		
鴿 鸽 gē 196 17 [54]	領 领 lǐng 181 14 [48]	敘 叙 xù 66 11 [31]	敍 叙 xù 66 11 [31]
頌 颂 sòng 181 13 [48]	頒 颁 bān 181 13 [48]	殺 杀 shā 79 11 [69]	

豆 冂 冓

矛 牙 豕

甲 果 票

县 県 原

我 奚

角

令 余

分 杀

厂 尸 广

厂

歷	曆	厲	壓	厭	脣
历 lì	历 lì	厉 lì	压 yā yà	厌 yàn	唇 chún
77 16 [32]	72 16 [32]	27 15 [32]	32 17 [32]	27 14 [32]	130 11 [78]

尸

層	屬	屢	屍	屜	屆
层 céng	属 shǔ zhǔ	屡 lǚ	尸 shī	屉 tì	届 jiè
44 15 [32]	44 21 [32]	44 14 [32]	44 9 [39]	44 11 [32]	44 8 [32]

广

庫
库 kù
53 10 [33]

廂	廁	廟	廚
厢 xiāng	厕 cè sī	庙 miào	厨 chú
53 12 [32]	53 12 [32]	53 15 [33]	53 15 [32]

廠	龐	廳
厂 chǎng	庞 páng	厅 tīng
53 15 [39]	53 19 [33]	53 25 [32]

廣	廈	廬
广 guǎng	厦 shà xià	庐 lú
53 15 [38]	53 13 [32]	53 19 [33]

廢	麼	應	鷹	慶	塵
废 fèi	么 me	应 yīng yìng	鹰 yīng	庆 qìng	尘 chén
53 15 [33]	200 14 [77]	61 17 [33]	196 24 [33]	61 15 [33]	32 14 [75]

疒 虍 产

痹	瘓	療			
痹 bì	痪 huàn	疗 liáo			
104 13 [33]	104 14 [33]	104 17 [33]			
瘉	瘡	癒	癢		
愈 yù	疮 chuāng	愈 yù	痒 yǎng		
104 14 [72]	104 15 [33]	104 18 [72]	104 20 [33]		
癡	癮	癱			
痴 chī	瘾 yǐn	瘫 tān			
104 19 [33]	104 22 [33]	104 24 [33]			
瘧	瘋				
疟 nüè yào	疯 fēng				
104 14 [33]	104 14 [33]				
慮	膚	虜	處	盧	廬
虑 lù	肤 fū	虏 lǔ	处 chǔ chù	卢 lú	庐 lú
61 15 [33]	130 15 [27]	141 13 [33]	141 11 [35]	108 16 [66]	53 19 [33]
彥	產				
彦 yàn	产 chǎn				
59 9 [62]	100 11 [62]				

辶

連
连 lián
162 11 [34]

進　　遊　　遜
进 jìn　游 yóu　逊 xùn
162 12 [34]　162 13 [7]　162 14 [34]

這　　適　　遠　　達　　違　　遺
这 zhè zhèi　适 shì　远 yuǎn　达 dá　违 wéi　遗 yí wèi
162 11 [34]　162 15 [34]　162 14 [34]　162 13 [34]　162 13 [34]　162 16 [34]

遼　　邊　　邁　　遙
辽 liáo　边 biān bian　迈 mài　遥 yáo
162 16 [34]　162 19 [34]　162 17 [34]　162 14 [34]

還　　邏　　遷　　過
还 hái huán　逻 luó　迁 qiān　过 guò guo guō
162 17 [34]　162 23 [34]　162 15 [34]　162 13 [34]

運　　選　　蓮
运 yùn　选 xuǎn　莲 lián
162 13 [34]　162 16 [34]　140 15 [65]

遞　　遲　　週　　迴
递 dì　迟 chí　周 zhōu　回 huí
162 14 [34]　162 16 [34]　162 12 [36]　162 10 [37]

走

趙　　趕　　趨
赵 zhào　赶 gǎn　趋 qū
156 14 [35]　156 14 [35]　156 17 [35]

...

題　　翹　　颱　　麵　　麪
题 tí　翘 qiào qiáo　台 tái　面 miàn　面 miàn
181 18 [35]　124 18 [35]　182 14 [78]　199 20 [39]　199 15 [39]

直　　置　　眞
直 zhí　置 zhì　真 zhēn
24 8 [67]　122 13 [68]　109 10 [67]

貳
贰 èr
154 12 [36]

幾
几 jǐ
52 12 [39]

載
载 zāi zài
159 13 [36]

飛
飞 fēi
183 9 [39]

馬
马 mǎ
187 10 [73]

鳥
鸟 niǎo
196 11 [58]

烏
乌 wū
86 10 [58]

區 匯
区 qū ōu   汇 huì
23 11 [37]   22 13 [57]

齒
齿 chǐ
211 15 [66]

岡 風 鳳
冈 gāng   风 fēng   凤 fèng
46 8 [36]   182 9 [36]   196 14 [36]

門 閃 閉 閑 開 閏
门 mén   闪 shǎn   闭 bì   闲 xián   开 kāi kai   闰 rùn
169 8 [1]   169 10 [36]   169 11 [36]   169 12 [36]   169 12 [39]   169 12 [36]

問 間 閒 聞 閘 悶
问 wèn   间 jiān jiàn   闲 xián   闻 wén   闸 zhá   闷 mēn mèr
30 11 [36]   169 12 [36]   169 12 [36]   128 14 [36]   169 13 [36]   61 12 [36]

閨 閡 閣 閱 闡 闖
闺 guī   阂 hé   阁 gé   阅 yuè   阐 chǎn   闯 chuǎng
169 14 [36]   169 14 [36]   169 14 [78]   169 15 [36]   169 20 [36]   169 18 [36]

闊 閥 關 闆 闢
阔 kuò   阀 fá   关 guān   板 bǎn   辟 pì bì
169 17 [36]   169 14 [36]   169 19 [58]   169 17 [17]   169 21 [54]

鬥 鬧
斗 dòu   闹 nào
191 10 [1]   191 15 [36]

兩 為 歲 蘭 繭
两 liǎng   为 wéi wèi   岁 suì   兰 lán   茧 jiǎn
11 8 [60]   86 9 [38]   77 13 [76]   140 21 [58]   120 19 [65]

■□ ▮ ⊞ ■

園	圍	圓	國	圖	團
园 yuán	围 wéi	圆 yuán	国 guó	图 tú	团 tuán
31 13 [37]	31 12 [37]	31 13 [37]	31 11 [37]	31 14 [37]	31 14 [37]

囂	蠶
嚣 xiāo	蚕 cán
30 21 [68]	142 24 [79]

術	衔	衝	衛
术 shù zhú	衔 xián	冲 chòng	卫 wèi
144 11 [41]	167 14 [10]	144 15 [52]	144 15 [39]

辮	辯	辦
辫 biàn	辩 biàn	办 bàn
120 20 [54]	160 21 [37]	160 16 [1]

務	殼	穀	殺	隸	歸
务 wù	壳 ké qiào	谷 gǔ	杀 shā	隶 lì	归 guī
19 11 [76]	79 12 [71]	150 14 [59]	79 11 [69]	171 17 [77]	77 18 [1]

鬆	鬚	鬍
松 sōng	须 xū	胡 hú
190 18 [16]	190 22 [1]	190 19 [53]

艷	豔	豐艶
艳 yàn	艳 yàn	艳 yàn
139 24 [30]	151 28 [30]	151 27 [30]

夾	來	氷
夹 jiā jiá gā	来 lái lai	冰 bīng
37 7 [38]	9 8 [38]	85 5 [3]

車	東	肅	甚
车 chē jū	东 dōng	肃 sù	什 shén shèn
159 7 [38]	75 8 [38]	129 13 [69]	99 9 [43]

弔	亞	兩	冊
吊 diào	亚 yà	两 liǎng	册 cè
57 4 [68]	7 8 [39]	11 8 [60]	12 5 [39]

■ 、 丶 ノ 丨 卜 ㇗ 刂

、

祕	跡	嚇	掛
秘 mì	迹 jī	吓 hè xià	挂 guà
113 10 [18]	157 13 [34]	30 17 [47]	64 11 [55]

恥	減	滅	鍬
耻 chǐ	减 jiǎn	灭 miè	锹 qiāo
61 10 [25]	0 12 [43]	85 13 [60]	167 17 [21]

□少 → A20
□代 → A20
□戈 → A20
□犬 → A21
□甫 → A24

ノ

冰	鍬
冰 bīng	锹 qiāo
85 5 [3]	167 17 [21]

丨

訓	糾
训 xùn	纠 jiū
149 10 [4]	120 8 [15]

卜

掛
挂 guà
64 11 [55]

㇗

誹
诽 fěi
149 15 [4]

刂

刪	剝
删 shān	剥 bāo bō
18 7 [31]	18 10 [42]

剛	劇	劉	測	側
刚 gāng	剧 jù	刘 liú	测 cè	侧 cè
18 10 [42]	18 15 [42]	18 15 [42]	85 12 [42]	9 11 [9]

劃	劑	別	則	廁
划 huà huá	剂 jì	别 bié biè	则 zé	厕 cè si
18 14 [42]	18 16 [42]	18 7 [42]	18 9 [42]	53 12 [32]

劍	創
剑 jiàn	创 chuàng chuāng
18 15 [42]	18 12 [42]

■ ㄴ ㄴ 屯 也 丁 A19

軋	亂
轧 yà zhá gá	乱 luàn
159 8 [19]	5 13 [26]

訛
讹 é
149 11 [42]

純	鈍
纯 chún	钝 dùn
120 10 [42]	167 12 [21]

牠	馳
它 tā	驰 chí
93 7 [70]	187 13 [28]

術	衘	衝	衛	虧
术 shù zhú	衔 xián	冲 chòng	卫 wèi	亏 kuī
144 11 [41]	167 14 [10]	144 15 [52]	144 15 [39]	141 17 [60]

十　寸　少　弋　戈

十

針	計
针 zhēn	计 jì
167 10 [21]	149 9 [4]

寸

討	謝	樹	對	廚	財
讨 tǎo	谢 xiè	树 shù	对 duì	厨 chú	财 cái
149 10 [4]	149 17 [4]	75 16 [17]	41 14 [1]	53 15 [32]	154 10 [28]

少

鈔	紗
钞 chāo	纱 shā
167 12 [21]	120 10 [44]

弋

試	賦	膩	貳
试 shì	赋 fù	腻 nì	贰 èr
149 13 [4]	154 15 [43]	130 16 [27]	154 12 [36]

戈

戰	戲	餓
战 zhàn	戏 xì	饿 è
62 16 [30]	62 17 [1]	184 15 [43]

誡	絨	賊
诫 jiè	绒 róng	贼 zéi
149 14 [43]	120 12 [15]	154 13 [43]

誠	滅	減	鹹
诚 chéng	灭 miè	减 jiǎn	咸 xián
149 13 [4]	85 13 [60]	0 12 [43]	197 20 [36]

識	織	鐵	殲
识 shí zhì	织 zhī	铁 tiě	歼 jiān
149 19 [4]	120 18 [15]	167 21 [46]	78 21 [26]

註 注 zhù 149 12 [44]	駐 驻 zhù 187 15 [28]		
較 较 jiào 159 13 [19]	餃 饺 jiǎo 184 14 [20]	絞 绞 jiǎo 120 12 [15]	紋 纹 wén 120 10 [15]
訪 访 fǎng 149 11 [44]	紡 纺 fǎng 120 10 [44]		
該 该 gāi 149 13 [4]	駭 骇 hài 187 16 [28]		
涼 凉 liáng liàng 15 11 [54]	諒 谅 liàng 149 15 [54]	鯨 鲸 jīng 195 19 [29]	

羊　并

羊	**詳** 详 xiáng 149 13 [4]	**鮮** 鲜 xiān xiǎn 195 17 [29]
并	**餅** 饼 bǐng 184 14 [20]	**併** 并 bìng 9 8 [74]

臥 臥 wò 131 8 [41]	夾 夹 jiā jiá gā 37 7 [38]	來 来 lái lai 9 8 [38]		
狹 狭 xiá 94 10 [46]	俠 侠 xiá 9 9 [9]	挾 挟 xié 64 10 [13]	峽 峡 xiá 46 10 [14]	陝 陕 shǎn 170 10 [46]
狀 状 zhuàng 94 8 [3]	獻 献 xiàn 94 20 [46]	獄 狱 yù 94 14 [46]	獸 兽 shòu 94 19 [58]	馱 驮 tuó duò 187 13 [28]
鋤 锄 chú 167 15 [21]	動 动 dòng 19 11 [46]	勁 劲 jìn jìng 19 9 [46]	勵 励 lì 19 17 [31]	勸 劝 quàn 19 20 [1]
執 执 zhí 32 11 [13]	軌 轨 guǐ 159 9 [19]			
決 决 jué 15 7 [46]	訣 诀 jué 149 11 [46]			

丁 干 几 長 壬 氏

丁	訂 订 dìng 149 9 [4]	釘 钉 dīng dìng 167 10 [21]			
干	軒 轩 xuān **159 10 [19]**	汙 污 wū 85 6 [7]			
几	凱 凯 kǎi 16 12 [48]	汎 泛 fàn 85 6 [48]			
長	帳 帐 zhàng 50 11 [14]	張 张 zhāng 57 11 [43]	脹 胀 zhàng 130 12 [43]	賬 账 帐 zhàng 154 15 [14]	漲 涨 zhǎng zhàng 85 14 [7]
壬	餁 饪 rèn 184 12 [20]	姙 妊 rèn 38 9 [48]			
氏	祇 只 zhǐ 112 8 [68]	紙 纸 zhǐ 120 10 [15]			

靭	靭	
韧 rèn	韧 rèn	
178 12 [49]	177 12 [49]	

紀	記	
纪 jì	记 jì	
120 9 [15]	149 10 [49]	

詞	飼	
词 cí	饲 sì	
149 12 [49]	184 13 [20]	

釣	約	喲
钓 diào	约 yuē yāo	哟 yo yō
167 11 [21]	120 9 [50]	30 12 [24]

鉋	飽	
刨 bào	饱 bǎo	
167 13 [42]	184 13 [20]	

鉤	夠	詢
钩 gōu	够 gòu	询 xún
167 13 [21]	36 11 [57]	149 13 [4]

欠 夂 反 斤 殳

欠

軟	欽	飲	歐
软 ruǎn	钦 qīn	饮 yǐn yìn	欧 ōu
159 11 [50]	76 12 [50]	184 12 [20]	76 15 [28]

款	歎	歡	畝
款 kuǎn	叹 tàn	欢 huān	亩 mǔ
76 11 [50]	76 15 [24]	76 22 [50]	102 10 [62]

夂

敗	敘	敵	數	
败 bài	叙 xù	敌 dí	数 shù shǔ shuò	
66 11 [28]	66 11 [31]	66 15 [26]	66 15 [51]	

倣	徵	徹	轍	敍
仿 fǎng	征 zhēng	彻 chè	辙 zhé	叙 xù
9 10 [8]	60 15 [10]	60 14 [10]	159 18 [51]	66 11 [31]

繳	緻	廠		
缴 jiǎo	致 zhì	厂 chǎng		
120 19 [51]	133 15 [51]	53 15 [39]		

反

販	飯
贩 fàn	饭 fàn
154 11 [28]	184 12 [20]

斤

斬	斷	漸	慚	訴
斩 zhǎn	断 duàn	渐 jiàn jiān	惭 cán	诉 sù
69 11 [51]	69 18 [51]	85 14 [51]	61 14 [2]	149 12 [4]

殳

設	殺	穀	殼	沒
设 shè	杀 shā	谷 gǔ	壳 ké qiào	没 méi mò
149 11 [55]	79 11 [69]	150 14 [59]	79 12 [71]	85 7 [6]

緞	鍛	澱	毆	蝦
缎 duàn	锻 duàn	淀 diàn	殴 ōu	虾 xiā
120 15 [55]	167 17 [21]	85 16 [5]	79 15 [28]	142 15 [29]

鋅	辭	辦	辯	辮	倖
锌 xīn	辞 cí	办 bàn	辩 biàn	辫 biàn	幸 xìng
167 15 [21]	160 19 [54]	160 16 [1]	160 21 [37]	120 20 [54]	9 10 [67]

瑪	馮	媽	嗎	螞	碼
玛 mǎ	冯 féng	妈 mā	吗 ma má mǎ	蚂 mǎ mà	码 mǎ
96 14 [49]	187 12 [3]	38 13 [49]	30 13 [24]	142 16 [29]	112 15 [26]

鴉	鴨	鳴	嗚		
鸦 yā	鸭 yā	鸣 míng	呜 wū		
196 15 [19]	196 16 [54]	196 14 [54]	30 13 [24]		

鵝	鶴	鴿	鵲	鷄	
鹅 é	鹤 hè	鸽 gē	鹊 què	鸡 jī	
196 18 [31]	196 21 [30]	196 17 [54]	196 19 [54]	196 21 [54]	

鴻	鵬	鷗			
鸿 hóng	鹏 péng	鸥 ōu			
196 17 [54]	196 19 [54]	196 22 [28]			

維	誰	進	確		
维 wéi	谁 shuí shéi	进 jìn	确 què		
120 14 [15]	149 15 [55]	162 12 [34]	112 15 [26]		

雖	雜	離	雞	難	
虽 suī	杂 zá	离 lí	鸡 jī	难 nán nàn	
172 17 [79]	172 18 [69]	172 19 [62]	172 18 [54]	172 19 [55]	

灘	攤				
滩 tān	摊 tān				
85 22 [7]	64 22 [55]				

占			
佔	貼	黏	點
占 zhàn zhān	贴 tiē	粘 zhān nián	点 diǎn
9 7 [66]	154 12 [28]	202 17 [18]	203 17 [72]

由	
鈾	軸
铀 yóu	轴 zhóu
167 13 [21]	159 12 [19]

甫		
鋪	輔	補
铺 pū pù	辅 fǔ	补 bǔ
167 15 [21]	159 14 [19]	145 12 [20]

見			
視	規	現	狽
视 shì	规 guī	现 xiàn	狈 bèi
147 11 [20]	147 11 [48]	96 11 [48]	94 10 [14]
親	襯	觀	
亲 qīn qìng	衬 chèn	观 guān guàn	
147 16 [74]	145 21 [43]	147 25 [48]	

且	
詛	組
诅 zǔ	组 zǔ
149 12 [53]	120 11 [15]

丑	
鈕	紐
钮 niǔ	纽 niǔ
167 12 [21]	120 10 [53]

鬥					
門	憫	潤	嫻	嫺	鬥
门 mén	悯 mǐn	润 rùn	娴 xián	娴 xián	斗 dòu
169 8 [1]	61 15 [49]	85 15 [7]	38 15 [22]	38 15 [22]	191 10 [1]
們	擱	攔	欄	爛	
们 men	搁 gē gé	拦 lán	栏 lán	烂 làn	問 → A
9 10 [9]	64 17 [49]	64 20 [11]	75 21 [16]	86 21 [3]	

頃	頂	項	頓	賴	偵
顷 qǐng	顶 dǐng	项 xiàng	顿 dùn	赖 lài	侦 zhēn
181 11 [48]	181 11 [19]	181 12 [48]	181 13 [48]	154 16 [30]	9 11 [8]

頰	頗	頤
颊 jiá	颇 pō	颐 yí
181 16 [48]	181 14 [48]	181 16 [48]

煩	順	傾	噸	懶
烦 fán	顺 shùn	倾 qīng	吨 dūn	懒 lǎn
86 13 [3]	181 12 [48]	9 13 [48]	30 16 [42]	61 19 [2]

頻	穎	顛	類
频 pín	颖 yǐng	颠 diān	类 lèi
181 16 [48]	115 16 [48]	181 19 [48]	181 19 [59]

額	顏	顫
额 é	颜 yán	颤 zhàn chàn
181 18 [48]	181 18 [48]	181 22 [48]

頑	頭	頸	預
顽 wán	头 tóu tou	颈 jǐng gěng	预 yù
181 13 [48]	181 16 [74]	181 16 [48]	181 13 [48]

顆	顯	題	籲
颗 kē	显 xiǎn	题 tí	吁 yù
181 17 [48]	181 23 [68]	181 18 [35]	118 32 [24]

須	頹	頌	頒	領
须 xū	颓 tuí	颂 sòng	颁 bān	领 lǐng
181 12 [1]	181 16 [48]	181 13 [48]	181 13 [48]	181 14 [48]

碩	頗	顏	願	顧
硕 shuò	颇 pō	颜 yán	愿 yuàn	顾 gù
112 14 [48]	181 14 [48]	181 18 [48]	181 19 [32]	181 21 [48]

頤
颐 yí
181 16 [48]

卩

卻 却 què 26 9 [54]	腳 脚 jiǎo 130 13 [54]	氾 泛 fàn 85 5 [48]

阝

郵 邮 yóu 163 12 [54]	鄉 乡 xiāng 163 12 [38]	綁 绑 bǎng 120 13 [54]	擲 掷 zhì zhī 64 18 [54]
郤 隙 xì 170 10 [22]	鄰 邻 lín 163 15 [31]	鄭 郑 zhèng 163 15 [54]	鄧 邓 dèng 163 15 [54]

艮

銀 银 yín 167 14 [53]	艱 艰 jiān 138 17 [53]

鬼

塊 块 kuài 32 13 [10]	醜 丑 chǒu 164 17 [39]

風

楓 枫 fēng 75 13 [17]	諷 讽 fěng 149 16 [4]	飄 飘 piāo 182 20 [57]

冊

柵 栅 zhà shān 75 9 [17]	珊 珊 shān 96 9 [19]

區

樞 枢 shū 75 15 [17]	摳 抠 kōu 64 14 [13]	嘔 呕 ǒu 30 14 [52]	驅 驱 qū 187 21 [52]

令

各

鈴	齡		
铃 líng	龄 líng		
167 13 [21]	211 20 [30]		

絡	駱	賂	銘
络 luò	骆 luò	赂 lù	铭 míng
120 12 [15]	187 16 [56]	154 13 [28]	167 14 [21]

永文亦它宅	詠 咏 yǒng 149 12 [23]	紋 纹 wén 120 10 [15]	跡 迹 jī 157 13 [34]	駝 驼 tuó 187 15 [28]	詫 诧 chà 149 13 [4]
才巾隶盍盇	財 财 cái 154 10 [28]	帥 帅 shuài 50 9 [1]	隸 隶 lì 171 17 [77]	豓 艳 yàn 151 28 [30]	豔 艳 yàn 151 27 [30]
丩甘井弗	糾 纠 jiū 120 8 [15]	拑 钳 qián 64 8 [21]	鉗 钳 qián 167 13 [21]	畊 耕 gēng 102 9 [18]	佛 佛 fú 60 8 [9]
大九女糸	馱 驮 tuó duò 187 13 [28]	軌 轨 guǐ 159 9 [19]	妝 妆 zhuāng 38 7 [3]	絲 丝 sī 120 12 [73]	
攴虎皮内	敍 叙 xù 66 11 [31]	號 号 hào háo 141 13 [68]	皺 皱 zhòu 107 15 [51]	納 纳 nà 120 10 [15]	
中史虫申	沖 冲 chōng 15 7 [52]	駛 驶 shǐ 187 15 [57]	蝕 蚀 shí 142 14 [52]	紳 绅 shēn 120 11 [52]	
車東柬	陣 阵 zhèn 170 10 [22]	陳 陈 chén 170 11 [22]	棟 栋 dòng 75 12 [45]	練 练 liàn 120 15 [15]	鍊 链 liàn 167 17 [21]
午乍布畢	許 许 xǔ 149 11 [4]	詐 诈 zhà 149 12 [50]	飾 饰 shì 184 13 [20]	輝 辉 huī 159 15 [18]	
久色	畝 亩 mǔ 102 10 [62]	艷 艳 yàn 139 24 [30]			

工正丐丏

紅	証	鈣	麪
红 hóng gōng	证 zhèng	钙 gài	面 miàn
120 9 [15]	149 12 [4]	167 12 [21]	199 15 [39]

亐平牙

汙	評	訝
污 wū	评 píng	讶 yà
85 6 [7]	149 12 [47]	149 11 [4]

丂帀面

虧	師	緬	麵
亏 kuī	师 shī	缅 miǎn	面 miàn
141 17 [60]	50 10 [1]	120 15 [15]	199 20 [39]

吕貝田里

鋁	狽	細	裡
铝 lǚ	狈 bèi	细 xì	里 li lǐ
167 15 [21]	94 10 [14]	120 11 [15]	145 12 [75]

卩艮⺕

氾	報	蝦
泛 fàn	报 bào	虾 xiā
85 5 [48]	32 12 [13]	142 15 [29]

凡及尋

訊	級	歸
讯 xùn	级 jí	归 guī
149 10 [4]	120 10 [49]	77 18 [1]

乇禾乏舌斥

託	穌	貶	話	訴
托 tuō	稣 sū	贬 biǎn	话 huà	诉 sù
149 10 [13]	115 16 [29]	154 12 [28]	149 13 [4]	149 12 [4]

系我

係	孫	縣	縣	餓
系 xì	孙 sūn	县 xiàn	县 xiàn	饿 è
9 9 [60]	39 10 [41]	120 16 [77]	120 16 [77]	184 15 [43]

令参仐全余

於	診	幹	詮	餘
于 yú	诊 zhěn	干 gàn	诠 quán	馀 余 yú
70 8 [39]	149 12 [4]	51 13 [39]	149 13 [4]	184 15 [59]

有爻

賄	駁
贿 huì	驳 bó
154 13 [28]	187 14 [28]

丶 丿 丶 丷 八 业 人

烏	島	鳥	樂	衆
乌 wū	岛 dǎo	鸟 niǎo	乐 yuè lè	众 zhòng
86 10 [58]	46 10 [58]	196 11 [58]	75 15 [60]	143 12 [59]

氷	為
冰 bīng	为 wéi wèi
85 5 [3]	86 9 [38]

並	義	養
并 bìng	义 yì	养 yǎng
1 8 [74]	123 13 [71]	184 15 [58]

爺	貧
爷 yé	贫 pín
88 13 [59]	154 11 [59]

糞
粪 fèn
119 17 [71]

賞	嘗	黨	當
赏 shǎng	尝 cháng	党 dǎng	当 dāng dàng
154 15 [77]	30 14 [59]	203 20 [59]	102 13 [59]

傘	貪	倉	會
伞 sǎn	贪 tān	仓 cāng	会 huì kuài
9 12 [59]	154 11 [77]	9 10 [79]	73 13 [77]

一 凹 二 一 夕

晉	爾	兩	盃	
晋 jìn	尔 ěr	两 liǎng	杯 bēi	
72 10 [79]	89 14 [72]	11 8 [60]	108 9 [17]	

亞	惡	頁	貢	憂
亚 yà	恶 è ě wù	页 yè	贡 gòng	忧 yōu
7 8 [39]	61 12 [72]	181 9 [60]	154 10 [77]	61 15 [2]

爭	愛	覓
争 zhēng	爱 ài	觅 mì
87 8 [61]	61 13 [60]	147 11 [77]

氣	氫	無
气 qì	氢 qīng	无 wú
84 10 [61]	84 11 [61]	86 12 [33]

軍
军 jūn
159 9 [61]

魚	負	魯	龜
鱼 yú	负 fù	鲁 lǔ	龟 guī jūn
195 11 [61]	154 9 [61]	195 15 [61]	213 16 [61]

亠 宀 穴

亠

棄	牽	齊	齋	裏	贏
弃 qì	牵 qiān	齐 qí	斋 zhāi	里 li lǐ	赢 yíng
75 11 [62]	93 11 [75]	210 14 [62]	210 17 [62]	145 13 [75]	154 20 [62]

彥	產
彦 yàn	产 chǎn
59 9 [62]	100 11 [62]

宀

宮	寢
宫 gōng	寝 qǐn
40 10 [63]	40 14 [63]

寧	憲	寫	審
宁 níng nìng	宪 xiàn	写 xiě xiè	审 shěn
40 14 [63]	61 16 [63]	40 15 [73]	40 15 [63]

寬	賽	賓	實	寶	寵
宽 kuān	赛 sài	宾 bīn	实 shí	宝 bǎo	宠 chǒng
40 15 [63]	154 17 [77]	154 14 [71]	40 14 [63]	40 20 [63]	40 19 [63]

穴

窯	窩	竄	窮	竊
窑 yáo	窝 wō	窜 cuàn	穷 qióng	窃 qiè
116 15 [63]	116 14 [63]	116 18 [63]	116 15 [63]	116 23 [63]

十			
直 直 zhí 24 8 [67]	專 专 zhuān 41 11 [38]	喪 丧 sāng sàng 30 12 [77]	麥 麦 mài 199 11 [67]

吉				
壺 壶 hú 33 12 [73]	賣 卖 mài 154 15 [74]	臺 台 tái 133 14 [78]	壽 寿 shòu 33 14 [33]	堯 尧 yáo 32 12 [71]

大	
奪 夺 duó 37 14 [67]	奮 奋 fèn 37 16 [67]

歩	
齒 齿 chǐ 211 15 [66]	歲 岁 suì 77 13 [76]

山					
豈 岂 qǐ 151 10 [66]	巖 岩 yán 46 23 [66]	嶺 岭 lǐng 46 17 [56]	崗 岗 gǎng 46 11 [66]	嶺 岭 lǐng 46 17 [56]	嶄 崭 zhǎn 46 14 [66]

艹

艹	萊 莱 lái 140 12 [65]	華 华 huá huà 140 12 [70]	蕭 萧 xiāo 140 17 [64]	黃 黄 huáng 201 12 [67]	
艹	茲 兹 zī 140 10 [58]	菸 烟 yān 140 12 [3]	莊 庄 zhuāng 140 11 [33]	蔣 蒋 jiǎng 140 15 [65]	蘋 苹 píng 140 20 [64]
	蕩 荡 dàng 140 16 [65]	陰 荫 yìn yīn 140 15 [65]	薩 萨 sà 140 18 [65]	蘇 苏 sū 140 20 [65]	蘊 蕴 yùn 140 20 [65]
					藹 蔼 ǎi 140 20 [65]
苫	葉 叶 yè 140 13 [24]	蓋 盖 gài 140 14 [58]	蒐 搜 sōu 140 14 [11]	蔥 葱 cōng 140 15 [64]	蕭 萧 xiāo 140 16 [64]
	莖 茎 jīng 140 11 [64]	夢 梦 mèng 36 14 [76]	蘿 萝 luó 140 23 [76]	萬 万 wàn 0 13 [39]	薑 姜 jiāng 140 17 [58]
					黃 黄 huáng 201 12 [67]
	蒼 苍 cāng 140 14 [79]	舊 旧 jiù 134 18 [53]	藍 蓝 lán la 140 18 [64]	藥 药 yào 140 19 [65]	藝 艺 yì 140 19 [65]
艹	薦 荐 jiàn 140 17 [65]	蘆 芦 lú lǔ 140 20 [64]	蒼 苍 cāng 140 14 [79]		
苫	蔔 卜 bo 140 15 [1]				
艹	蓮 莲 lián 140 15 [65]				
苫	蘭 兰 lán 140 21 [58]	繭 茧 jiǎn 120 19 [65]			

竹 羽 火火

筆
笔 bǐ
118 12 [76]

篤
笃 dǔ
118 16 [66]

範
范 fàn
118 15 [65]

節
节 jié jiē
118 13 [65]

篩
筛 shāi
118 16 [66]

籠
笼 lóng lǒng
118 22 [66]

籬
篱 lí
118 25 [66]

籲
吁 yù
118 32 [24]

箏
筝 zhēng
118 14 [66]

簽
签 qiān
118 19 [73]

質
质 zhì
154 15 [32]

築
筑 zhù zhú
118 16 [66]

籮
箩 luó
118 25 [76]

籌
筹 chóu
118 20 [66]

籃
篮 lán
118 20 [66]

筍
笋 sǔn
118 12 [66]

籤
签 qiān
118 23 [73]

簾
帘 lián
118 19 [63]

簡
简 jiǎn
118 18 [66]

習
习 xí
124 11 [36]

勞
劳 láo
19 12 [64]

榮
荣 róng
75 14 [64]

螢
萤 yíng
142 16 [64]

營
营 yíng
86 17 [64]

鶯
莺 yīng
196 21 [64]

口　口口　四　目　目　田

口

吴 吳
吴 wú
30　7　[74]

呂
吕 lǚ
30　7　[68]

員
员 yuán
30　10　[77]

口口

單
单 dān
30　12　[58]

嚻
嚣 xiāo
30　21　[68]

嚴
严 yán
30　20　[60]

四

買
买 mǎi
154　12　[69]

罵
骂 mà
122　15　[68]

罰
罚 fá
122　14　[68]

罷
罢 bà
122　15　[68]

羅
罗 luó luō
122　19　[68]

置
置 zhì
122　13　[68]

眾
众 zhòng
109　11　[59]

目

昇
升 shēng
72　8　[60]

暈
晕 yūn yùn
72　13　[75]

疊
叠 dié
72　19　[61]

目

貝
贝 bèi
154　7　[36]

見
见 jiàn
147　7　[36]

田

異
异 yì
102　11　[69]

畢
毕 bì
102　11　[70]

壘
垒 lěi
32　18　[61]

疊
叠 dié
102　22　[79]

貫
贯 guàn
154　11　[77]

西				
賈 贾 gǔ 154 13 [68]				
雷				
雲 云 yún 173 12 [77]	電 电 diàn 173 13 [38]	靈 灵 líng 173 24 [69]	霧 雾 wù 173 19 [68]	
畫				
書 书 shū 73 10 [41]	晝 昼 zhòu 72 11 [73]	畫 画 huà 102 12 [37]	盡 尽 jìn 108 14 [36]	肅 肃 sù 129 12 [69]
髟				
髮 发 fà 190 15 [41]	鬆 松 sōng 190 18 [16]	鬚 须 xū 190 22 [1]	鬍 胡 hú 190 19 [53]	

⼘ ⼟ ⺀ ⼔	貞 贞 zhēn 154 9 [77]	堯 尧 yáo 32 12 [71]	責 责 zé 154 11 [67]	眞 真 zhēn 109 10 [67]
⾀ ⾀ 朿	肅 肃 sù 129 12 [69]	盡 尽 jìn 108 14 [36]	棗 枣 zǎo 75 12 [70]	
虫 虫 車	貴 贵 guì 154 12 [77]	蟲 虫 chóng 142 18 [38]	轟 轰 hōng 159 21 [69]	
五 且 女 血	韋 韦 wéi 178 9 [38]	彙 汇 huì 58 13 [57]	姦 奸 jiān 38 9 [22]	眾 众 zhòng 143 12 [59]
戈 力 厶	盞 盏 zhǎn 108 13 [80]	脅 胁 xié 130 10 [27]	參 参 cān cēn shēn 28 11 [70]	
其 廿 弗 业	甚 什 shén shèn 99 9 [43]	黃 黄 huáng 201 12 [67]	費 费 fèi 154 12 [77]	叢 丛 cóng 29 18 [73]
非 曲 冊	輩 辈 bèi 159 15 [75]	農 农 nóng 161 13 [77]	帶 带 dài 50 11 [75]	

工 不 ヨ 巨

貢	盃	尋	長
贡 gòng	杯 bēi	寻 xún xín	长 cháng zhǎng
154 10 [77]	108 9 [17]	41 12 [70]	168 8 [38]

⊞ 耳 凡

貫	聶	骨
贯 guàn	聂 niè	骨 gǔ gú gū
154 11 [77]	128 18 [69]	188 1 [69]

禾 匆

喬	忽
乔 qiáo	cōng
30 12 [60]	61 9 [3]

巛

災
灾 zāi
86 7 [63]

凶 臼

兇	兒
凶 xiōng	儿 ér
10 6 [37]	10 8 [42]

斑,

學	覺
学 xué	觉 jué jiào
39 16 [59]	147 20 [59]

狙

譽	與	輿	興	釁
誉 yù	与 yǔ yù yú	舆 yú	兴 xīng xìng	衅 xìn
149 21 [78]	134 14 [35]	159 17 [71]	134 16 [59]	164 25 [30]

癶 丽 旡旡 栴林

發	麗	蠶	鬱
发 fā	丽 lì	蚕 cán	郁 yù
105 12 [41]	198 19 [60]	142 24 [79]	192 30 [54]

八　儿　彡　一

八

貝	頁	黃	異	糞
贝 bèi	页 yè	黄 huáng	异 yì	粪 fèn
154 7 [36]	181 9 [60]	201 12 [67]	102 11 [69]	119 17 [71]

與	輿	興	眞
与 yǔ yù yú	舆 yú	兴 xīng xìng	真 zhēn
134 14 [35]	159 17 [71]	134 16 [59]	109 10 [67]

儿

兇	兒	見
凶 xiōng	儿 ér	见 jiàn
10 6 [37]	10 8 [42]	147 7 [36]

堯	蒐
尧 yáo	搜 sōu
32 12 [71]	140 14 [11]

彡

彥	參
彦 yàn	参 cān cēn shēn
59 9 [62]	28 11 [70]

一

豈	豎	豐
岂 qǐ	竖 shù	丰 fēng
151 10 [66]	151 15 [73]	151 18 [38]

畫	薑	晝	疊	疊
画 huà	姜 jiāng	昼 zhòu	叠 dié	叠 dié
102 12 [37]	140 17 [58]	72 11 [73]	102 22 [79]	72 19 [61]

並	亞	莖	壺	靈	
并 bìng	亚 yà	茎 jīng	壶 hú	灵 líng	壺 → A3
1 8 [74]	7 8 [39]	140 11 [64]	33 12 [73]	173 24 [69]	壼 → A3

灬 心

魚 鱼 yú 195 11 [61]	無 无 wú 86 12 [33]	馬 马 mǎ 187 10 [73]	烏 乌 wū 86 10 [58]	鳥 鸟 niǎo 196 11 [58]	為 为 wéi wèi 86 9 [38]
熱 热 rè 86 15 [72]	黨 党 dǎng 203 20 [59]	窯 窑 yáo 116 15 [63]	嚥 咽 yàn yān yè 30 19 [24]		
寫 写 xiě xiè 40 15 [73]	薦 荐 jiàn 140 17 [65]	鶯 莺 yīng 196 21 [64]	鷹 鹰 yīng 196 24 [33]		
罵 骂 mà 122 15 [68]	篤 笃 dǔ 118 16 [66]	駕 驾 jià 187 15 [73]	驚 惊 jīng 187 23 [2]		
嗎 吗 ma má mǎ 30 13 [24]	嗚 呜 wū 30 13 [24]	鳴 鸣 míng 196 14 [54]			

惡 恶 è ě wù 61 12 [72]	忽 cōng 61 9 [3]	憲 宪 xiàn 61 16 [63]	蔥 葱 cōng 140 15 [64]		
憑 凭 píng 61 16 [71]	慾 欲 yù 61 15 [50]	態 态 tài 61 14 [72]	憊 惫 bèi 61 16 [72]	懲 惩 chéng 61 19 [72]	
戀 恋 liàn 61 23 [62]	懇 恳 kěn 61 17 [72]	懸 悬 xuán 61 20 [72]			
噁 恶 ě wù 30 15 [72]	唸 念 niàn 30 11 [59]	應 应 yīng yìng 61 17 [33]	癒 愈 yù 104 18 [72]	慮 虑 lǜ 61 15 [33]	

火 大 木 巾 山

火	災 灾 zāi 86 7 [63]	燙 烫 tàng 86 16 [74]			
大	吳 吴 wú 30 7 [74]	奬 奖 jiǎng 37 14 [74]	獎 奖 jiǎng 94 15 [74]		
木	棄 弃 qì 75 11 [62]	彙 汇 huì 58 13 [57]	樂 乐 yuè lè 75 15 [60]	槳 桨 jiǎng 75 15 [74]	
	業 业 yè 75 13 [40]	葉 叶 yè 140 13 [24]	藥 药 yào 140 19 [65]	築 筑 zhù zhú 118 16 [66]	榮 荣 róng 75 14 [64]
巾	帶 带 dài 50 11 [75]	幣 币 bì 50 14 [75]	幫 帮 bāng 50 17 [75]		
山	島 岛 dǎo 46 10 [58]				

準 准 zhǔn 85 13 [3]	傘 伞 sǎn 9 12 [59]	華 华 huá huà 140 12 [70]	畢 毕 bì 102 11 [70]	單 单 dān 30 12 [58]
尋 寻 xún xín 41 12 [70]	專 专 zhuān 41 11 [38]	奪 夺 duó 37 14 [67]	導 导 dǎo 41 16 [69]	
舉 举 jǔ 134 17 [74]				
犂 犁 lí 93 12 [75]	牽 牵 qiān 93 11 [75]			
堅 坚 jiān 32 11 [75]	塗 涂 tú 32 13 [6]	墊 垫 diàn 32 14 [75]	墾 垦 kěn 32 16 [75]	墜 坠 zhuì 32 15 [75]	墮 堕 duò 32 15 [75]
壟 垄 lǒng 32 19 [75]	壘 垒 lěi 32 18 [61]	臺 台 tái 133 14 [78]			
壓 压 yā yà 32 17 [32]	塵 尘 chén 32 14 [75]				

糸 水 氏 衣

糸	絷 扎 zhá zā 120 11 [13]	縶 扎 zhá zā 120 10 [13]	緊 紧 jǐn 120 14 [66]	繋 系 xì 120 19 [60]
水	漿 浆 jiāng jiàng 85 15 [77]	眾 众 zhòng 143 12 [59]	眔 众 zhòng 109 11 [59]	
氏	喪 丧 sāng sàng 30 12 [77]	農 农 nóng 161 13 [77]	長 长 cháng zhǎng 168 8 [38]	
衣	裝 装 zhuāng 145 13 [77]	製 制 zhì 145 14 [42]	襲 袭 xí 145 22 [77]	裏 里 li lǐ 145 13 [75]

又	隻 只 zhǐ zhī 172 10 [68]	雙 双 shuāng 172 18 [1]	髮 发 fà 190 15 [41]			
夂	愛 爱 ài 61 13 [60]	麥 麦 mài 199 11 [67]	憂 忧 yōu 61 15 [2]	變 变 biàn 149 23 [76]	廈 厦 shà xià 53 13 [32]	慶 庆 qìng 61 15 [33]
	髮 发 fà 190 15 [41]	夢 梦 mèng 36 14 [76]				
女	嬰 婴 yīng 38 17 [76]	屢 屡 lǚ 44 14 [32]				
力	勞 劳 láo 19 12 [64]	勢 势 shì 19 13 [76]				
手	摯 挚 zhì 64 15 [76]	擊 击 jí 64 17 [67]				

口　日　田　月　皿

口

呂	宮	啓	營	譽
吕 lǔ	宫 gōng	启 qǐ	营 yíng	誉 yù
30 7 [68]	40 10 [63]	30 11 [32]	86 17 [64]	149 21 [78]

倉	蒼
仓 cāng	苍 cāng
9 10 [79]	140 14 [79]

日

書	習	暫	響
书 shū	习 xí	暂 zàn	响 xiǎng
73 10 [41]	124 11 [36]	72 15 [79]	180 21 [23]

晉	會	嘗	魯
晋 jìn	会 huì kuài	尝 cháng	鲁 lǔ
72 10 [79]	73 13 [77]	30 14 [59]	195 15 [61]

曆	層	簡
历 lì	层 céng	简 jiǎn
72 16 [32]	44 15 [32]	118 18 [66]

田

奮	審	當
奋 fèn	审 shěn	当 dāng dàng
37 16 [67]	40 15 [63]	102 13 [59]

月

腎	脅	骨	脣	膚
肾 shèn	胁 xié	骨 gǔ gú gū	唇 chún	肤 fū
130 12 [79]	130 10 [27]	188 1 [69]	130 11 [78]	130 15 [27]

皿

盃	盡	盞
杯 bēi	尽 jìn	盏 zhǎn
108 9 [17]	108 14 [36]	108 13 [80]

盪	監	鹽	盤
荡 dàng	监 jiān jiàn	盐 yán	盘 pán
108 17 [65]	108 14 [66]	197 24 [80]	108 15 [80]

蓋	藍	籃	盧	廬	蘆
盖 gài	蓝 lán la	篮 lán	卢 lú	庐 lú	芦 lú lǔ
140 14 [58]	140 18 [64]	118 20 [66]	108 16 [66]	53 19 [33]	140 20 [64]

虫

螢	蠻
萤 yíng	蛮 mán
142 16 [64]	142 25 [79]

車

輩	暈	軍	單
辈 bèi	晕 yūn yùn	军 jūn	单 dān
159 15 [75]	72 13 [75]	159 9 [61]	30 12 [58]

貝

頁	貢	員	貞	負
页 yè	贡 gòng	员 yuán	贞 zhēn	负 fù
181 9 [60]	154 10 [77]	30 10 [77]	154 9 [77]	154 9 [61]

貴	買	賈	責	費	貫
贵 guì	买 mǎi	贾 gǔ	责 zé	费 fèi	贯 guàn
154 12 [77]	154 12 [69]	154 13 [68]	154 11 [67]	154 12 [77]	154 11 [77]

貪	貧	賣	貳
贪 tān	贫 pín	卖 mài	贰 èr
154 11 [77]	154 11 [59]	154 15 [74]	154 12 [36]

賞	賓	實	賽	寶
赏 shǎng	宾 bīn	实 shí	赛 sài	宝 bǎo
154 15 [77]	154 14 [71]	40 14 [63]	154 17 [77]	40 20 [63]

貸	貨	資
贷 dài	货 huò	资 zī
154 12 [77]	154 11 [77]	154 13 [77]

貿	賀	質	賢	贊
贸 mào	贺 hè	质 zhì	贤 xián	赞 zàn
154 12 [77]	154 12 [77]	154 15 [32]	154 15 [66]	154 19 [77]

見

覓	覺	覽	寬
觅 mì	觉 jué jiào	览 lǎn	宽 kuān
147 11 [77]	147 20 [59]	147 21 [66]	40 15 [63]

耳 酉 馬 鳥

耳

聲	聾	聳
声 shēng	聋 lóng	耸 sǒng
128 17 [67]	128 22 [80]	128 17 [80]

酉

醫	醬
医 yī	酱 jiàng
164 18 [37]	164 18 [80]

馬

罵	篤	駕	驚
骂 mà	笃 dǔ	驾 jià	惊 jīng
122 15 [68]	118 16 [66]	187 15 [73]	187 23 [2]

鳥

鶯	鷹
莺 yīng	鹰 yīng
196 21 [64]	196 24 [33]

白 向 言 鹿

習	嚮	譽	麗
习 xí	向 xiàng	誉 yù	丽 lì
124 11 [36]	30 18 [78]	149 21 [78]	198 19 [60]

束 犬

棗	獎
枣 zǎo	奖 jiǎng
75 12 [70]	94 15 [74]

止 革

歷	鞏
历 lì	巩 gǒng
77 16 [32]	177 15 [48]

丁 工 王 死

寧	莖	聖	斃
宁 níng nìng	茎 jīng	圣 shèng	毙 bì
40 14 [63]	140 11 [64]	128 13 [61]	66 17 [80]

云 示

雲	藝	禦
云 yún	艺 yì	御 yù
173 12 [77]	140 19 [65]	113 16 [54]

子 分 弓

學	釁	彎
学 xué	衅 xìn	弯 wān
39 16 [59]	164 25 [30]	57 22 [62]

匹 厘 叩 蚰

甚	釐	囂	蠶
什 shén shèn	厘 lí	嚣 xiāo	蚕 cán
99 9 [43]	166 18 [32]	30 21 [68]	142 24 [79]

且 电 甲

疊	疊	電	單
叠 dié	叠 dié	电 diàn	单 dān
102 22 [79]	72 19 [61]	173 13 [38]	30 12 [58]

夕 升 我 臼

夢	昇	義	舊
梦 mèng	升 shēng	义 yì	旧 jiù
36 14 [76]	72 8 [60]	123 13 [71]	134 18 [53]

食 金

養	鑒	鑿
养 yǎng	鉴 jiàn	凿 záo zuò
184 15 [58]	167 22 [66]	167 28 [69]

Table 1: Characters which sometimes simplify

The characters in the first row do occur in simplified text, even though they have simplified forms. Hence they are included in the main section of the Fast Finder. The simplified forms as shown by the bottom row are mostly used, but in some contexts, or to avoid ambiguity, the traditional forms can be retained.

Table 2: Numbers

Numbers are usually written in simple characters, as shown by the middle row. However, to avoid mistakes or guard against alterations, more complex characters (bottom row) are often used in relation to money. Note that the relationship between the characters in the rows is different from that of simplified versus traditional characters.

1	2	3	4	5	6	7	8	9	10		100	1,000	10,000
一	二	三	四	五	六	七	八	九	十		百	千	万
壹	貳	叁	肆	伍	陆	柒	捌	玖	拾		佰	仟	萬

Table 3 : 'Heavenly Stems' and 'Earthly Branches'

This table lists the 10 'Heavenly Stems' and 12 'Earthly Branches': characters which were used in historical methods of writing dates (related to the 'year of the tiger' and so on), and which have traditionally been linked with times of day, directions and various other things. (For example, 丑 is associated with the period 1 a.m. to 3 a.m., the 12th lunar month, and a north-easterly direction.) Apart from being of general interest, these characters (especially the first few Heavenly Stems characters) are used for numbering, in the same way that English uses letters (a), (b), (c) ... or Roman numerals (i), (ii), (iii) ...

Heavenly Stems		Earthly Branches			
1	甲	1	子	鼠	rat
2	乙	2	丑	牛	ox, cow
3	丙	3	寅	虎	tiger
4	丁	4	卯	兔	hare, rabbit
5	戊	5	辰	龍	dragon
6	己	6	巳	蛇	serpent, snake
7	庚	7	午	馬	horse
8	辛	8	未	羊	goat, sheep
9	壬	9	申	猴	monkey
10	癸	10	酉	鸡	cock, hen, rooster
		11	戌	狗	dog
		12	亥	豬	pig, boar

Table 4: Traditional Radical Chart

Table 4 give the traditional 214 radicals, their variant forms, and (where applicable) their modern equivalents (referring to the numbers in Table 5). Unlike the situation for modern radicals, the numbering of these traditional radicals is universally agreed.

Traditional	Mod.	Traditional	Mod.	Traditional	Mod.	Traditional	Mod
1 一	2	23 匚 匚	15	45 屮	61	67 文	8
2 丨	3	24 十	12	46 山	60	68 斗	8
3 丶	1	25 卜	16	47 巛 川	78	69 斤	11
4 丿 丿	4	26 卩 㔾	32	48 工	48	70 方	8
5 乙 乛 乚	5, 6, 7	27 厂 厂	13	49 己 巳	72	71 无 旡	
6 亅	-	28 厶	37	50 巾	57	72 日	10
7 二	11	29 又	35	51 干	-	73 曰	10
8 亠	9	30 口	58	52 幺	76	74 月	11
9 人 亼 亻	20,21,23	31 囗	59	53 广	44	75 木	9
10 儿	29	32 土	49	54 廴	36	76 欠	12
11 入	23	33 士	49	55 廾	51	77 止	10
12 八 丷 八	24	34 夂	65	56 弋	56	78 歹	9
13 冂 冂	19	35 夊	65	57 弓	71	79 殳	11
14 冖	18	36 夕	64	58 彐 彐 彑	70	80 母 毋 毌	
15 冫	8	37 大	52	59 彡	63	81 比	12
16 几 几	30	38 女	73	60 彳	62	82 毛	11
17 凵	38	39 子 孑	74	61 心 忄 忄	41, 81	83 氏	12
18 刀 刂	17, 27	40 宀	45	62 戈	101	84 气	10
19 力	28	41 寸	54	63 戶	86	85 水 氺 氵	40,12
20 勹	26	42 小 ⺌ ⺍	79	64 手 扌	55, 111	86 火 灬	80, 8
21 匕	39	43 尢	53	65 支	-	87 爪 爫	11
22 匚	15	44 尸	67	66 攴	113	88 父	10

Table 4 (continued)

Traditional	Mod.	Traditional	Mod.	Traditional	Mod.	Traditional	Mod.
89 爻	-	121 缶	175	153 豸	198	185 首	-
90 爿	42	122 网 罒 罓	145	154 貝	106	186 香	215
91 片	114	123 羊 羌 羋	157	155 赤	190	187 馬	75
92 牙	99	124 羽	183	156 走	189	188 骨	214
93 牛	110	125 老 耂	92	157 足 𧾷	196	189 高	218
94 犬 犭	69, 96	126 而	169	158 身	200	190 髟	220
95 玄	-	127 耒	176	159 車	100	191 鬥	46
96 玉 王	88, 131	128 耳	163	160 辛 辛	186	192 鬯	-
97 瓜	151	129 聿 肀 聿	124	161 辰	187	193 鬲	219
98 瓦	98	130 肉 月	118	162 辵 辶	47	194 鬼	216
99 甘	135	131 臣	164	163 邑 阝	34	195 魚	210
100 生	-	132 自	180	164 酉	193	196 鳥	152
101 用	-	133 至	171	165 釆	197	197 鹵	-
102 田	142	134 臼	179	166 里	195	198 鹿	222
103 疋 疋	156	135 舌	177	167 金	147, 209	199 麥	188
104 疒	127	136 舛	-	168 長	-	200 麻	221
105 癶	154	137 舟	182	169 門	46	201 黃 黄	-
106 白	150	138 艮 艮	184	170 阜 阝	33	202 黍	-
107 皮	153	139 色	-	171 隶	-	203 黑	223
108 皿	146	140 艸 艹	50	172 隹	208	204 黹	-
109 目	141	141 虍	173	173 雨	204	205 黽	207
110 矛	155	142 虫	174	174 青	202	206 鼎	-
111 矢	148	143 血	181	175 非	205	207 鼓	224
112 石	136	144 行	-	176 面	-	208 鼠	225
113 示 礻	87, 132	145 衣 衤	129, 161	177 革	212	209 鼻	226
114 禸	-	146 西 覀 襾	166	178 韋	91	210 齊 斉	-
115 禾	149	147 見	107	179 韭	-	211 齒	206
116 穴 穴	128	148 角	201	180 音	211	212 龍 竜	137
117 立	126	149 言	10, 185	181 頁	170	213 龜	-
118 竹 ⺮	178	150 谷	199	182 風	121	214 龠	-
119 米	159	151 豆	191	183 飛	-		
120 糸	77	152 豕	194	184 食 𩙿	68, 217		

Table 5: Modern Radical Chart

This table lists the 'modern' radicals used in the Fast Finder, with their alternative forms, and (where applicable) the corresponding traditional radicals (see Table 4). This set of modern radicals is used in *'A Chinese English Dictionary'* and many modern dictionaries use this set of radicals or a close approximation – albeit allocating to them numbers which differ slightly from dictionary to dictionary.

Modern		Trad.	Modern		Trad.	Modern		Trad.	Modern		Trad
1	丶	3	25	乂	-	49	土 士	32, 33	73	女	3
2	一	1	26	勹	20	50	艹	140	74	子 孑	3
3	丨	2	27	刀 ⺈	18	51	卝	55	75	马	18
4	丿	4	28	力	19	52	大	37	76	幺	5
5	㇇	5	29	儿	10	53	尢	43	77	纟 糸	12
6	丁	5	30	几 八	16	54	寸	41	78	巛	4
7	乙 乚乁	5	31	冖	-	55	扌	64	79	小 ⺌	4
8	冫	15	32	卩	26	56	弋	56	80	灬	8
9	亠	8	33	阝	170	57	巾	50	81	心	6
10	讠	149	34	阝	163	58	口	30	82	斗	6
11	二	7	35	又	29	59	囗	31	83	火	8
12	十	24	36	廴	54	60	山	46	84	文	6
13	厂	27	37	厶	28	61	屮	45	85	方	7
14	𠂇	-	38	凵	17	62	彳	60	86	户	6
15	匚	22, 23	39	匕	21	63	彡	59	87	礻	11
16	卜 ⺊	25	40	氵	85	64	夕	36	88	王	9
17	刂	18	41	忄	61	65	夂	34, 35	89	生	
18	冖	14	42	爿	90	66	丸	-	90	天 夭	
19	冂 几	13	43	亡	-	67	尸	44	91	韦	17
20	勹	9	44	广	53	68	夂	184	92	耂	12
21	亻	9	45	宀	40	69	犭	94	93	廿 㞢	
22	厂	-	46	门	169	70	彐 彐 㞢	58	94	木	7
23	入 入	9, 11	47	辶	162	71	弓	57	95	不	
24	八 八 丷	12	48	工	48	72	己 巳	49	96	犬	9

Table 5 (continued)

Modern	Trad.	Modern	Trad.	Modern	Trad.	Modern	Trad.
97 歹	78	130 夬	-	163 耳	128	196 足 足	157
98 瓦	98	131 玉	96	164 臣	131	197 釆	165
99 牙	92	132 示	113	165 戋	-	198 豸	153
100 车	159	133 去	-	166 西 西	146	199 谷	150
101 戈	62	134 丗	-	167 東	-	200 身	158
102 止	77	135 甘	99	168 亚	-	201 角	148
103 日	72	136 石	112	169 而	126	202 青	174
104 曰	73	137 龙	212	170 页	181	203 卓	-
105 中	-	138 戊	-	171 至	133	204 雨	173
106 贝	154	139	-	172 光	-	205 非	175
107 见	147	140	-	173 虍	141	206 齿	211
108 父	88	141 目	109	174 虫	142	207 龟	205
109 气	84	142 田	102	175 缶	121	208 隹	172
110 牛	93	143 由	-	176 耒	127	209 金	167
111 手	64	144 申	-	177 舌	135	210 鱼 鱼	195
112 毛	82	145 皿	122	178 竹 竹	118	211 音	180
113 攵	66	146 皿	108	179 臼	134	212 革	177
114 片	91	147 钅	167	180 自	132	213 是	-
115 斤	69	148 矢	111	181 血	143	214 骨	188
116 爪 爫	87	149 禾	115	182 舟	137	215 香	186
117 尺	-	150 白	106	183 羽	124	216 鬼	194
118 月 月	74, 130	151 瓜	97	184 艮 艮	138	217 食	184
119 殳	79	152 鸟	196	185 言	149	218 高	189
120 欠	76	153 皮	107	186 辛 辛	160	219 鬲	193
121 风	182	154 癶	105	187 辰	161	220 影	190
122 氏	83	155 矛	110	188 麦	199	221 麻	200
123 比	81	156 疋	103	189 走	156	222 鹿	198
124 聿 聿 聿	129	157 羊 羊 羊	123	190 赤	155	223 黑	203
125 水	85	158 类	-	191 豆	151	224 鼓	207
126 立	117	159 米	119	192 東	-	225 鼠	208
127 广	104	160 齐	-	193 酉	164	226 鼻	209
128 穴	116	161 衣	145	194 豕	152	227 -	-
129 礻	145	162 亦 亦	-	195 里	166		